The
Proving
Ground

The Proving Ground

A SEASON ON THE FRINGE
IN NFL EUROPE

Lars Anderson

ST. MARTIN'S PRESS ❧ NEW YORK

www.stmartins.com

All photos courtesy of Dave McRitchie, except where noted

Library of Congress Cataloging-in-Publication Data

Anderson, Lars.
    The proving ground : a season on the fringe in NFL Europe / Lars
Anderson.—1st U.S. ed.
        p. cm.
    ISBN 0-312-26975-7
    1. NFL Europe (Football league) 2. Football—Europe. I. Title.

GV955.5.N355 A53 2001
796.332'64'094—dc21

                                                        2001034944

First Edition: October 2001

10 9 8 7 6 5 4 3 2 1

For my father, Robert I. Anderson, Esq. I now agree: Johnny Rodgers was the best football player that man, woman, or child ever saw.

Contents

CONTENTS

Foreword

I'll never forget my first day in NFL Europe. I played defensive tackle for the Barcelona Dragons in spring 1996, and when we arrived at our hotel in the resort town of Sitges, Spain, one thought popped into my mind: This is pretty cool. We lived on a nude beach right on the Mediterranean. The first thing I did was go to a restaurant on the beach, have a nice meal, and just sit back and take in the scene. That was when I realized how fun—and how meaningful—NFL Europe would be for me.

Simply put, if I hadn't played in Europe, I would be out of football right now. I never would have led the NFL in sacks, been voted to the Pro Bowl, and been named an All-Pro. You probably never would have heard of La'Roi Glover.

Before I suited up for Barcelona, I was a practice squad player for the Oakland Raiders. When the Oakland coaching staff first asked me to go to Europe, I didn't want to go. But then I called guys like Mike Jones—yes, the same Mike Jones who made the tackle on the last play of Super Bowl XXXIV to seal the win for the Rams—who had NFL Europe experience. They all said the same thing: If you really want to make it in the NFL, if you're willing to do whatever it takes, then you should go. They said it would give me experience and allow me to travel the world. Looking back, I'm glad I followed their advice.

So I went to Europe and played for the Dragons. Our team won the World Bowl and I led the league in sacks. The guys on our team had a blast the entire season. We'd take day trips on our days off and we even went to Paris once. Other times we'd just hang out on the beach. We'd rent paddleboats, go swimming in the aqua waters of the Mediterranean, relax in the sun, and just try to make each other laugh. I have some great memories of the NFL Europe—memories that will last a lifetime.

I also got to know some of the local fans in Barcelona. I'll never forget the way they'd stare at me the first time they saw me. It was as if they had never seen someone so big. I taught English at different schools a few times, and by the end of my three months in Barcelona, I really felt that the city was my home.

When I came back from Europe, I thought I had a good camp with the Raiders. But then they cut me. I was shocked. I thought my career was over. I started to look into finishing up my degree at San Diego State and getting on with the rest of my life. Then, out of the blue, the Saints called and offered me a tryout. The only reason they made that call, I found out later, was because they had tape of me playing in NFL Europe. To a football player struggling to make it in the league, your tape is your résumé. If you don't have fresh tape, you're going to have a difficult time making it in the league. That's why NFL Europe is so valuable: NFL coaches can see on film exactly what you can do.

It's hard to explain in a few words the depth of my experience in Europe. It had such a deep effect on me professionally and personally. I suggest to any fan who wants to know what the league is really like—and to any player who's considering going to NFL Europe—that they pick up *The Proving Ground* and give it a close read. Lars Anderson has captured the essence of the league in this book. You'll enjoy it because, like life in NFL Europe itself, you never quite know what's going to happen next.

—LA'ROI GLOVER
New Orleans, Spring 2001

1 The Dream

Glasgow, Scotland. Morning of Game Seven

EVERYTHING WAS SET. The woman was scheduled to arrive at
three o'clock. She would enter the stadium, walk through the
crowd, and emerge on the field behind the home team's bench.
There she would wait, trying to blend quietly into the shadows.
Then, if all went according to plan and she got the signal from a
player on the sidelines, she would slip out of her clothes and take
off running into the cool spring afternoon—and straight into
professional football history.

For a week, whispers of the event had circulated among the Scottish Claymores. The anticipation grew by the hour, the players becoming as agog as seniors on prom night waiting to see what will be exposed by evening's end. No two Claymores had more at stake in the streak than Matt Finkes and Rob Hart, the brains behind the brave act. They had negotiated the fee, plotted the getaway, and even crafted a few backup plans to ensure that the world's largest peepshow would go off as smoothly as a Broadway production. "If we do it with class, we can pull it off," said Hart, the team's place kicker to Finkes, a linebacker. "We just have to make sure that she doesn't get caught."

"If this works," said Finkes, "it will be our legacy."

Fans sprint onto professional playing fields all the time in Scotland. But Gillian Stevenson, a twenty-six-year-old with auburn-colored hair and a double-D chest, was willing to take it a step further. A waitress in Glasgow, Stevenson had a break-your-heart smile and sparkling green eyes. In those eyes, if you looked closely, was the glimmer of mischief. This partly explained why Stevenson, in all of her model beauty, agreed to gallop across the field naked in the third quarter of the Claymores game against the Barcelona Dragons. Not only that, she consented to rent out space on the curves and swerves of her body on which the players could either write messages to friends back home in the States or print their uniform number. If it all worked out then football, at least for a few moments, would be the sexiest sport on this green earth.

Yet the flesh show would cause more than just heavy breathing. For Finkes and Hart were betting that the $450 they were paying Stevenson would also accomplish something on a grander, worldwide scale. They hoped the stunt would grab the attention of folks back home. Attention—when you're an NFL Europe player—is the one commodity that's as precious as a bag of jewels. "When we pull this off, it will be the highlight of my career," said Finkes, who in 1996 was an All-Big-Ten player at Ohio State.

Orlando, Florida. First Day of Training Camp. March 13, 2000

Three months earlier at the NFL Europe orientation, Finkes and Hart were among the 450 players sitting in the Reflection Ballroom at Orlando's Harley Hotel. These were the players who would compete for roster spots on the six teams of NFL Europe for the 2000 season. Each of these men—141 of whom had been loaned to the league by NFL teams; all the others were free agents—had his own reason for being here. Some were veterans trying to salvage their waning careers. Others were younger players, green on and off the field, looking to gain experience. Yet others were past-their-prime graybeards, there because they didn't want their dream of playing professional football to die.

It was 8:30 in the evening. The room was quiet, everyone hushed in expectation. Outside the tall windows of the fourth-floor ballroom, the last blush of sunlight licked the Florida sky. Inside, Bill Peterson, the thirty-five-year-old president of the league, stepped up to the dais. Peterson, who was named president in November 1999 after spending three years as general manager of the Amsterdam Admirals, cleared his throat and then put forth an all-out sales pitch, trying to convince these players that NFL Europe mattered. "Welcome to our league," Peterson said. "One of the first things you all should know is that videos of every game we play are sent back to every NFL team. If you play well, you'll get noticed. It's certainly happened before."

Peterson then stirred the echoes of past NFL Europe greatness, showing the players a five-minute video. Sitting in the darkness, the players saw on a big screen highlights of quarterback Kurt Warner, Jon Kitna, and Brad Johnson playing in Europe. They saw wide receiver Marcus Robinson, who reeled in 84 receptions for the Chicago Bears in 1999, catching passes for the Rhein Fire. They saw defensive tackle La'Roi Glover, now an All-Pro for the New Orleans Saints, rush the quarterback for the Barcelona Dragons. More than anything, though, what the players really saw on the screen was hope—for their careers, their futures, and their bank accounts.

"Just knowing that players have gone on from Europe to become stars in the NFL gives you a lot of motivation," said Aaron Stecker, a running back for the Claymores. "That's why I came, to help my career and make people know my name."

In the year 2000, NFL Europe would field teams in Amsterdam (the Admirals), Barcelona (the Dragons), Berlin (the Thunder), Düsseldorf (the Rhein Fire), Frankfurt (the Galaxy), and Glasgow (the Scottish Claymores). Each team would play each other twice, which made for a 10-game season between April and June, with a three-week training camp in Orlando. At the end of the season the teams with the two top records would play in the World Bowl, which is NFL Europe's equivalent to the Super Bowl.

"This isn't a holiday you're on," continued Peterson. "In these next three months, you'll be expected to act like a professional and play like a professional. If you do that, I promise only good things will happen for you."

THE NEXT AFTERNOON, at 3 P.M. sharp, the Scottish Claymores officially began their season with a team meeting back in the Reflection Room. Most of the players had never met, so before Coach Jim

Criner and his staff spoke to the team the players introduced themselves to each other. There were players from big schools (Nebraska
and Ohio State) and small (Murray State and Western Illinois). They
were from the North (Michigan), the South (Clemson), the East
(University of Massachusetts), and the West (USC). Some even came
from outposts as far away as England and Japan to try out for the
Claymores, a team named after a large, double-edged broadsword
once used by Scottish Highlanders. For all the players, this moment
before the coaches marched in the room was rich with meaning.
Because there before all of them, dangling like an apple waiting to be
plucked from the tree, was something that most people never get: a
second chance.

In the room there were sixty-two souls. They were competing for
forty-three roster spots. Twenty-one of the players had been allocated to the Claymores by NFL teams; the rest were free agents.
Some would eventually make it to the NFL, some would quietly slip
back into anonymity, and one would suffer a life-altering injury
before the season was done.

Forty-two of the players were black. Eighteen were white. Two
were Asian. This team was an ethnic cocktail, and racial tension
would eventually flare. Players would segregate themselves—black
players would sit in the back of the bus, white players in the front. In
the most frustrated moments of the season, whites would accuse
blacks of playing dirty on the field, and blacks would resent them
for it.

But as players sat in the Reflection Room on that soft afternoon,
they were full of optimism. Near the front of the room was linebacker
Matt Finkes, who had waved goodbye to his fiancée in Columbus,
Ohio, to play for the Claymores. One of the brightest players on the
team, Finkes was a voracious reader of fiction, riveted by the sound-
less song of the printed word. Before practice every morning he

would breeze through crossword puzzles and study stock reports. In training camp, he tried to convince players to buy stock in a company that he had heard was on the verge of a most magical discovery: finding a cure for cancer. "It could be the easiest million you ever make," Finkes told his teammates.

Finkes, who played with the Jets for eight games in 1997, came to NFL Europe because he wasn't ready to start his real, nine-to-five life just yet. "I pretty much know that my football career is over," said Finkes. "I really just want to have a good time in Scotland and see if we can win a championship." Before the season was over, Finkes would have the time of his life—especially when he visited the sumptuous city of Amsterdam. Nowhere in Europe were forbidden fruits more plentiful, as Finkes and a few of his teammates would soon discover.

Sitting close to Finkes was tight end Willy Tate, who had left his job as a cowhand on a ranch in Oregon to give football one last shot. Tate's father had passed away recently, succumbing to a diseased colon. This had a profound impact on Willy, largely because he had enjoyed a bond with his old man that ran deeper than blood: They shared an unconditional love of football. Tate's father had played college ball at Cal-Polly and instilled a passion for the sport into Willy when he was a small boy. But, after his father passed away, Tate wasn't sure if he wanted to return to Scotland again—he had been a Claymore in 1996 and '98. After spending over one hundred hours driving and thinking as he steered his beat-up pickup across America's highways and byways, Tate decided that the best way to honor his father would be to keep on playing. "My dad and I loved to talk about football," said Tate, twenty-eight, who played at the University of Oregon. "The sport really brought us closer. I guess that's why I didn't want to give it up just yet."

Also in the room was cornerback Duane Hawthorne, who played

in fourteen games with the Dallas Cowboys in 1999. The twenty-three-year-old Hawthorne had all the tools be a top cover corner in the NFL: speed, agility, and wits. That was why he wished he wasn't here, that he was back at his home in St. Louis and living the care-free life of a professional athlete in his offseason. But when Cowboys coach Dave Campo told him that he should go to Europe to improve his coverage skills, that he should go and set the first stones in the building of his career, Hawthorne felt he had little choice but to pack his bags. It would turn out to be one of the best decisions of Hawthorne's young life.

Running back Aaron Stecker was also there. A few years earlier Stecker looked like he was on a path to become a starter in the NFL. Then, at the 1999 scouting combine, his lifelong goal was obliterated in less than five seconds. His time in the forty-yard dash just wasn't good enough. At the end of this short season, though, Stecker would be named the top offensive player in the league, proving that he belonged in that shining city on the hill, the NFL.

Coach Criner finally entered the Reflection Room and strolled up to the podium. Around the room the players were scattered and silent. "Well, gentleman, we've got a great team put together," said the fifty-nine-year-old Criner. "Everything is in place to win a championship. We're going to be especially strong on defense. Our offense won't be as crisp as our defense in the beginning, but we believe in all of our offensive guys. But the only way for us to achieve our goal of winning a championship is for us to play together and go about our business on the field in a professional manner. We run, we hustle, we finish everything we do on the field. I'll treat everyone the same. It doesn't matter if you've been allocated or drafted. I'll play the best players. I hope everyone leaves the program a better player, but I also hope you leave with a championship."

Criner's season begins in July, when he visits as many as eighteen

NFL training camps. On these stop-ins, Criner looks for players who have the talent to play in the NFL but are still works-in-progress. This genre of player usually ends up spending the NFL season on a team's practice squad, working out with his team but never seeing any game action. To give this kind of player some game experience, NFL coaches will often allocate him to NFL Europe for a season or two. Precisely which NFL Europe team gets that particular player, however, usually depends on what kind of relationship the NFL head coach has with coaches in NFL Europe. This is why Criner's visits to preseason camps are as much about schmoozing as they were about scouting.

"The only way we can get a player allocated to us that we really want is to have a relationship with an NFL coach," said Richard Kent, the Claymores' defensive backs coach, who usually attends ten training camps himself. "Take our best cornerback, Duane Hawthorne of the Cowboys, for example. The only reason we got him was because Coach Criner and Dave Campo, the coach of the Dallas Cowboys, worked together at Boise State twenty years ago. If Criner didn't have that relationship with Campo, there's no way we get Hawthorne. We could have asked the league to allocate him to us, but it's much more powerful when the NFL coach asks the league to allocate his player to a certain team. Probably nine times out of ten, the league will honor a request like that."

Criner and his staff also tour the camps to find the best players who don't make an NFL roster. The coaches take copious notes at the camps and use these notes to determine whom they should select in the NFL Europe free-agent draft, which is twenty rounds long and is held a few weeks before the start of training camp. The other primary way to acquire a player in NFL Europe is to put him on a protected list. A team can only put a player on this list if he was on their roster the previous season.

THE PROVING GROUND

"There is a science to putting an NFL Europe team together," said Kent. "You really need a head coach who knows a lot of people in the league, which is usually why the successful head coaches in NFL Europe tend to be a little older. As in life, sometimes it's more about who you know than what you know."

In cobbling together a team, every NFL Europe coach first concentrates on acquiring three things: a good, accurate quarterback; defensive ends who can rush the passer; and cornerbacks who can handle man-to-man coverage. These three positions are the pillars that success—or failure—rests upon in this league. A team needs a talented signal-caller because he's the most important player on the field, and in a short season in which the teams are theoretically balanced, one player can mean the difference between being a winner or a washout. Pass-rushing defensive ends are also crucial because if a team can apply pressure on the quarterback without blitzing its linebackers, it allows them to drop more players into pass coverage. This is the key to success for every defense in the league because precious few good cornerbacks fall to NFL Europe. So if a team can land one or two cornerbacks who have the skills to blanket wide receivers man-to-man, it enables the team's defense to plug holes elsewhere.

"Things in this league hinge on such little things," said Criner. "You just have to hope that your weaknesses aren't at quarterback or on defense. Then at least you'll have a chance."

A team's success in NFL Europe—more so than in the NFL—also depends on the talent of its head coach. A good coach in this league must be many things: teacher, recruiter, counselor, organizer, cultural liaison, and, in some instances, a discerning map-reader. Criner got his first job in coaching in 1963 as an assistant at Charter Oaks (California) High under Jim Hanifan, the future head coach of the St. Louis Cardinals. Since then, the life story of Jim Criner has been filled with a few sweet chapters, a few sad chapters, and one very dangerous chapter.

West Yellowstone, Montana, Jim Criner's Home

Nestled in a valley of the Rocky Mountains, the town of West Yellowstone, Montana, rests on the border of Yellowstone National Park. With the silvery brooks that wind through the area and the distant mountaintops that rise to kiss the sky, the landscape in West Yellowstone appears lifted from an Ansel Adams photograph. Eight miles outside this picture-perfect town you can find Jim and Ann Criner's slice of paradise on a six-acre swath of forested land filled with lodgepole pines and firs. Jim likes to call the place his "Golden Pond," and he seems as natural here as the deer that glide through the trees at dusk.

The Criners acquired the land in an auction held the day after the stock market crashed in 1987. Golfer Johnny Miller had planned to buy the property, but he was hit hard by Blue Monday. His bad luck was the break of a lifetime for the Criners. "We came within a few hundred dollars of all the money that we had saved, but we won the bid," said Ann. "A trapper built a cabin on the property back in the 1920s and the main structure of it still stands today. The original logs are still there."

The cabin is also close to the shallows of Duck Creek. This is Jim's sanctuary, the place he escapes to go fly-fishing. The Criners came to Montana in the mid-1980s after Jim was fired as head coach at Iowa State. Criner enjoyed moderate success as the Cyclones coach from 1983 to '86, guiding the moribund program to a winning record in 1986. Criner was a no-nonsense coach in Ames, never afraid to speak precisely what was on his mind. In the middle of the 1986 season, for example, Iowa State was beating Missouri 34–14 with five seconds remaining in the game. The Cyclones had the ball on the Tigers' 8-yard line. Instead of running the clock out—which basic football etiquette demands—Criner called a timeout to allow his team to kick a 25-yard field goal. After the 37–14 win, Criner defended the excess, saying he was upset that Missouri coach Woody Widenhofer had accused him of sending spies to Missouri's practices the previous year. "I wanted to make sure that Woody had it in his mind who won the game," Criner explained afterward.

That controversial win marked the high point of Criner's 1986 season. The low point would come soon after, as a couple of major twisters blew through the Cyclones' coaching office that year and tore the program apart. For starters, a few players got arrested and then one player, who had grown depressed after he was told that he would lose his scholarship for academic reasons, committed suicide. And a handful of more players were kicked off the team for various violations. "If I knew we were going to have those kinds of problems," Criner said. "I don't think I'd have gone into coaching."

It didn't take long for the NCAA to investigate these brushfires. Eventually the NCAA, largely based on the testimony of four players, charged the school with thirty-four different violations, ranging from giving cash to players to coaches paying for players' meals. Three days before Iowa State met with NCAA officials in Mission, Kansas, school president Gordon Eaton asked Criner to resign. Criner refused, so the next day Eaton fired him, with two games remaining in the '86 season. The NCAA investigation didn't accuse Criner of any major wrongdoing, but he was the coach, the one in charge. He'd recruited the players and he'd hired the assistants. He was, ultimately, responsible.

The NCAA hit Iowa State hard: the school got two years probation and lost four football scholarships. Criner claimed that an overzealous assistant coach was to blame for most of the violations. "They should have hung him by his toes," Criner said. "But I am the only one they let go." In the aftermath of his firing, Criner took numerous lie-detector tests, and he maintains that they all vindicated him. But regardless of Criner's culpability in the matter, a scarlet letter was branded on his chest by this incident. He was, in effect, banished from college football.

So the Criners moved to the beautiful big-sky country of Montana, to a quieter life. Jim opened a store called Bud Lilly's Trout Shop and became one of the premier fly fishermen in the country. He made fishing videos. He led guided tours of the area. And he watched the movie *A River Runs Through It* a hundred times, entranced by the notion of a river being the main character of a film. "It's one of the few videos I've ever bought," said Jim.

Yet during these days, Criner still pined for football, for its fellowship, its competition. So in 1992, six years after he was fired from Iowa State, he found what he thought was the perfect job when he landed a position as an assistant coach with the Sacramento Surge of the fledgling World League of American Football. This new line of football work allowed Criner to coach and still enjoy the fruits of West Yellowstone, since he'd only have to coach a few months each year. He loved it, being back in the action. Three years later, Criner was hired to coach the offensive line of the Scottish Claymores, a team that was entering its first season in the WLAF. He couldn't have been happier.

But trouble was brewing in Scotland, too. The Claymores' head coach in the franchise's first year was Larry Kuharic, who had most recently been the head man of the Tampa Bay Storm of the Arena League. Almost immediately after taking the job, Kuharic ran into problems. In training camp, which was held in Atlanta in 1995,

THE PROVING GROUND

Kuharic worked the players so hard that a NFL scout who attended a few practices told a Claymores' front-office staffer, "They don't work players anywhere near this hard in the hardest of all the camps in the NFL. What the hell is he doing?"

What Kuharic was doing was running his players into the ground. He had his players sprint up and down hills until a few of them vomited. He had them do pushups throughout practice. He had players jog in place, then when a whistle blew, they went down on their bellies, then jumped back up—for twenty-five minutes at a time. Quartererbacks coach Doug Williams, now the head coach at Grambling, was privately critical of Kuharic's intensive, militaristic style. And Kuharic didn't make many friends in the Scottish press, either. On the first day of practice in Scotland, he told a few members of the media who had showed up to watch, "It's a beautiful day, so go enjoy your time at the pool."

"We want to watch practice," replied one member of the press. "We want to learn more about this game of American football."

"I said go enjoy your time at the pool," said Kuharic.

But what really caught the attention of the league was that players were getting sick. One player suffered from dehydration and Kuharic, according to several sources, told the trainers not to help him, to let him recover by himself in his room. Finally, with the players on the verge of a mass walkout, the league intervened and fired Kuharic five days before the Claymores' first-ever game. At a meeting held in Edinburgh, World League President Marc Lory, a Frenchman, told Kuharic and the Claymores' front office that it was in the best interests of the league that Kuharic be removed as head coach. Lory never gave a detailed explanation behind the move to the press, but every sports reporter in Scotland knew why Kuharic was sent home.

The situation was disastrous. Some members of the Scottish

press believed that Kuharic's public flogging was a conspiracy to generate publicity, but that seemed farfetched, given that the league was already struggling to appear legitimate. The entire incident was an embarrassment to NFL Europe, as the league was renamed in 1996. But from the dust of the rubble left by Kuharic arose an opportunity for Criner to rebuild his career. With only a few days to go before the start of the season, the league couldn't hire someone outside the team as coach, so they promoted from within and gave the head job to Criner. One man's downfall was Criner's good fortune.

"That first season was rough," recalled Criner. "We just didn't have much talent and we finished 2–8. Everything was thrown together so quickly at the beginning that it was difficult for us to get into some sort of a rhythm. But really, what I felt really badly about was how we didn't come through for the people of Scotland, because they came out and supported us and we just weren't that good. That's part of the reason I came back and that's why I have kept coming back, because I want to give the people of Scotland, who are so great in their support of us, a winner. Maybe that sounds corny, but it's true."

MOST MORNINGS IN the offseason Criner woke up at 5 AM and then, as he watched the glow of dawn outside of his West Yellowstone window, he made phone calls to his front office staff in Scotland or the league office in London. He then had coffee and toast. At six, he phoned whomever he needed to speak with on the East Coast, whether it was potential players or someone in the NFL office in New York. After that, he took a break. He either drove into town to run errands or went cross-country skiing with Ann. On December 29, 1999, during this break time, he traveled to town with Ann to drop off some Christmas presents for friends who had been away for the holiday.

It was a clear, sunlit morning. Criner drove his pickup truck the eight miles into town and then, arriving at his friend's house, pulled over on the snow-covered road. He stepped out and looped around to the back of the tuck to get the presents out. Just as he reached the back, though, something terrible happened. He didn't see it coming, but an out-of-control snowmobile blindsided Criner at about 30 miles per hour, sending him flying 10 feet into the air.

Criner hadn't been paying attention to the snowmobiles in the area, because there were so many buzzing around. But 30 yards behind him, just as Criner was getting out of his truck, a middle-aged woman was mounting one of the machines, which she had rented only a few minutes earlier. When the woman started the snowmobile, the throttle was apparently on full, because the machine shot out into the winter afternoon. The woman, who was an inexperienced snowmobiler, froze as the machine lurched forward. Seconds later Criner was catapulted forward, wondering if he was going to die. He landed on a patch of frozen ice, which nearly knocked him unconscious and shattered his right femur. The pain was excruciating. About ten minutes later, a team of paramedics was on the scene.

"My wife was still in the truck when I got hit and she heard this big thud and she came right over to me," recalled Criner. "The first thing out of my mouth was: 'Are the presents okay? You gotta deliver them.' Then I felt a funny sensation that the bottom of my leg was higher than the top. I asked the paramedics where my feet were. Well, the ambulance took me to a local clinic and pulled the leg out and twisted the ankle just right and everything fell back into place. It was very, very painful."

Criner winced as he retold the story a few days after the 2000 training camp had kicked off. The memory was still fresh in his mind, and he seemed to be using it as a motivational tool for this season. Only three months had passed since the day the music nearly stopped for Criner, and now here he was, trying to mold a team together that could win a championship. If he could coach through this, he believed he could coach through pretty much anything.

2 Camp Life

Head Coach Jim Criner.

Orlando, Florida. Two Weeks into Training Camp

THE PAIN OF his injuries still plagued Criner as he hobbled around with the help of a cane at the Citrus Bowl in March of 2000. Jim Criner was an old-school coach. He believed that a strong defense and a strong offensive line were the bricks and mortar of championships. He also believed in physical play and physical practices. But despite his demands, Criner was a cheery presence, bopping along with a big, lopsided grin and dispensing aphorisms about life and football to his players. His approach to the game was similar to that of Dick Vermeil, the former St. Louis Rams and Philadelphia Eagles coach, whom Criner worked with at UCLA back in the early 1970s. In fact, Vermeil had offered Criner a job to be his offensive line coach when Vermeil took over the Rams in 1997. But Criner declined, foregoing, as it turned out, a Super Bowl ring.

At age fifty-nine, Criner was in the autumn of his coaching career, but he still took the game as seriously as a first-year assistant trying to make an impression, which was why he had such a sense of urgency in training camp. "If we don't get the job done this year, then it may be time for a change," said Criner, sitting amid the clutter in room 330 at the Harley Hotel that served as the coaches' meeting room. "We haven't won the World Bowl since 1996, so we need to get back on top. But, I'll tell you, winning in this league is harder than in any other league I've ever coached in because you start with an entirely new team each year."

As Criner predicted, the Claymores' offense in training camp lagged behind the defense like a three-legged dog. The offense was led by running back Aaron Stecker, who'd been allocated to the Claymores by the Tampa Bay Buccaneers. The two quarterbacks were Kevin Daft, who was the third-string quarterback for the Tennessee Titans during their run to Super Bowl XXXIV, and Marcus Crandell, a free agent from the Kansas City Chiefs who, at East Carolina, broke most of the records held by Jeff Blake. Neither quarterback, much to the displeasure of offensive coordinator Vince Alcalde, was having a particularly strong training camp.

"Right now I have no idea who we will start," said Alcalde, the night before the team's third and final scrimmage of training camp, against the Frankfurt Galaxy. "I'm leaning a little toward Kevin because he doesn't make mistakes as often as Marcus, but he also doesn't make things happen the way Marcus can make things happen. We'll just have to see. We may end up playing both of them." The next afternoon at the scrimmage, Daft had his worst day of camp. Played at the Disney Studios complex under an azure sky on a breezy, palm tree–swaying day, Daft was high, wide, or short on nearly every pass. Crandell wasn't much better, but he did guide the team to a score on his second series under center.

The most memorable play of the scrimmage took place on the very first snap. That was when Scotland's Rasheed Simmons, a defensive end, saw the Galaxy's Dorrick Roy, a tight end, punch one of his Claymore teammates flush in the groin during the play. Though the whistle had blown, Simmons sprinted five yards and crushed Roy with a hard hit to the sternum. This triggered an all-out brawl in which fifteen players participated. It lasted for a full minute, which in fight-time is as long as an ice age. "Come on, motherfucker," Simmons yelled at Roy. "You can't play with me, you can't play with me."

"At that point, I knew football in NFL Europe was going to be taken serious by everyone," said Claymore cornerback Duane Hawthorne. "I mean, the first few scrimmages weren't so bad, but on that third scrimmage, there was a fight on nearly every play. It was some of the dirtiest football I've ever seen. You can't get away with that crap in the NFL. If you play dirty like that, you'll eventually pay the price."

After the so-called controlled scrimmage, Criner met the Scottish press for the first time of the season. Six reporters had flown over to check out the team and—more importantly—have a good time in the Sunshine State. "Hey guys," yelled Criner to the six press members. "Who's got the beer?"

Everyone pointed to Andy Colvin of *The Scottish Sun*, the largest daily paper in Scotland. Colvin had the long blond hair of a 1980s heavy-metal guitar player and he liked to party as if he were a rock star. Colvin was quick to tell the story of what took place during the 2000 Super Bowl at a party that the Claymores' front office had organized back in Glasgow. From 9 AM to 3 PM local time, Colvin sucked down exactly thirty-five longneck bottles of Budweiser. Perhaps more astonishing, Colvin made it out of the bar under his own power, staggering only slightly.

Criner knew the local press liked to have a good time. He'd seen this firsthand in Berlin during the 1999 season. After a 48–14 Scotland win, Criner gave his players the green light to drink in the hotel bar. He normally prohibits this, fearful of the potential problems it can cause, but on this night, after such a big win, Criner thought, What the hell, I'll let the boys have some spirits at the bar.

It was a night for the ages, as Colvin recounted. After the hotel bartender told Barry Stokes, an offensive lineman, that he'd stay open as long as they'd stay drinking, Stokes phoned virtually the entire team and told them to come on down. About thirty-five players did, and the soirée was in full swing. At about 5 AM, Matt Finkes decided it would be a good idea to show off his skills on the piano in the lobby. He played and crooned, "You've Lost that Loving Feeling," and soon everyone in the bar was singing along. It was a nice bonding moment for the team, as the players swayed back and forth to the music. But it was not a nice moment for the other hotel guests, most of whom were still sleeping. The partying got so loud that Criner eventually got wind of it. The coach walked down to the bar and told his players that it was time for bed. That was when a Scottish television producer stumbled up to Criner and slurred, "Ayee, come on, Jimmy. The boys are just blowing off a little steam. Can't you cut them some slack?"

But Criner was not swayed. Again he ordered his team to hit the sack. This time the players shuffled into their rooms in an eye-blink. The next afternoon one of the reporters, who requested that his name not be revealed, discovered that he had spent all of his money buying drinks and had no way to get to the airport. He missed his flight and had to buy another ticket at a premium. By the time he touched down in Scotland, he figured out that, in the last twelve hours, he had spent his entire season's budget. He missed every away game for the rest of the season, as the news organization he worked for punished him for his indulgence. Not that he had any regrets.

"That night in Berlin was one of the better nights of the season," he said. "That's why European journalists love this league. It's one big rolling party."

THIS STORY HAS become part of the Claymores' lore. Criner told it to his assistants as a cautionary tale with a straightforward moral: Don't spend too much time with the Scottish press. Criner felt that local press often played the role of enabler when they got around his players in bars. Despite this, Criner had cultivated good relations with local reporters over the years. In Criner's first year, the Claymores stumbled to a league-worst 2–8 record. But never during that woebegone season was Criner lampooned as a loser in the press. Rather he was canonized as a revolutionary, as the man who brought American football to the shores of Scotland. The local writers were diehard fans of the Claymores—a bias that was *not* taught in sport journalism 101—and they wanted American football to flower in their country. For his part, Criner understood that the league needed to have the press on its side if the American sport was ever going to flourish in Scotland. So the Criner-press relationship was, at its core, based on mutual self-interest.

After meeting the local reporters for five minutes at the end of the scrimmage in Orlando, Criner and the Claymores went back to the peachy-pink Harley Hotel. For the players, life at the Harley was no bowl of cherries. During training camp the Harley was being renovated and construction was ongoing everywhere. Starting at 8 AM every weekday, the cacophony of drills, jackhammers, sanders, and electric saws filled the halls of the hotel. This constant noise made it impossible for the Claymores to nap in their rooms in the afternoon, which is a necessity in any training camp.

"If you think it's bad now, you should have seen this place last year," said Finkes, who played for the Claymores during the 1999 season. "This is a five-star hotel compared to how awful it used to be."

One night during camp, the fire alarm in the hotel went off from 3 to 4:15 in the morning, forcing the players to scurry from their rooms to escape the noise. The next afternoon the Claymores had a scrimmage with Frankfurt. Not surprisingly, Scotland was a step slower than the Galaxy and was destroyed on the field. It wouldn't be the last time this season that the players would be awakened by the shrill of a fire alarm.

A few days before the Frankfurt scrimmage, linebackers Jon Hesse and Dave Menard returned to their room and found that their air-conditioner didn't work. That evening they told the front desk, and the next day the air-conditioner was fixed. But in their bathroom, Menard discovered that one of his muscle magazines had been opened to a picture of a steamy redhead in a string-bikini and there was a gooey, milky substance on the rim of the toilet. Menard quickly yelled out to Hesse, accusing his roommate of, let's say, singing solo. But in a matter of minutes Menard and Hesse determined that neither of them was responsible for that mess. Menard and Hesse then went down to the front desk to complain to the hotel manager.

"Can I help you?" asked the woman behind the front desk.

"Uh, I can't talk to you about this," Menard said. "I need to talk to a gentleman."

"Is it a boy problem?" asked the woman.

"You could say that," said Menard.

A male employee then walked over to speak with Menard. "We really should go outside to talk about this," said Menard. "I can't do this public."

The two went outside and talked. Menard said he suspected the air-conditioning repairman.

"That's really bizarre," the hotel manager said. "Do you need some disinfectant?"

"No," replied Menard, "I already, um, used a hot washcloth."

It was such a ridiculous situation that Hesse lost it. He collapsed on the ground in a fit of laughter. This incident revealed two things: The Harley was no Four Seasons, and Hesse was going to enjoy his time in NFL Europe. Daily life in this league is a struggle. If players can't laugh their way through some of the hard times off the field, it is difficult for them to be successful on the field.

For all its deficiencies, though, the Harley Hotel did offer one benefit to the players: It was only five minutes away from the Citrus Bowl, where the Claymores practiced. That bus ride, however, took the team through one of the poorest neighborhoods in Orlando. From both sides of the bus, players saw shirtless men on street corners tipping back 40-ounce beers hidden in brown paper bags—at nine in the morning. They saw bug-eyed junkies, just killing time between fixes. They saw leggy prostitutes loitering and proffering their services. They saw hopelessness in its ugliest form, and some of the players could relate to this scene personally. As Noel Scarlett, a defensive tackle on the Claymores, said during training camp, "I'm playing to eat, dawg. It's that motherfucking simple."

THE CLAYMORES' NATIONAL COACH, Stephen McCusker, knew firsthand how physically hard NFL Europe can be on players. When he first walked into the lockerroom at the Citrus Bowl in 1996 as a lightweight offensive guard, one thought entered his mind: Get me the hell out of here. His body was like a weeping willow compared to all the redwoods in the room. "I couldn't believe how big everyone was," recalled McCusker. "That night I went home and wrote a letter to my girlfriend back in Glasgow. I told her that I'd probably be home before that letter. I was so scared."

Every NFL Europe team is required to have a national coach on its coaching staff—a position that must be filled by a non-American—and eight national players. These players are also non-American and they must be active for every game. McCusker, who was from Glasgow, weighed only 240 pounds when he was a national player in 1996. The next lightest lineman that season tipped the scales at 285 pounds. At training camp, McCusker had as much success as Custer did at Little Big Horn. "The most painful experience of my life," was how he described it.

One of his responsibilities as national coach was to inform players on the day of cuts that Criner needed to see them—a job known as the "Turk." Cutting players is something that every coach in every league hates to do, but in NFL Europe it is an even more depressing task, because it usually means the end of a player's career. "It is devastating, I mean really devastating, for guys to be cut from our team," said Criner. "I feel so bad doing it, but it's just the reality of the business."

At training camp, the first round of cuts started at 6:30 AM. One of the first players to be let go was 6'4", 340-pound Bob Sapp, a massive defensive tackle who was originally a third-round draft selection of the Chicago Bears in 1997. Since then he'd bounced around from Minnesota, to Baltimore, and then to Oakland. Things just hadn't worked out for him. And now Sapp's career appeared to be over. McCusker worried for days about how Sapp would take the news, and as McCusker knocked on his door in the predawn light, he trembled.

"Bob, Coach needs to see you. Please bring your playbook," said McCusker. When McCusker looked at Sapp, it was as if he was looking at a ghost. He tried to look through Sapp while talking to him. This was McCusker's attempt at disassociating himself from the grimness of this task. Every Turk knows this trick.

"Okay, coach. No problem," replied Sapp.

Sapp then met with Criner. Instead of being upset, Sapp tried to console Criner, who got grandfatherly and emotional when relaying the news. Criner can be compassionate when he needs to be, even though he is conservative by nature when it comes to showing his emotions. "It's okay, Coach," said Sapp. "I'll be okay."

But not all of the players handled such news with the dignity of Sapp. Shawn McWashington, a wide receiver who the past season had led the Amsterdam Admirals in receiving with 39 catches, was shocked. At first he didn't accept that he could be cut. "Coach, there must be a mistake," he told Criner. He then wandered the halls of the Harley, dazed and a little crazed. He refused to have his exit physical that each player was required to undergo before heading home, and he refused to get on the bus that would take him to the Orlando International Airport. Finally, after three separate meetings with coaches, he agreed to get onto a bus that left the hotel at 1:30 PM. He was supposed to leave at 8:30 AM. "He just couldn't believe it," said Criner. "He just couldn't grasp that this was maybe the end of the line for him."

Another player who had trouble dealing with the news was a back-up wide receiver. As soon as Criner cut him and handed him back his passport—the coaching staff held onto all the passports of all the players, so they didn't get lost—this player summarily ripped it in half. Though Criner had told the player that he might get a call at any time during the season to rejoin the team if someone got hurt, he didn't seem to care. "I've never seen anyone so mad after he got cut," said Damon Gibson, a receiver for the Claymores. "He felt like, if you cut me now, I don't ever want to play for you. And I guess he took care of that by ripping up that passport."

This player wasn't so much throwing away a chance to earn money as he was an opportunity to get back to the NFL. Players who make the roster only earn about $1,000 a week during the season. (One NFL Europe player, who attended a Big-Ten school, was paid more than that in each of his four years in college.) In training camp the wages were even more paltry. Players were paid only $14 a day during camp. During one night out at Scruffy Murphy's, an Irish pub that was the team's favorite swizzle stick during camp, Matt Finkes nearly spent his entire training camp per diem by buying drinks for his teammates.

"NFL Europe is all about getting into the NFL and not about the money," said Antonio Dingle, a defensive tackle for the Claymores. "I'm calling it a stairway to the NFL, because that's what it's going to be for me. If you care about the money, you shouldn't be here. You just shouldn't."

Indeed, by the end of training camp every player knew that NFL Europe was more about dreams than dollars. For guys like Dingle, it was a quixotic attempt to recapture past glory—and, for some lucky players, it would be a path to future greatness.

3 The Ingredients

Quarterback Kevin Daft holds the Royal Flag of Scotland.

Orlando, Florida. The Last Day of Training Camp

THE CLAYMORES BROKE camp in Orlando on April 4, 2000. The team spent the morning in small meeting rooms at the Harley and the afternoon was devoted to packing. As the players stuffed their lives and dreams into a few suitcases, most of them were both scared and excited. Scared of the unknown, of leaving the land of their boyhoods, of traveling to places they'd never been before. But excited to play again, to be back in the action, to have that second chance to prove to the scouts that they were NFL-worthy. "This is both good and bad," said defensive end Chris Ward, who played at the University of Kentucky and spent the 1999 preseason with the Tennessee Titans. "I wish I wasn't leaving the States, but I know it's my only way back to the NFL."

That night, at 7 PM, the Claymores left summery Florida and boarded a British Airways 747 that was bound for wintry Scotland. There are no charters in NFL Europe; it is an economy-class league. Every player on this plane had made sacrifices to play in Europe. Punter Jon Ballantyne, a native of Australia, had left his fiancée in Melbourne, then taken a plane ride from hell. The league had found Ballantyne a cheap ticket to Orlando, but he was forced to have extended layovers in Los Angeles and Miami. It had taken Ballantyne more than thirty-five hours to complete his globe-trotting journey. "I became excellent at the game of solitaire," said Ballantyne. "Without cards, I would have gone nuts."

Ballantyne had a sinfully strong leg, and he'd believed he was going to have a chance to display his skill when the Broncos played the Chargers in Australia during the 1999 preseason. Late in the fourth quarter, Ballantyne, who was signed by the Broncos as a third-string punter for that one game, thought he would finally get a chance to kick. The Broncos faced a 3rd and 10 in their own territory. But that was when he saw a familiar figure jog out onto the field from the Chargers' sidelines—his old Claymores' roommate from the 1999 NFL Europe season, cornerback Clifford Ivory. "I just said to myself, please don't throw at Clifford," recalled Ballantyne, who had seen Ivory get repeatedly toasted when the two played together with the Claymores.

Ivory promptly got burned for a first down. A few plays later, the Broncos faced a 3rd and 35. Ballantyne once again assumed his dream would finally happen, that he'd get to kick in an NFL game in front of his friends and family. But Ivory was still on the field, which meant that anything could—and likely would—happen. Incredibly, Ivory got beat and Denver made another first down. Ballantyne never punted in the game. "I'm going back to NFL Europe because I want that chance to kick in the NFL," said Ballantyne. "Hopefully, Clifford won't be around when my time comes again."

Another player who'd had a long trip to Orlando was tight end Nachi Abe, a national player from Tokyo. Abe didn't possess much talent—he had only played football for a few years—but he'd stopped his life in Japan to participate in NFL Europe. Even though his biggest contribution to the team would be to teach players how to say dirty words in Japanese, Abe would savor every second of the season. "Football is the greatest game on the planet," said Abe. "I even like practices."

The American players liked to have fun with Abe. One time at a fan party in Glasgow during the season, free safety Blaine McElmurry told a crowd of people that Abe's real name was Sachi Hatchi, which in Japanese means "cocksucker." Abe didn't know that McElmurry had done this. So as Abe sat at a table, fans would approach him with a pen in their hands and ask Mr. Sachi Hatchi for an autograph. The bewildered look on Abe's moon-bright face was priceless, one of the best memories that McElmurry would take from the season. "The funniest thing I ever saw," said McElmurry.

Another player on the plane was Rickey Brady, a tight end who'd played at Oklahoma. Brady had left behind his wife in Norman, Oklahoma, to be a Claymore. A religious, friendly player, Brady was on the scene in Oklahoma City minutes after the bombing of the federal building in 1995. One of his high-school friends perished in the tragedy and Brady could tell stories from that April afternoon that brought tears to your eyes. "It was just awful," said Brady. "The destruction was everywhere. I don't even like to think about it." Brady would miss his wife profoundly during the season. The first time he laid eyes on her, years ago in his youth, Brady's heart nearly stopped. This season his heart would break when she was forced to undergo emergency surgery in Norman. Quitting football suddenly became a real possibility.

Sitting close to Brady was offensive tackle Ben Cavil, who'd played with him at Oklahoma. Cavil had left his wife, child, and his job as a car salesman in Houston, Texas, to be on this plane. Big Ben, as his teammates called him, was as plump as a Christmas goose and, at age twenty-eight, one of the oldest players on the team. Cavil would rarely leave his hotel room in Scotland, but his constant smile and easygoing demeanor would make him a favorite among the players in the locker room. In the darkest hour of the season, his encouraging words would save the Claymores. He would be the man who came riding into town on the white horse.

Glasgow, Scotland. Two Weeks Before the Claymores' Home Opener

"British Airways really screwed up," said Criner, referring to the team's flight to Scotland. "We always try to get our lineman in aisle seats so they can stretch out a little, but they didn't honor our requests and they wouldn't let our guys move around. Travel is so important in this league and when it doesn't go well, it can have a tremendous effect on your team. Hopefully, that won't happen again."

The Claymores touched down in Glasgow on an early-spring afternoon. A wet chill hung in the air. The team took a bus to the Quality Central Hotel, where the Claymores would live for the next three months, and then Criner gave his players a day off. He wanted to give them a chance to recover from their jet lag and acclimate to their new surroundings. This wasn't easy, because the first thing the players noticed when they stepped off the plane in Glasgow was that, while technically English is spoken there, to the American ear, it's extremely difficult to understand. "I think we were given some bad information," said defensive tackle Antonio Dingle. "The people here may as well be speaking French for all I can tell."

When Criner had a chance to review his notes from the last days of training camp, he felt good about his players. As he did when he first addressed them, Criner still believed that the Claymores had all the ingredients of a championship team. And many league officials agreed. Based on what they'd seen in Orlando during training camp, most NFL Europe executives were privately betting that the Claymores would be one of the two teams to advance to the World Bowl.

The Claymores' defense, led by an outstanding defensive line and two quality cornerbacks in Duane Hawthorne and Kory Blackwell, had a chance to be the best in the league. And their offense, while it wouldn't be the most productive in NFL Europe, would be serviceable if either Kevin Daft or Marcus Crandell could merely be ordinary at quarterback. The offensive line was strong, and running back Aaron Stecker, Criner felt, was the most talented back in the league. "I'm the kind of coach who adapts gameplans to the types of players I have," said Criner. "But I gotta admit that I love this kind of football, having a tough defense and a strong running game."

Criner was also in high spirits when the team arrived in Glasgow simply because another season was set to begin, one replete with delicious possibilities. The flowers were shouting their colors in Scotland, the grass was growing greener by the hour, and it was almost time to kick off NFL Europe's season. To see Criner on the days leading up to Scotland's first game was like seeing a young boy before his birthday. The excitement lit up his face.

"All things considered, we came out of training camp in pretty good shape," said Criner. "We lost six offensive lineman who we thought we'd have before camp even started. Three were allocated to us and just didn't show up and three failed their physicals, so we really had to rebuild our line. I think we're close to doing that. Also, I think our defense could be really special. We've got players at every position. What I'm not sure about is our quarterback situation."

Over the years, NFL Europe has acquired a reputation for developing and delivering quarterbacks to the NFL. In 1999, for example, seventeen former NFL Europe signal-callers were on NFL rosters. NFL Europe executives like to boast, with some validity, that the most fertile breeding ground for NFL quarterbacks is not the NFL draft, but NFL Europe. In 1999, four of the eight highest-ranked passers in the NFL were alumni of Europe: Kurt Warner of the Rams, Brad Johnson of the Redskins, Jon Kitna of the Seahawks, and Damon Huard of the Dolphins.

"Each year we've had quarterbacks come over and they've done well, and I think that will continue," said Ray Willsey, NFL Europe's director of operations. "That's one of the positions where you can see marked improvement in a player by his playing in NFL Europe."

NFL Europe lends itself to being a quarterback-friendly league. Cornerbacks and safeties tend to be a step slow in NFL Europe, which means wideouts can usually get separation from defensive backs one to two seconds into each play. Also, there are precious few defensive linemen who go to Europe who are dominating. This means defensive coordinators, if they want to pressure the quarterback, will employ various blitzes. Since league rules mandate that the defense can only rush six players, the best defensive coordinators will design relatively complex blitz packages. But if the quarterback can read this quickly, he should be able to find an open running back or tight end. Kurt Warner learned this skill in Europe and now he's the top blitz-busting quarterback in the NFL.

Most of all, though, it's a good league for quarterbacks simply because it gives them a chance to get on the field and play. "When you're an undrafted quarterback in NFL training camp, you don't get many repetitions," said Jim Kubiak, a quarterback for the Amsterdam Admirals. "You might get a couple of reps, and based on those limited opportunities, teams will either decide to keep you around or not. But here everybody plays. You're part of a team and everybody works hard. You get better."

You also get known, which was what happened to Jon Kitna, who won a World League championship and MVP award with Barcelona in 1997. "I wouldn't be where I'm at right now without going over there," said Kitna, who went to college at Central Washington, a NAIA school. "For guys like me who have no chance at the NFL, Europe was my big chance. Guys who take the Europe league seriously can use it to help their future."

No one on the Claymores' roster took the game more seriously than quarterback Kevin Daft. On the day after Super Bowl XXXIV, Titans coach Jeff Fisher called Daft into his office. He told his third-string quarterback that he'd like him to go play in Europe, but the decision was ultimately his. Fisher then gave him twenty-four hours to decide. "I slept on it and then told Coach Fisher that I'd go," said Daft. "He clearly wanted me to go and I wanted a chance to actually play. Even though I was tired and was really looking forward to some time off, I just thought coming to Europe would be the best thing for my career."

A few weeks later, Daft was on vacation in California when his father called and told him that the NFL Europe quarterback allocation had taken place. This is the event in which Ray Willsey distributes the eligible quarterbacks to the six teams. Willsey is a matchmaker of teams and players, trying as much as possible to accommodate each coach's wish list. "There are surprisingly few arguments when it comes to the quarterback allocation," said Willsey. "It usually goes fairly smoothly."

After being given the news by his father, Daft then logged onto the Internet and found out that he'd been allocated to Scotland. With his girlfriend Kesa Koida, they looked up Scotland and Glasgow in various encyclopedias, trying to learn as much as they could about their future home. "We really had no idea what Scotland was like," said Kesa. "Neither of us had been to Europe before, so we had to do our research."

Kevin and Kesa met at Division II UC-Davis, where Daft started 23 games at quarterback during his junior and senior years. Playing in front of crowds of about 5,000 a game at tiny Tommey Field, Daft set school records for career passing yards (7,601), 300-yard games (11), attempts (982), completions (566), touchdowns (68), and total offense (7,696 yards). But even though the 6'1", 200-pound Daft was putting up big-league numbers, he still thought of himself as more of a little-league quarterback, as he wasn't planning on a career in the NFL. Daft, who'd majored in biological sciences, was preparing to go to medical school and study to become an orthopedic surgeon when the Titans surprisingly selected him in the fifth round of the 1999 draft. Daft made the Titans' roster by beating out quarterback Steve Matthews, who played for the Scottish Claymores in 1996, for the third-string job.

Daft didn't see any action for Tennessee during their Super Bowl season, but he did make an impression on Les Steckel, the Titans' offensive coordinator. On several occasions, Steckel pulled his rookie quarterback aside to tell Daft that he had the tools to play in the NFL—for a very long time. Daft needed to hear this, because he's not the type of player who oozes confidence. But Steckel's encouragement helped Daft believe in himself. One season removed from Division II, Daft eventually grew comfortable with being under the bright lights of the NFL. "Coming from a small school you question whether or not you belong in the NFL," said Daft. "But I really feel like I belong now."

Daft, who grew up in Orange Country, California, was refreshingly innocent. He retained the look of a wide-eyed teenager and was genuinely floored by the size of the bonuses he received in the playoffs—all for just holding a clipboard on the sidelines. He brought his video camera with him everywhere during Super Bowl week to record the event and he and Kesa still marvel at the perks of being a professional football player. "It's unreal," said Kesa. "People seem to just give you stuff—shirts, shorts, whatever—all the time. But we're not complaining."

Many quarterbacks in the NFL possess larger-than-life personalities, lighting up rooms and arenas just by their presence. Daft was not one of these guys. When he walked into a room or an arena, he was usually the quietest person there. During the Claymores' season, Daft was one of the most reticent players on the team. When offensive coordinator Vince Alcalde would tell Daft something over his headset during a game, Alcalde would frequently be surprised by how little Daft contributed to their dialogue. "I'd tell him something and then it would just be quiet on the other end," said Alcalde. "I mean, he usually just wasn't that inquisitive." Worse, sometimes Daft's stony demeanor would get misinterpreted by his teammates as aloofness. This is not good for the morale of a team, especially when things start to fall apart on the field.

"What Kevin excels at is protecting the ball and making smart decisions," said Criner. "That's why we targeted him as a guy we wanted. We don't need him to pass for four touchdowns and 300 yards each game. We just need him to be smart and be a good game manager."

Daft was a conservative quarterback, usually opting to throw the safe pass. At the other end of the spectrum was Marcus Crandell. A shade under 6 feet and about 200 pounds, Crandell was an undersized quarterback by NFL standards. But when a play broke down, Crandell had that special ability to create something out of nothing. He was quick enough to pick up yards with his feet, like a Donovon McNabb, and he had a strong enough arm to complete those dangerous, across-the-field throws, like a Daunte Culpepper. The only reasons he wasn't playing on Sundays in the States were that he had a propensity to be intercepted and he wasn't as accurate as most NFL quarterbacks. "When Marcus is on, he can really move our team," said Alcalde. "But when he's off, he can really hurt our team."

Crandell had not lived a charmed life. Raised in Robersonville, North Carolina, which is thirty minutes northeast of Greenville, Crandell lost his mother when he was five to diabetes and hypertension. Soon after she passed away, his father split for Charlotte, leaving Crandell and his three older siblings. Latricia, the oldest of the four, became Marcus's guardian. "Marcus has always been quiet," said Latricia, who is seventeen years older than Marcus. "Then again, we all are."

Latricia always taught Marcus the importance of maintaining his composure, no matter how explosive the situation. Growing up, he took that lesson and applied to it to baseball, where as a teenager he was a standout pitcher and shortstop. "Marcus was a big baseball player," said Latricia. "I didn't want him to play football because of the injuries. But the coaches at Roanoke High convinced him, and me, that playing football was okay."

Crandell quickly emerged as the star of the Roanoke Redskins. At the high school level, he turned running the option into an art form, leading his team to the state title game in 1990. Recruiters showed up at his games and were smitten with what they saw. They all viewed Crandell as a blue-chip recruit—but as a defensive back. Crandell chose East Carolina because it was one of the few schools that said it would give him a chance to play quarterback. "I really don't think

East Carolina thought he was going to be a quarterback either," said Doc Avery, Crandell's coach at Roanoke High. "They offered it to him because he was close and he was a great athlete."

In his first year at ECU, Crandell ran the scout team during practice. It was during these practices that it became clear he would not be moving to defensive back. "He was wearing out the defenses," said Avery. Crandell was named outstanding scout team player his freshman season. The next year he became the starting quarterback. By the time he was done at ECU, Crandell had set a career record with 7,198 yards passing. "Marcus is a natural quarterback and natural leader," said ECU coach Steve Logan. "People put too much stock on a player's size and height. I think the NFL made that mistake with Jeff Blake, and I think they're making the same mistake with Marcus."

Crandell wasn't drafted, so he headed north to the football badlands and played for three seasons for the Edmonton Eskimos of the CFL. He was never able to win a starting job, however. That was why he decided to give Europe a shot when Criner called and told him he'd be given a fair opportunity to earn the starting job for the Claymores. The money wasn't as good as it was in Canada, but Crandell believed that if he could start, the experience he got in Europe would be more valuable than a few paychecks from the Eskimos. "I believe in my ability," said Crandell one day in the lobby of the Central, his voice barely louder than a whisper. "I believe I'm good enough to be in the NFL. I just want a chance to play, to show people what I can do."

Before the season was done, that chance would be stripped away from Crandell—not because of what would happen on the field but off of it.

DAFT WAS UNDERWHELMING in training camp, falling slightly behind Crandell in the coaches' minds. But then at a practice in Glasgow a week before the Claymores' season opener against Amsterdam, Daft outperformed Crandell in a two-minute drill. Because the offense was sputtering, Alcalde didn't believe that they would score many points against Amsterdam. He thought that the game would be decided in the final two minutes, so he recommended to Criner that Daft, based on Tuesday's drill, be named the starter. The coach agreed.

"We are basically running the Titans' offense here," said Alcalde. "Kevin knows it and he won't lose the game for us. Honestly, we don't feel pressure to play Kevin because he was a big-name allocation. We're playing him simply because we think he gives us a better chance to win."

Alcalde and Criner also knew one simple fact: In the short NFL Europe season, no team had ever lost their first game and then gone on to play in the World Bowl. Daft may not have been a sexy quarterback, but he wouldn't make a stupid play that would cost them the game—or so they hoped.

4 History

Criner greets NFL Commissioner Paul Tagliabue.

New York. 1989

IT BEGAN WITH a simple question, asked more than a decade ago. Network television officials, who are always in search of reasonably priced nonbaseball sports programming in the spring, asked the NFL in January 1989 if the league could begin April-to-June football by 1990. Intrigued, the league decided to investigate the possibility. So the NFL hired Tex Schramm and gave him three months and $1.4 million in seed money to find out if the idea, which included teams in other countries, could work.

Schramm seemed like the right man for the job. As president and general manager of the Dallas Cowboys, he was responsible for turning Dallas into one of the game's marquee franchises. He had also brought Pete Rozell into the NFL and headed the league's competition committee for years. The fact that he was experienced and respected in every NFL circle gave legitimacy to the entire endeavor.

Schramm packed his bags and lit a blue streak around the globe, scouting cities for potential franchises. Many cities gave Schramm the royal treatment. In Birmingham, Alabama, a thousand local residents greeted Schramm at the airport and chanted, "We want a team! We want a team!" Orlando, Florida and its business community promised Schramm it would move heaven and earth—read: provide tax relief—if they got a team. But the most impressive sales pitch came in Nashville, Tennessee, where Johnny Cash left his wife June's sixtieth birthday gala for two hours to meet Schramm's chartered jet. Yes, for a few weeks Schramm seemed to be as popular as the Pope as he jumped from city to city.

The world was Schramm's laboratory. He had some bold ideas he wanted to implement in his new league. He dreamed of putting a radio receiver in the quarterback's helmet so that coaches could give him the plays directly (which is now standard practice in the NFL) instead of through hand-signals. He also wanted to ban huddles (which now *isn't* standard practice in the NFL or NFL Europe), a move aimed at speeding up play and making the game more appealing to European audiences.

But almost from the beginning, Schramm and NFL officials had different visions of what the World League of American Football, as it was then called, should look like. Schramm envisioned the WLAF to be big and bold and profitable; all the NFL wanted was a little spring football league, which would feed the parent league some players, make it a nominal amount of money, and expand interest in the NFL throughout Europe—maybe someday the world. In October 1990, with their views increasingly colliding, the NFL fired Schramm. "I know this sounds corny," said Schramm at the time, "but if you dare to be great, dare to do something different and unique, it's possible that something like this can happen. I wasn't going to sit by, knowing we've got a good league. It's not my nature. I wanted this league to be great."

Mike Lynn, who had been general manager of the Minnesota Vikings, replaced Schramm as president of the WLAF. Lynn shared the same view as the majority of the NFL owners, who believed that the WLAF should have a narrower focus than what Schramm had wanted. A month after Lynn was hired, with the NFL and the WLAF executives in agreement over what the league should look like, the NFL owners gave final approval for the startup of the WLAF. The great international experiment was underway.

"We're in this to make money," announced Lynn in 1990 at a press conference in New York City. "We're motivated by what happened when we tested the market in 1983 and our tests since then. When the Vikings went to Great Britain in 1983 [for an exhibition game], we had zero marketing sales. Last year [1989], the NFL sold $50 million in Great Britain alone. *One country.* Take that and multiply it by thirty, and you see what we're looking at. Imagine two hundred million Chinese wearing World League stuff. No, five hundred million Chinese."

If you're going to dream, you may as well dream big.

WHEN THE INAUGURAL WLAF season kicked off on March 23, 1991, teams were based in such disparate locales as Frankfurt, Germany; Birmingham, Alabama; and Sacramento, California. The ten-team league spanned two continents, five countries, and nine time zones. This presented more than just logistical problems. In Barcelona, for example, the endzones at Montjuic Stadium were only 7 feet deep. But what really caused migranes among league officials in the early days of WLAF was trying to answer this question: How do you translate the nuances of American football to a European audience raised on soccer while at the same time convincing Americans to watch minor-league football? The answer: You can't—at least not overnight.

From day one, league executives had believed that the game could flourish overseas. This would take time, they all agreed, and they had to take steps to slowly infiltrate the European sporting culture. It was Schramm who'd first envisioned each foreign team as having "national" players. These would be home-grown heroes who would give the local fans a source of pride, a sense of identity with the teams. The original program to get this started was called "Operation Discovery," which was a three-month worldwide search for players that was conducted by former Denver Broncos assistant coach John Ralston. Operation Discovery faced a daunting task before the league's first season opened. To wit: "One of the foreign guys we had was 6'6", 250 pounds, and he was running full speed down the field," related Lee Corso, who in 1991 was the general manager of the Orlando Thunder. "Then he got cracked under the chin. He said this wasn't anything like soccer. He went home and never came back."

The era of global football opened in Frankfurt with the Galaxy taking on the London Monarchs. Oliver Luck, who at the time was the general manager of the Galaxy and later became the president of NFL Europe, watched the game's initial possession in disbelief. Luck had to laugh as he and all of Frankfurt watched the London Monarchs' offense move backward into its own endzone, while the scoreboard rang up 2 points for the team without the ball. Oh no, thought Luck. Is anyone going to know what's going on here?

But even in those early days, when many of the Europeans in the crowd didn't have a clue as to what was happening on the field, Luck bore the look of a conquering hero when he would mingle with the fans before the games at Frankfurt's Waldstadion. Even though it would be two-and-half hours before kickoff, there would be tens of thousands of fans on the grounds, tossing rubber footballs and listening to rock music blaring from a 10-foot high sound system shaped like a football helmet. This was all Luck's idea, to make football into a daylong experience. As Luck would walk through the crowds, hundreds of fans would stop and wave. He'd shake hands, catch a football, chat with sausage vendors; he'd even kiss a baby every now and then.

"The fans want a slice of American life," said Luck at the time. "That includes tailgate parties and cheerleaders. They're fascinated with all things American. Our biggest challenge is convincing people who don't know anything about American football that this will be a fun sport. We want to mix entertainment and sport and I think we have. These pregame parties are a blast for everyone."

But not all of Luck's experiences proved as positive, as *Sports Illustrated* recounted in August 1993. Back in the early 1990s, Luck conducted a series of football clinics in the former East Germany. Afterward, he stayed to watch two local teams clash in the first football game ever played in the city of Cottbus, near the Polish border. In the crowd he noticed one boy in a Los Angeles Raiders cap and another in a San Francisco 49ers jersey. The NFL had done it, Luck thought to himself, it had won the hearts and pocketbooks of people living in the former Soviet bloc. Luck approached the boys and introduced himself, a lieutenant from the world-renowned NFL. "Ah," said one of the boys in German, clearly impressed. "The NFL—it is a clothing company?"

"That told me two things," Luck told *SI*. "That NFL properties has done a great job in merchandizing over here. But it also said that, in other areas, we still have a long way to go."

Indeed they did. In 1992, after two seasons and $20 million in losses, the league shut down. A worldwide recession had hit and fans in the United States had failed to warm to the idea of spring football, so the venture collapsed. The NFL didn't really seem to mind at the time. The league was distracted by labor unrest and by the lack of a television contract. With those issues looming, the NFL let the WLAF, which had sent thirty-two players on to NFL rosters, die a quiet death.

THREE YEARS LATER, the league was back with a different vision. Gone was the effort to force minor-league football on the American ticket-buying public. This time there were just six European teams—all jointly owned and funded by the NFL and FOX television—and a lean budget of $40 million for four years. The NFL embarked on a double-barreled approach: the return of an NFL-backed professional league and the development of foreign interest in the game through more sponsorship of high-school level football in the cities where the teams were based. Also, the NFL changed its expectations of the league. Instead of being an instrument for profit, it was now looked upon as a testing ground for possible expansion overseas. "We see the league as a tool to make American football more popular," said one NFL official. "Ultimately, we'd like to expand the World League to the Far East and Latin America."

The league was rechristened NFL Europe and is now gaining more credibility in the NFL every season. No longer seen as merely a public-relations arm of the NFL, NFL Europe more closely resembles a minor-league than a throwaway league. At the start of the 2000 NFL regular season, there were 159 players on NFL rosters who had NFL Europe experience.

"The talent and competition are getting better every year in the Europe league," according to Bill Kuharic, former Saints president and general manager. "If we can get one or two every year from the people we send over there to be a role player or a special teams standout, we've strengthened our team. And it becomes like dominoes. The more success such players have in the NFL, the more receptive future players will be to going to Europe."

"You've got to keep all of this in perspective, of course," added Giants' General Manager Ernie Accorsi. "It is a developmental league, so we see it differently than the fans do. But all of us are getting much more enthusiastic about it. We scout the heck out of the league. Players need to realize that we are treating it seriously, and if they play well, they might have a chance when they return home."

The next step is expansion, which many NFL Europe executives in early 2001 believed was just a year or two away. Sites in Italy, France, and Poland are among those under consideration. "We have six teams now, and that's pretty much the minimum you can run a league on," said David Tossell, an NFL Europe spokesman. "We're starting to get pressure from NFL owners to add two more teams. They look at the way players are developing, but there can only be six starting quarterbacks developed in NFL Europe each season. They want to get more of their guys a chance to have the opportunity that Kurt Warner had."

Though NFL Europe has consistently lost money over the years, the actual bottom line is difficult to gauge. The league has expanded interest in the NFL abroad, which has caused the sale of NFL merchandise in Europe to mushroom. "The league is getting closer to profitability and we continue to grow toward a positive number," claimed Bill Peterson, president of NFL Europe. "The current growth percentage is very acceptable to our people."

Pure profits, though, won't determine the fate of the league. In the short term, that depends on how many Kurt Warners can emerge from the sideshow in Europe and prosper on the main stage in the States. Warner was undoubtedly the best thing to ever happen to the league, but now there is an expectation that the league can produce more similarly gifted players. Can NFL Europe do that? The answer will decide how long the league lasts.

5 The Central

Pre-game prayer session.

Glasgow, Scotland. Two Days Before Game One

IN SOUTHWEST SCOTLAND, on the banks of the River Clyde, lies the blue-collar city of Glasgow, a place that can be both brutal and beautiful. Situated in the country's lowlands, Glasgow is Scotland's largest city (population 611,600) and principal seaport. Because Glasgow is the shipbuilding center of the entire United Kingdom, it is a largely working-class town and its citizens are notoriously hard-boiled.

The soul of the city is its downtown, an aging area that wages a daily battle between development and decay, and swarms with folks at all hours of the day. Pubs sit on nearly every street corner. Sallow-skinned homeless people, including many children, pander aggressively on the streets. Men in business suits walk in a quick, purposeful gait. Laborers, dirty and tired, stand around and chat about their hard life and times. And in both the light of day and dark of night, there are intoxicated people stumbling around and looking for trouble. This was the environment that the Scottish Claymores would live in for three months during their stay at the Quality Central Hotel.

The players and their families had had problems in Glasgow in the past. One night in the 1999 season, linebacker Jon Hesse—who returned to the Claymores for the 2000 season—and his wife, Amy, went on a late-night pizza run. When they arrived at the pizzeria, Hesse realized he didn't have any money. He told his wife to stay put and went off into the night in search of an ATM. A few minutes after Hesse left, a drunk man in his twenties who said he was from Amsterdam stumbled in. Amy, a petite blonde, tried to ignore him. But after arguing with the store manager behind the counter, the man unzipped his pants and started waving around his most private part. He then started toward Amy, who pushed him away. At this point another man waiting for pizza intervened and shoved the intoxicated foreigner backward. The predator, who was only about 5'6" and 150 pounds, challenged him to a knife fight. Right then Hesse, a towering 6'4" and 250 pounds, returned to the pizzeria. Not wanting to tussle with Hesse, the man disappeared into the darkness, screaming at the top of his lungs that he wanted to kill someone as he brandished a switchblade he had pulled out of his back pocket. No one was hurt that time, but such unsettling occurrences happen with disturbing frequency on the cobblestone streets of downtown Glasgow.

49

THE PROVING GROUND

According to several players who were on the 1999 Claymores' roster, one of the reasons why the team stumbled to a 4–6 record that year was that too many players had bouts with the bottle and spent too much time in the pubs. Players frequently showed up hung-over at practice—and occasionally even at games. In order to prevent the same thing from happening in the 2000 season, Criner did two things: he tried to pack his roster with "players of character," even at times sacrificing talent; and he set up numerous activities in Glasgow for the players that were both free of charge and free of booze. By simply waving a laminated card with the Claymores' logo on it, players could get into movies and a bowling alley for free and they also received discounts from many stores and restaurants. "We needed to give them something to do rather than just go and sit in a bar," explained Criner. "These activities at least gave them some alternatives."

Ah, but boys will be boys, and on the night before their opener at home against Amsterdam, three players snuck out of the Central after curfew. They were in their rooms for bedcheck, which was at 11 PM, and then went out to a club until one in the morning. When they returned to the hotel, they passed by Coach Kent, who happened to be sitting in the lobby. The next morning at a defensive unit meeting, Myrel Moore, the team's defensive coordinator, exploded at them.

"Do not fuck with me!" Moore yelled at his defense. "I'll send your fucking ass home in a heartbeat if you do. Next time anyone sneaks out after bedcheck, you'll get a $1,000 fine."

THE QUALITY CENTRAL Hotel encompasses six floors and houses 220 single, double, and triple rooms. The high ceilings and massive stairway in the hotel lobby give it the look and feel of the Overlook Hotel in *The Shining*. And Stephen King would do well to research this place as a setting for another horror story. Many of the players believed that the Central was haunted.

"I'm a hundred percent positive that spirits live in this hotel," said Antonio Dingle. "A couple of really strange things have happened in my room. The windows will steam up and I'll see a small child's hand print. The first night I was here I felt like I was pinned in my bed for five minutes. I tried to get up, but I couldn't. When you walk on the fifth floor it feels like something overhead is taking the same steps that you are taking. You can hear it. It's spooky. I respect all things, even spirits. At first I made wisecracks about this, but no more."

Back in the 1970s, one of the hotel chefs committed suicide by jumping out of a sixth-floor window. Local legend has it that the chef haunted the sixth floor, which, because of financial considerations, is no longer in use. "Strange things have always happened in this hotel," said Scott Couper, a wide receiver who is a national player from Glasgow.

Couper holds a Ph.D. in Polymer Chemistry from Strathclyde University in Glasgow. His teammates called him "Dr. Scoops" and he was one of the top national players in NFL Europe. He ran the 40 in 4.38 and had sure hands. He also had a keen sense of humor, and he liked to scare his teammates by regaling them with tales of demons residing in the Central. Most players dismissed these stories as nonsense, but some of the more gullible found them unsettling. "It's fun to joke with the guys about the Central," said Couper. "It's surprising how many of them actually believe the stuff I say."

Couper picked up the sport when he was in high school, tossing around a football with friends after the school days were done. Couper learned the game quickly and beat out hundreds of other local players to earn a roster spot with the Claymores in 1995, the first year of the team's existence. In the offseason he worked for the Claymores' front office, trying to spread the gospel of American football to as many people in his homeland as possible. And like many of the guys on the team, Couper clung to football because it made him feel young and free. "I just like the life of a football player," said Couper. "Being in the locker room and being around the guys is much more fun to me than sitting behind a desk all day. That's why I never want to give this up. I'll probably play as long as they let me. Then I guess I'll have to look for a real job."

Couper showed the players around the Central when they first arrived. One of the first stops was the basement, which during World War II served as a morgue. Though the bodies had long since been removed, the basement of the Central still had an eerie, death-chamber quality to it. It was dank, unfinished, and the place where the Claymores' weight and training rooms were located. Many of the players were so spooked by the area that they wouldn't go down there alone.

Next to the weight room, which was about the size of a typical junior-high weight room, was the trainer's office. This was where players came for treatment and received their medication. It was alarming how frequently this place would be choked with players throughout the season. Even at this level, football is more brutal and more violent than most fans can fathom.

The coaches didn't have it much better than the players. The team rented out a wing of rooms on the second floor that served as both coaches' offices and team meeting rooms. These spaces were small, poorly lit, and not well ventilated, which often made the meetings seem achingly long. The quarters were so tight that it made the day-to-day interactions among the coaches stressful. Eventually, a few assistants would confess that by late in the season it was a minor miracle that they tolerated the daily upbraidings Criner gave them in these meetings. "He is too hard on us," said one coach. "We don't make that much money, but he seems to think that we are as well-paid as NFL coaches. I don't know how long we can put up with it."

Each player had his own room in Central—a luxury the Claymores didn't have in the 1999 season. The furniture in the rooms was vintage 1950 and the shower water was sometimes green. Most of the players' rooms were smaller than a typical college dorm room. The wallpaper was flaking and the carpet, more often than not, had water stains. There was enough space in each room for a single bed and desk, but that was it. When the players' wives or girlfriends came to Scotland during the season, players would frequently sleep on the floor because two people couldn't fit on a bed. "It's tough to get a good night's rest when you're on the floor," said punter Jon Ballantyne, who was forced to the floor when his fiancée Vicki visited Glasgow during the season. "But it is physically impossible for two people to sleep on most of these beds."

Each player had an old, tiny television that got four channels in English; they also had a radio. A few players brought laptop computers to Scotland, but they couldn't access the Internet from the rooms because the phones were rotary. There was no voice mail on the phones, either. If someone tried to get in touch with a player and he wasn't in his room, a hotel receptionist would jot down a message. The receptionist would then write the player's name down on a big chalkboard that was in the lobby, informing them that they had a message. "It's kind of like we're living in the 1940s," observed Finkes. "The technology gap between Scotland and the United States is pretty remarkable."

Glasgow, Scotland. Game One

At 11:45 AM two buses carrying the Claymores pulled out of the Central for Murrayfield Stadium, a cavernous place that seated 67,500 and was located forty-five minutes away in Edinburgh. Back in 1975 over 104,000 people poured into Murrayfield to watch a rugby match, which today still stands as a world-record rugby crowd. This season the Claymores, even though they lived and practiced in Glasgow, played their first three home games in Edinburgh's Murrayfield Stadium; their last two games were played in Glasgow. The reason for this splitting of their home games was because the Claymores' front office was hoping to build their fan base. Last season the team drew about 10,000 to each of their home games.

As the buses navigated through the narrow streets of Glasgow bound for Murrayfield, a hard rain started to fall. The rain then turned to hail. As the players looked out the window at the misery outside, few words were uttered. "You'll have to start enjoying the bad weather boys," said national coach Stephen McCusker to the players on the second bus, trying to lighten the mood, "because in Scotland it's the only kind of weather we have."

Ten minutes before kickoff, the rain stopped. Sunshine poured through the torn sky. Inside the Claymores' locker room, Coach Criner flitted from player to player. He implored everyone to play with passion and, more importantly, to play with class. These would be the recurring themes of Criner's pregame speeches throughout the season. "We know we have a great team here," Criner said to his players. "Let's make a statement to the league about what the Scottish Claymores are all about."

The players then ran out into the heavy, cold afternoon. Even though this wasn't the most critical game any of these players had ever suited up for, they showed their nervousness early on. In the first series of the game, Amsterdam marched quickly down the field as a few missed tackles and an assortment of blown assignments undid Scotland's defense. But the Claymores' defense finally stiffened and stopped the Admirals at the 5-yard-line, forcing Amsterdam to settle for a field goal.

The Claymores began their first offensive possession of the season at the 32-yard-line. Alcalde wanted to begin with a simple pass over the middle, a play so rudimentary that a kindergartner could have drawn it up in finger paint: Daft was supposed to hit a wideout cutting across the middle. Since this was Daft's first action in a professional game—he didn't take a single snap with the Titans in the '99 season—Alcalde wanted to start with something easy to jump-start Daft's confidence, to make him feel like he belonged on the field. But instead of throwing to Damon Gibson, Daft was intercepted by the Admirals' Antonio Banks, who returned it to Scotland's 35-yard-line. There wasn't a Claymore within five yards of Banks when he picked off the pass.

"I'll admit it, I had my doubts about Kevin after that play," said Alcalde after the game. "I mean, it was just a terrible, terrible pass."

Six plays after the interception, Amsterdam had the ball first and goal at the Claymores 4-yard-line. Scotland defensive line coach, Jim Tomsula, knew that if Amsterdam pushed the ball into the endzone right here it could signal the end of the game—and, maybe, given the league's history, an end to the Claymores' chance at advancing to the World Bowl. If the Claymores went down 10–0, Tomsula feared that his team wouldn't be able to make up the deficit. This was why Tomsula yelled at his players from the sidelines. "This could be our season right now," Tomsula screamed. "Make this the best four downs of your life!"

Suddenly—surprisingly—Scotland's defenses came alive. Three straight running plays by running back Ralph Dawkin netted just three yards, so the Admirals had to settle for an 18-yard field goal from kicker Silvio Dilberto. That defensive stand, just as Tomsula suspected, was the turning point of the game.

"If we're down more than 6–0 at that point, all of the sudden our offensive guys might start to press and make mistakes," said Criner in retrospect. "But our offense finally got in a groove."

THE PROVING GROUND

The rest of the afternoon belonged to the Claymores. Daft threw four touchdown passes as the offense suddenly awakened from its preseason slumber. The Claymores won 28–9. In the locker room after the game, Coach Criner burst with pride. This game proved that the intensive, physical practices he had been running since the first days of training camp had been worthwhile, as Scotland physically manhandled the Admirals. This game was won on the line of scrimmage, which was where Criner wanted to win every game. "Men, you did a great, great job of sticking with it even though we got off to a slow start," Criner told his troops. "You whipped them physically and they gave up."

When Criner entered the pressroom after the game, he was aglow. And for good reason. Based on the Claymores' strong performance, he knew he had a team that could challenge for a championship. There was an appreciable difference in talent between the Claymores and the Admirals. Suddenly, all those hours spent scouting players at training camp and nurturing relationships with NFL coaches were worth it. Also, Criner sensed something else quietly developing between his boys. "One of the big things in NFL Europe is how you come together as a team," observed Criner. "We're lucky because right now we're building a great team environment."

One week into the 2000 NFL Europe season, there was promise in the air. Things couldn't have been any sweeter in Scotland.

6 The Loudest Place in Football

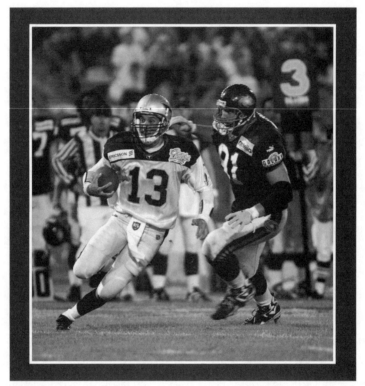

Quarterback Kevin Daft during the game at Frankfurt.

Glasgow, Scotland. Two Days Before the Claymores' Game at Frankfurt

A SOFT MIST fell from the mottled Scotland sky as the two buses pulled out of Glasgow at 11:30 AM on April 21. The Claymores were embarking on their longest road trip of the season, a journey deep into Germany that would span nine days and include twenty-three bus rides, four flights, two hotels, and two games. Scotland was scheduled to play the Frankfurt Galaxy on a Saturday and then a week later they would take on the Berlin Thunder. Instead of traveling back to Scotland between games, Criner decided to keep his team in Germany and prepare to play the Thunder on the road.

"The idea is to give my players variety," said Criner, sitting in the first row on the lead bus, his customary perch. "One of the main things you have to do for your players in this league is keep things different, don't allow them to get in a rut. If they do get in a rut, they quit playing and just want to go home. Hopefully, being in Germany for ten days will mix things up for them."

As the buses drove through the gloom to Edinburgh, where the team would catch a flight to Frankfurt, the players did a good job of occupying themselves. Some played dominoes, others checkers, others chess. Duane Hawthorne, one of a few Claymores wearing a suit, held a boom box up to his ear. He listened to soft soul music as he stared out of the window at the fallow fields of the Scottish countryside, its lush hills and hollows.

Finally the buses pulled into the Hilton Hotel located next to the Edinburgh airport. Since the Frankfurt game was about thirty hours away, Criner had organized a team walk-through practice in the Hilton ballroom before boarding the plane. A walk-through is what almost every football team has the day before a game. It's a simple exercise: The players act out different formations and alignments with their coaches. When Myrel Moore, for example, called a formation that he thought the Frankfurt offense would show during the game, his defense had to respond with an appropriate formation. Even though this was a mundane task, the players were sharp. "I guarantee you this, fellas," said Moore to his players. "The game will be won or lost with our goal-line defense."

At lunch the players sat at tables segregated by color—as they had since the beginning of training camp. The same dynamic existed on the buses: black players sat in the rear, white players sat up front. So far in the season, there hadn't been any overt racial problems on the team. But, as is the case in much of society, there was tension. "If I try to hang out with the white guys, many of the black players will give me a really hard time," said defensive tackle Tom Tovo, who is black. "This is as bad a race problem as I've seen since I've been playing football. It's not really talked about, but you can sense it. I just hope it doesn't blow up."

In the hotel lobby after lunch, Criner looked intense—and tense. He viewed the Frankfurt game as one of the most important of the season. Though Criner and his coaching staff wouldn't say it publicly, they believed that the league had tried to stack Frankfurt with the best players because the Galaxy was NFL Europe's top draw. The evidence suggested that the Claymores' coaches may have been right: In each of the previous two seasons, Frankfurt had played in the World Bowl.

Aside from the Galaxy's talent, though, what made Frankfurt such a difficult team to beat at home was its fans. The 35,000 people who filled up Waldstadion, which was built in 1925 and once hosted a Muhammad Ali title fight, were as loud as any crowd in the United States, mostly because everyone brought a whistle to the stadium and did a Dizzy Gillespe impersonation for three hours. The screechy noise was so ear-splitting that it would often disorient the visiting team, which wasn't used to it.

"If you win at Frankfurt, it's really like winning two games," said Criner on the trip. "Not only do you get a 'W' in the win column, but more likely than not, Frankfurt will beat a team at home that you need beaten later on in the season. That's why this game could really catapult us in the standings."

Frankfurt, Germany. Twenty-four Hours Before Kickoff

After the Claymores landed in Frankfurt, the players were greeted in the terminal by about twenty Galaxy fans who showed up to heckle the team. But, this being NFL Europe, the hecklers were unseasoned. They shouted in English such things as, "You're not going to play well" and "We like you very little." The players just laughed at these innocuous jabs.

On the third and final bus ride of the day, to the Marriott Courtyard Hotel just outside of Frankfurt, linebackers Phil Glover and Ryan Taylor and defensive back Hurley Tarver talked in the back of the bus. "I want to win and all, but I'm more than ready to go home, get back to my crib," said Taylor, squinting his eyes as he looked out the window at the sinking sun. "It's like nine days of prison, being in Germany."

Nearly every NFL Europe player has to deal with the issue of homesickness at some point during the season. But it was unusual to feel the desire to be States-bound so early. When Criner and his staff notice that a player has the blues, they talk to him immediately, acting more like counselors than coaches. Myrel Moore is particularly adept at this. Though he can reduce grown men to tears with his sharp tongue when he's upset about something, the sixty-six-year-old Moore can also effectively slip into the role of grandfather. A few days earlier, defensive back Kory Blackwell was sitting alone while eating breakfast. Just by looking at Blackwell's sad eyes, Moore could tell that his player was having a rough morning. So he went up to Blackwell, put his arm around him, and asked him what the problem was. "Just a little homesick, Coach," said Blackwell quietly.

Moore then leaned in close to him and whispered a few encouraging words. Blackwell smiled weakly and said, "Thanks, Coach, I needed that."

At 8:30 PM, the team arrived at the Marriott. After eating from a gut-busting buffet of undercooked hamburgers and greasy french fries, the team broke into groups for meetings. At the defensive meeting, in a small first-floor room off of the lobby, Moore told his linemen to stay low to the ground until they made contact with the offensive linemen. Once they did that, they needed to explode into them. "Bring the mother-fucking violence to them!" yelled Jim Tomsula, the defensive line coach. "Get after them and make the fucking play."

One room over, Vince Alcalde met with his quarterbacks. As they watched video from the Amsterdam game, Alcalde told Daft to trust his wide receivers. In their Week One win, Daft only threw downfield on a few occasions, opting instead to throw safer, shorter passes to his running backs and tight ends. "You gotta have faith in your receivers," Alcalde told him. "They can make plays." In the next breath, Alcalde then instructed Daft not to be afraid to dump the ball off to running back Aaron Stecker. "The more we get the ball to 27 [Stecker], the better off we'll be," said Alcalde. "We want to give him 35 touches. Also, don't be afraid to tuck the ball away and run. Nothing scares a defense more than a quarterback who can run."

After the meetings ended, producers from FOX television summoned defensive lineman Michael Mason to give a pregame interview. During these sessions, game commentators talk to players to try to unearth interesting color for the telecast. FOX uses these broadcasts to test out new talent. Players such as Troy Aikman, Bill Maas, Michael Strahan, and Daryl Johnston have all cut their broadcasting teeth by commentating on NFL Europe games for FOX.

Sitting before Mason tonight was Kevin Greene, the former NFL linebacker who led the league in sacks in 1994 with the Pittsburgh Steelers and again in 1996 with the Carolina Panthers. In his playing days, Green was known as one of the most intense players in the league, as a carnival barker extraordinaire. That intensity was now being channeled into his new job—with awkward results. "I want to know," asked Green, who conducted his interview in the hotel bar, "who's the most vocal, jacked, geeked, excited, pumped, barking, ready-to-play, in-your-face player on your defensive line?"

After a moment of silence, a sheepish grin lit up Mason's face. "I'm sorry, but what are you asking?" Mason asked with a laugh.

THE PREGAME PARTY at Frankfurt started three hours before the 7 PM kickoff. Located on the large grassy fields in front of Waldstadion, the party was equal parts carnival and barbecue. A band played cheesy American music from the '80s and a bucking bronco was set up next to a booth that sold Wrangler jeans. Thousands of rubber footballs flew through the air, thrown by Germans who practiced their long, Bobby Layne-like windups. There were karaoke tents. There was a rock-climbing wall. And, of course, there were beer tents that recorded brisk sales. It was a rollicking party, with everyone drinking massive amounts of Apfelwein (a potent German specialty) and, of course, Budweiser. More than a few Germans were completely soused before kickoff.

For better or worse, this was a celebration of Americana. Throughout the Cold War, Frankfurt was a bastion of U.S. Air Force and Army bases. The presence of Americans and their way of life eventually seeped into German culture, which was purposefully wiped out at the end World War II. Over the years American pop culture has become trendy in Frankfurt. Though there has been a movement away from this recently with German reunification, the American way of life is still a source of fascination to many Germans. That's why football thrives here.

The fans in Frankfurt were pigskin savvy. This was obvious in the '99 season when, before the Galaxy hosted the Claymores, Jamal

Anderson was interviewed down on the field. Anderson, the Pro Bowl running back for the Atlanta Falcons, was in Europe on a vacation and decided to check out the action. At the time he was negotiating a new contract with the Falcons and the talks between his agent and the team had turned acrimonious. The interview was broadcast over loudspeakers and on the scoreboard screen at both ends of the stadium. Though some people in the crowd didn't understand English well, it was clear that they understood enough.

Interviewer: So, Jamal, what do you think of the Falcons chances of winning the Super Bowl next year?

Anderson: Well, I can't really talk about the Falcons because I don't even know if I'll be playing for them next year. It's all up to them, if they want to pay me the money . . .

At this point, the crowd booed loudly. Anderson was flummoxed. He froze and the interview ended abruptly. This fan reaction showed that Germans are just as tired of the money-driven athlete as Americans. Greed, when you're an athlete, is not good—especially from a PR perspective.

THE LAST TIME the Claymores came to Frankfurt, in spring 1999, quarterback Dameyune Craig made history. A graduate of Auburn University, Craig passed for 2,932 yards and 21 touchdowns during his one season in Scotland. But he is best known for one game at Frankfurt in which he had the single most productive outing of any quarterback to ever play in the NFL of NFL Europe.

On the night of May 22, 1999, Craig was flawless. He started the game by completing his first 13 passes in leading the Claymores to a 21–14 halftime lead. Then, in the second half, he got even better. He wound up throwing for a league-record 611 yards and five touchdowns in leading Scotland to a 42–35 victory. His performance surpassed the NFL best of 554 yards set by Los Angeles Rams quarter-back Norm Van Brocklin in a game against the New York Giants on September 28, 1951. Wide receiver Donald Sellers was Craig's primary target that night, catching 14 passes for a league-record 265 yards and three touchdowns. "That was a magical evening," recalled Criner. "Everything just clicked perfectly for our passing game." And it paid off for Craig. Largely because of his tour-de-force performance that night, he became one of the most coveted NFL Europe players after the 1999 season. He signed a contract with the Carolina Panthers, where he is currently a backup.

Immediately after Craig had made history that evening in Frankfurt, team equipment manager Darren Becker asked Craig in the locker room after the game if he could have his helmet and shoes. Becker figured these items would be worth something someday, and he was never one to let a moneymaking opportunity slip through his fingers. But then Steve Livingstone, Scotland's public relations director, overruled Becker. Livingstone wanted Craig's uniform, helmet, and shoes because he was going to try to get them into the NFL Hall of Fame in Canton, Ohio. The next day Livingstone called the NFL's head office in New York and told them that the Hall of Fame should honor Craig's uniform. "I'll call you right back," a representative of the NFL told Livingstone.

Three weeks passed, and Livingstone still hadn't heard from the Hall. Craig's artifacts sat under Livingstone's desk in his Glasgow office in a large duffel bag, unwashed. Even though the NFL apparently wasn't interested, Livingstone didn't let the issue die. He mentioned the issue to Keith Webster, editor of *First Down,* the only weekly magazine in Europe exclusively devoted to football. Webster then wrote a cover story calling on the NFL to put Craig's jersey in the Hall, and a few publications in England and Scotland picked up on the story. Finally, Joe Horrigan, the curator of the Hall, called Livingstone and said he was interested in acquiring Craig's uniform. The next day, Livingstone shipped the large package overseas.

"Dameyune never believed he'd be in the Hall," said Livingstone. "I told him I'd get him there, but he was skeptical."

Three weeks after Livingstone shipped Craig's jersey, Horrigan phoned Livingstone and informed him that Craig's gear was on display in the Hall. When Livingston relayed the news to Craig, the young quarterback was in awe. At Carolina's training camp the following summer, which Craig attended three weeks after the Claymores' season had ended, Craig became fast friends with Nate Newton, a ten-time All-Pro offensive tackle who had taken Craig under his wing. One day Craig and Newton were shooting the breeze when Newton said, "You can't tell me nothing, Dameyune. You're just a kid."

"I may be just a kid," replied Craig, "But I'm a kid who's in the Hall of Fame."

Newton was incredulous. But then Craig pulled out a photo of the display he had in his wallet. "That shut him up real fast," said Craig.

To this day, Craig remains the only NFL Europe player who has made it to Canton—a fact that Nate Newton now knows well.

7 Talent

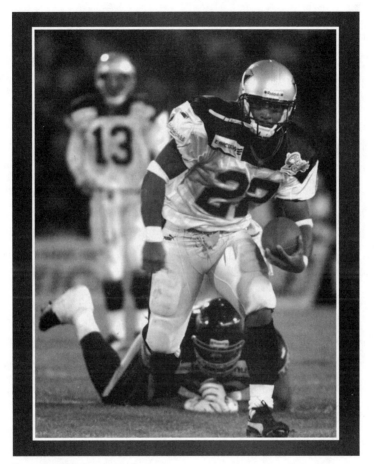

Running back Aaron Stecker.

Frankfurt, Germany. Game Two

INSIDE THE STADIUM fifteen minutes before kickoff, Coach Criner sat on a wooden bench in the locker room. His head was bowed, as if in prayer. Moore sat next to him. For five minutes, the coaches sat together but didn't speak. Nervous energy charged the air. Above them they could hear thousands of feet pounding on the concrete floor of the stadium stands as the fans stomped to the music. The walls shook.

Criner then called his players over and told them to take a knee. By the wide-eyed looks on the players' faces, it was clear that they hadn't expected this sort of electric atmosphere in NFL Europe. It was bedlam outside, and Criner tried to get his players to channel the energy of the moment into their play on the field. "Men, we've got a chance now to make another statement," Criner said, his voice rising with each word. "Do it our way. Make sure that when we hit the field that we lay it on the line. Play your butt off and have some fun. Let them know who they are playing against. Play our style of football and play with great leadership."

With his cane in his right hand, Criner walked his team to the portal that opened out on to the field. He was still using the cane as he recovered from his accident, and that cane came in handy now. As the team waited to be announced, Criner banged it on the 8-foot-high translucent, fiberglass walls. He wanted to rile his players and it worked. The players started jumping up and down, banging their helmets on the tunnel's ceiling. They were more than pumped.

From the tunnel, the players could see a potentially dangerous melodrama unfolding out on the field. Before home games, Galaxy officials often organize stunts to delight the crowd. This evening, a helicopter hovered about 75 yards above the field. An inflatable cushion sat on the 50-yard-line. Cheerleaders were holding it down with ropes, but they were struggling. The wind from the helicopter's propellers caused the cushion to lift off the ground. Several cheerleaders, desperately trying to hold the cushion down, were lifted as high as two feet into the air.

With the cushion flapping up and down, a man prepared to jump out of the helicopter. As defensive coordinator Myrel Moore, running out onto the field ahead of the team, saw this, his mind flashed back to a game in the mid 1970s played at the Houston Astrodome. That was the last time he saw a man fall from the sky. Moore was then an assistant defensive coach for the Oakland Raiders. Five minutes before the Raiders were to go out onto the field for warmups, a construction worker dropped from the rafters of the Astrodome to the carpeted concrete of the Astrodome floor. He died on impact. "There was a big pool of blood about 10 yards away from the exact center of the field," recalled Moore. "For the entire game, there was a noticeable stain."

In the coaches' box, Vince Alcalde and Richard Kent were going over the game plan when Alcalde saw the man prepare to jump from the helicopter. "Holy shit, that guy is gonna die," Alcalde told Kent. "They gotta abort."

It was an awkward jump. The stunt man caught his foot on something in the helicopter, then fell through the air. He hit the grassy field at about the 45-yard-line—fortunately landing on the slightly inflated cushion. He jumped up from the cushion right away and waved to the crowd. The place went bananas; it was as loud as any NFL stadium.

The players then ran out onto the field into a perfect spring dusk. A cool breeze strummed through the trees from the north and a red-orange sunset bled across the western sky. It was 72 degrees. The brushstrokes on the canvas couldn't have been finer.

The beauty of the moment, however, was quickly sullied by the play on the field. For the first twenty-five minutes of the game, the Claymores were terrible. They committed penalties, gave up sacks on offense and long plays on defense, generally looking like a bush-league team. They fell behind 7–0 early in the second quarter and it looked as if a blowout was at hand. Then one player—Aaron Stecker—saved the day.

Indianapolis, Indiana. 1999 NFL Scouting Combine

The artificial turf in the RCA Dome is springy, not the fast surface that players like when running the 40-yard dash. When Aaron Stecker lined up to run his sprint, he knew that this would be the most important event of his young football life. Stecker, a tailback, finished his college career at Western Illinois, an out-of-the way Division I-AA school. He was spectacular there, rushing for 1,957 yards his junior year and 1,124 yards his senior year. But not many scouts had made it to the small school to check out Stecker. So this was his big chance, his moment in the spotlight. "I knew it was important," said Stecker later. "I knew it was big opportunity for me."

On the morning of the combine, Stecker had been poked, prodded, X-rayed, and put on a platform in gym shorts while 300 scouts and NFL executives examined him. Then it was time to show his stuff. He crouched down and prepared to run the 40. Up in the stands, he could see coaches and player personnel directors from every team. Most were holding stopwatches and all were looking at Stecker. Bang! He took off, flying though the bright-white light of the Dome. When he crossed the finish line, Stecker knew he hadn't done well. He walked over to the official time-keeper and was given the terrible news: he had run the 40 in 4.82 seconds. That was a good time for a 300-pound lineman, but not for a 5'10", 207-pound back. In less than five seconds, his life-long hope of being a high-round NFL draft pick had evaporated.

If Stecker had clocked a time somewhere in the 4.5s, which is what he's capable of running on a good day, he certainly wouldn't be playing in Europe. "I'm still trying to forget that experience at the combine," said Stecker. "Before the combine it looked like I had a chance to be drafted pretty high. It all depended on my 40 time. I'm not a track-man, and I didn't do very well. I'm still trying to put it behind me."

THE PROVING GROUND

Stecker has shined on the field ever since his days at Ash-waubenon High in Green Bay, Wisconsin. In his senior year, Stecker rushed for 2,157 yards and scored 37 touchdowns in leading his team to the state finals. He was named the 1993 Wisconsin High School Player of the Year and was an A-list recruit. Eventually, he accepted a scholarship to Wisconsin. In his freshman year with the Badgers, Stecker rushed for 334 yards, which was the sixth-highest total ever for a freshman. He had moves that couldn't be taught. Like Barry Sanders, Stecker seemed to have an extra joint in his ankles, enabling him to make cuts that had to be seen to be believed. He could move sideways without taking any steps, gliding like an angel. He was a natural, able to create poetry with his legs.

But then along came Ron Dayne. When Stecker was a sophomore, he began summer practice with what he thought was a legitimate chance at winning the starting running back position. But Dayne, a big, bruising runner who is ideal for a between-the-tackles kind of conference like the Big Ten, quickly emerged. The future Heisman Trophy winner rushed for a record-setting 2,109 yards and 21 touch-downs as a freshman. His exemplary performance left Stecker with little choice but to transfer.

"I was never bitter about the situation," said Stecker. "I realized right away that Ron deserved to be playing. The decision to transfer really came down to me just wanting to have fun again with football. I certainly wasn't having fun watching the game from the sidelines. I realized that I'd have to go down a level and play. But if I played well enough, I always thought that the NFL would find me."

After the 1996 season, Stecker turned south and drove through 265 miles of corn and wheat fields to get to Macom and Division I-AA Western Illinois, choosing the school largely because it had sent six players to the NFL. His first year at Western—Stecker's junior season—was a memorable one. He scored 150 points, which was the fourth-highest total in I-AA history. During the season, he set twenty-three school records and seven conference records. In his senior year, despite missing two games because of an injury, Stecker gained 1,124 yards and scored 12 touchdowns.

Stecker wasn't drafted. He signed as a free agent with Chicago, but was released before the beginning of the 1999 season. He was picked up on waivers by the Buccaneers midway through the season. Coach Tony Dungy, after seeing Stecker play on the scout squad all season, thought he might just have a special player on his hands. So he sent Stecker to Europe.

"I really felt like I made Tampa's defense better last year," said Stecker. "And they made me better. It's hard to line up on the scout team every week knowing that you're never going to play in an actual game. You have to find ways to motivate yourself. And I did that by believing, and I really did believe it, that if I played well out there, I was making the team better. In the process, I think I impressed the coaches."

"He ran very well for us in practice," said Dungy. "He had to simulate a lot of different backs and he did a good job, and we could see the desire and quickness that he had."

Criner, who first saw Stecker when visiting the Bears training camp, asked the Bucs early on if they'd allocate Stecker to him. "As soon as I saw him I knew that I wanted Aaron," said Criner. "He's an outstanding cutback runner, and he has just enough juice and explosion to get the ball to the corner. Every so often, one of the coaches will say to me 'He ought to do this or that.' But I reply: 'You can tell me but don't you dare tell him.' Because when you have a guy with that kind of ability, you don't want him to be a robot runner going only one way. You just explain the philosophy of the play to him and get the ball deep enough to him so that he can use his vision."

Frankfurt, Germany. Final Moments of the First Half

It was third and goal from Frankfurt's 8-yard-line. Less than a minute remained in the half. Daft dropped back to pass. He looked right, then left, then back to his right. No one was open. Once the pressure finally reached him, he threw off his back foot to Stecker, who was in the right flat. All game long, two defenders had shadowed Stecker. Essentially, the Galaxy's defensive gameplan was wrapped around a single philosophy: if they stopped Stecker, they'd stop the Claymores. For the first twenty-nine minutes of the game, it worked.

Stecker caught the ball at the 9-yard-line. Three defenders stood in front of him. In a matter of two cuts and one spin, Stecker was past them. He then slanted toward the inside of the field. He spun off another tackle. He was now at the three. With one defender to beat, Stecker lowered his head and pushed the defensive back into the endzone. Stecker had broken five tackles total.

"When Kevin threw it out there I was thinking, Man, I gotta score," said Stecker after the game. "If we had come away with a field goal, we would have been pretty demoralized."

"It's so great to have Aaron out there," said Daft. "You know that if no one is open, you can just dump it to him and he'll make something happen."

The play seemed to re-energize the Claymores, who bounded into the locker room after the second quarter on a high. Once inside, players got treated for injuries or tried to hydrate themselves. Meanwhile, Criner met with his offensive coaching staff. Time got away from him, as he didn't have a chance to address the team in the locker room. But out on the field, about thirty seconds before the kickoff, Criner huddled his players into a tight a circle and yelled above the din, "Play with poise and play with class. And, goddamn it, play your asses off."

So the Claymores did. The penalties were eliminated. The offensive line started playing with passion and the defense was relentless. Thanks to a Daft touchdown run and a 42-yard field goal by Rob Hart, which made it over the crossbar by about an inch, Scotland was rolling toward victory when tragedy almost struck. Early in the fourth quarter, wide receiver Damon Gibson caught a pass from Daft along the Claymores' sideline. As soon as he turned up field, he was hit hard by the Galaxy strong safety. The momentum of the hit pushed Gibson deep into the Claymores' sideline.

Criner saw it coming. But the offensive lineman behind the coach—Rome Douglas—didn't move quickly enough, pinning his coach to the sideline. Criner got hit hard in the leg by Gibson and the Galaxy defender and crumbled down onto the turf, as if a man on stilts had gotten one of his wooden legs hit with a sledgehammer. It was painful to see, and the entire squad quickly ran over to their fallen coach.

Ever since training camp, defensive line coach Jim Tomsula had told the backup offensive linemen to stay close to Criner on the sideline. Tomsula had instructed them to throw themselves in front of Criner if a play ever came his way. "If Jim gets hit in his bad leg, that not only could be the end of his season, but also the end of his walking," said Tomsula. "He needs bodyguards out there."

As soon as Tomsula realized that Douglas hadn't protected Criner, he sprinted over to Douglas and grabbed him hard by the facemask. He yanked Douglas toward him once, then twice. Tomsula pressed his large, moon-shaped face within two inches of Douglas's. "You motherfucker!" Tomsula yelled. "You gotta protect your coach. Goddamn it."

Criner, who'd turned sixty during training camp, popped up as quickly as he could. Luckily, it was his good leg that got hit. "For as long as I've been coaching," Criner said later, "that's the first time I've ever been hit on the sideline. I just got pinned and I had nowhere to go."

Criner's pain was soothed by the fact that the Claymores went on to defeat the Galaxy 17–14. They were now 2–0 and were the only undefeated team in NFL Europe. In the locker room Coach Criner climbed back atop the wooden bench and delivered his most passionate speech of the season. He was not a naturally spellbinding speaker, but he dug down deep for this oratory.

"That was a sweet, sweet victory, men," Criner said. "Not very many teams can come in here and win. You saw what that crowd can do to a game. Now, let's learn from this. I gotta say that I'm a little disappointed, because we've got a lot of guys who all of a sudden decided to screw the team. You know who you are. You ran your mouths at the beginning of the game and then went out and played like a piece of shit.

"But once we settled down and started playing our brand of football, we were unbeatable. Even though we had penalties that were absolutely foolish. These things happen when an individual puts himself before the rest of the football team. Let's make a decision right now. I'm not going to coach a team that is going to do the shit we did tonight. I guarantee you I won't. Either they'll have to fire me or I'll make changes. But we're going to go back and play like a team and play with class and poise and let our shoulderpads do the talking. If we play our style of football, we can win this whole damn thing and then every one of you guys will profit from it. Anyone have a problem with that? Tell me right now. This is a championship football team— if you play your ass off and play like a family. If you are smart, men, we'll all get a ring. Hell of a comeback in extremely tough conditions. Hell of job. Enjoy it."

Enjoy it, they would. Frankfurt, known as the financial capital of Germany, is also considered the country's party capital. After taking the team bus back to the Marriott, thirty-five of the forty-three players on the roster dispersed into the night to blow off some steam. The players split into two different groups—the split was along racial lines—but everyone stayed out until sun-up.

Capitol, a multilevel disco club about twenty minutes away from Waldstadion, was teeming with hipsters when fifteen players from the Claymores walked through the doors without having to pay the cover charge. They met twenty or so players from the Galaxy. Over the years, Capitol has become the postgame club of choice for Frankfurt players. Here, players from both teams mingle with fans who know everything about them. But attention wasn't all that drew the players to the hot spot. Many of the guys came here, they said, because of the oh-so-sweet eye candy. At Capitol there was always an abundance of luscious German women wearing shrink-wrapped miniskirts— women who threw themselves at the feet of the players.

"I've never been to a night club where it's easier to pick up women," observed one Claymore player. "German women are infatuated with black guys. It's as if they've never seen one before. It's crazy."

Stecker had a long talk at Capitol with the Galaxy's Mario Bailey, who was a B-list celebrity in Frankfurt. The fans revered Bailey because for five years he had come back to Europe to play for the Galaxy. Bailey, a former Washington Husky star, is the all-time receptions leader in NFL Europe. But he was never able to make it in the NFL, mostly because at 5'9', 165 pounds, he is slightly built, and never possessed blazing speed. Still, he has been an upper-echelon NFL Europe receiver.

"There are guys like Mario who can really play here," said Stecker, "and they haven't made it to the NFL. It just goes to show that no matter how well you do over here, you're not necessarily going to make a team back home."

After a long night of dancing, drinking, and flirting (many of the women at the club became temporary roommates at the team hotel for the next week), the Claymores finally hopped into cabs just as the sun rose over Frankfurt. "I'll never forget that night," said Claymore wide receiver Damon Gibson. "That was just what we needed."

About five miles from Capitol is an area known as Saxxon House, located in the only part of Frankfurt that wasn't destroyed by bombs during World War II. In the five-block radius of Saxxon House, there are about twenty-five different bars. There are Spanish-style joints, discos, American saloons, German beer halls— every kind of drinking establishment imaginable. At just a little past one in the morning, twenty players and coaches from the Claymores walked into an Irish pub.

It was a night for gossip because once inside the pub, as everyone became full of cheer and beer, players told stories until dawn. There was talk about a possible mutiny by the assistant coaches, who had grown tired of the daily tongue-lashings administered by Criner. There was speculation about the continual dirty play by one defensive lineman of the Claymores, who poked players in the eye whenever the opportunity arose. And there were whispers about the red-hot libido of yet another defensive lineman, who was boffing his brains out and had gotten a girl pregnant in Glasgow—even though he had a wife back in the States. "There is some crazy stuff going on right now," said Finkes with a laugh the next day. "But that's what makes this league so intriguing."

8 The Night Prowler

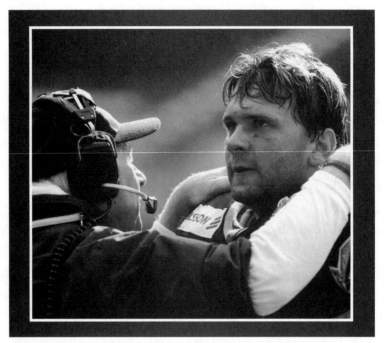

Linebacker Matt Finkes with defensive coordinator Myrle Moore.

Frankfurt, Germany. Six Days Before the Claymores' Game in Berlin

THE CLAYMORES CELEBRATED Easter dinner at Wäldches, a Frankfurt restaurant that serves traditional German fare. As the team strolled into the restaurant, you would have thought that Caesar was entering Rome, the way the patrons reacted to the sight of the team. Heads turned. Mouths dropped. A few people even reached for their video cameras to record the moment for posterity. "This is the weirdest feeling of my life," said guard Jason

Gamble as he walked toward his table. "Why are all these people flipping out?"

The team made its way to a reserved room in the rear. It was small and dim, as the only light came from flickering candles. The players sat on benches in front of long, wooden tables. It was a tight squeeze for everyone—except Rome Douglas, a backup offensive lineman, who sat alone with plenty of space on either side of him.

Douglas had done something that is blue-moon rare in football: He had alienated himself from the rest of the offensive line. On most professional teams, the players on the offensive line are inseparable, as close as any group on the team. They buddy up in the locker room together, eat their meals together, and socialize off the field. But at Wäldches, even though space was at a premium, not one lineman—or any other player, for that matter—sat next to Douglas. "Fuck Rome Douglas," said one lineman. "That guy's got the worst attitude on the team."

Since training camp, a feeling had spread among the offensive linemen that Douglas, who'd played at USC, was the one thing that a lineman simply can't afford to be: soft. That's the dirtiest four-letter word in football if you make your living in the trenches, but it's how both coaches and players described Douglas. The evidence against the offensive tackle was growing. Against Amsterdam in Week One, Douglas was bull-rushed by a defensive back, who weighed about 100 pounds less than Douglas, and, as a result, gave up a sack. Against Frankfurt, he was flagged for an unsportsmanlike conduct penalty for throwing a punch after an extra-point. Criner had lit into Douglas repeatedly for his ham-headed mistakes, but his words never sank in.

"I'm just trying to get back to the NFL," said Douglas, who was cut by Jacksonville in the '99 preseason. "I don't care about being friends with anybody, because I'm over here to work."

After dinner, the team went back to the Marriott on two double-decker buses. Everyone was in a merry mood, telling and retelling stories from the previous night's adventures. But in the back of the second bus was Douglas. He sat alone, staring out at the pulsing lights of downtown Frankfurt. The heart of the city was shining. But miles away from those shuffling lights, in the back of the Claymores' bus, all that came to light for Douglas was that playing football in Europe wasn't much fun at all.

THE MONDAY AFTER Easter was the players' day off. The city awaited them, rich with possibilities, spread out before them like an endless buffet of haute cuisine. But instead of indulging in the sights, more than half of the players took a bus to Waldstadion and lifted weights from 2 to 4 in the afternoon. Afterward, they spent the night holed up in the hotel. "I didn't come here to sightsee," said defensive tackle Antonio Dingle, who'd chosen to lift. "I came here to get better and play ball."

Not everyone shared that attitude. A few players took a boat ride up the Rhein River; some toured nearby castles and vineyards. Rob Hart and Jon Ballantyne—the team's kicker and punter—rode a train downtown, only to find that everything was closed because of a bank holiday. Then they went to a matinee showing of the movie *Godzilla* in 3-D. The fact that it was in German and incomprehensible to Ballantyne and Hart was of little consequence. The kickers just wanted to escape from the hotel—and from football—for one afternoon.

Kickers have long been known in the NFL as the odd men out on a team, as players who keep to themselves. But this stereotype doesn't fit any of the Claymores. Hart, from Southampton, England, was a quick thinker who liked to argue that the American style of government was more of an aristocracy than a democracy. Ballantyne was a

79

THE PROVING GROUND

rugged all-around athlete from Melbourne, Australia. In the Land Down Under, Ballantyne, at 6'3", 210 pounds, was a semi-famous Australian-Rules football player. He had a powerful leg, as he routinely blasted thunderbolts that traveled 75 yards in practice and could be heard from much farther away than that. But he was also inconsistent. For every 70-yard blast, he shanked it 15. "Punting is 90 percent mental," said Ballantyne, "and that's what I'm battling right now."

The team's practice squad kicker, Robert Grant, was easily the toughest kicker on the Claymores, if not in the entire league. Last season, in 1999, Grant was leaving a pub in Glasgow when he noticed a man slapping around a woman. Without thinking, Grant intervened. "You can't do that," Grant yelled. "Stop it right now." The man ignored Grant, a decision he will probably regret for the rest of his life. Partially fueled by multiple pints of Guinness, Grant headbutted the man in the face as hard as he could. "That guy's face went flying everywhere," recalled Hart.

When Grant returned to the Central Hotel, his hair was thick with blood. Hart told him to go see the team trainer, but Grant refused because he didn't want Criner to find out about the incident. Five days later, just as Grant's own dizziness was starting to fade away, he was at practice, kicking, when he felt an itch on the top of his head. He took off his helmet and started scratching his melon. He felt something hard embedded in his scalp. When he yanked it out, he was shocked to see, lying in his hand, his antagonist's front tooth. "He did all of that for the honor of a woman," said Hart. "I bet that guy hasn't slapped around another woman since. And that also goes to show you that you shouldn't mess with kickers. Somehow, some way, they'll get you."

Hart knows this from his own experience. After graduating from Murray State in 1997, he tried out for the Atlanta Falcons. On the first day of training camp, a kicker named Don Silvestri, who was also auditioning for the Falcons job, approached Hart. "You know, you're not the kicker here," Silvestri told him. "*I* am. You may kick an extra point or two, but *I*'m the kicker." Silvestri said this because he wanted to mess with Hart's head, to shatter his confidence. And it worked. The Falcons cut Hart during the preseason. But eventually, Silvestri was also let go.

At a tryout with the Albany Firebirds of the Arena League the next year, Hart thought he had won the job. The coach of the Firebirds called him and told Hart that he had narrowed the field of kickers from thirty-two down to two. "The coach then told me he'd call me back once he made his decision between myself and the other kicker," said Hart. "But my phone never rang." As it turned out, a fellow by the name of Don Silvestri got the job.

MATT FINKES SPENT the day off at a relative's house in nearby Pfedelbach. Matt's father, Heinz, had spent the first fifteen years of his life growing up in Germany, and this weekend he flew over from his home in Ohio to watch his son play against the Galaxy. After the game, father and son took a train two hours south to Pfedelbach and celebrated Heinz's forty-ninth birthday with thirty relatives. "We had a terrific time," said Finkes. "We stayed up all night talking and drinking great German beer—my favorite kind of evening."

It was also an evening for Finkes to explore his roots. The Finkes clan came from a town called Schwabisch Hall, located near Pfedelbach on the banks of the Kocher River, at the edge of the Black Forest. Schwabisch Hall was founded around 1100 AD and flourished as a salt-mining town for centuries. Many of Matt Finkes's ancestors toiled in the town's mines, earning enough money to survive. But after World War II the economic landscape finally changed. The money from the mines had dried up and life grew progressively more difficult. "I was born in '51 and later I remember living in an old horse barn with other refugees," said Heinz Finkes. "My parents had split up and my mom then decided to come to the United States with her four kids. Her mother and some brothers and sisters were working in the States on farms. When we came in 1966, none of us could speak English."

Heinz's mother, Ottile Cernyar, landed a job cleaning houses in rural Ohio. Heinz worked part-time on farms and on construction crews. It was hard work for everyone in the family but, like many new immigrants to the United States, they made the best of it. One day a social worker came to their house and began explaining food stamps and public assistance. Ottile didn't care to hear any of this. Politely, she told the worker she wasn't interested. "We didn't come here looking for handouts," Ottile said. "We'll work and we'll make it."

Ottile's toughness is evident in both Heinz and Matt. Heinz enrolled at Graham (Ohio) High, where he eventually was asked to try out for football. "Back home we called soccer 'football,' so I figured that's what I'd be playing," recalled Heinz. "The first day they gave me shoulderpads, kneepads, and a helmet, I thought, Boy, they must play a rough game over here."

Heinz learned the game quickly. He excelled in three sports at Graham High and was awarded a financial package that paid his way to Wilmington College, where he starred at football, track, and wrestling. Six years later, his brother Reinhold followed Heinz to the school and was a 1,000-yard rusher for the Quakers. A knee injury cut short Heinz's free-agent tryout with the Dallas Cowboys, but his younger brother lasted briefly with the Buffalo Bills and the Hamilton Tiger Cats of the Canadian Football League.

After his football career ended, Heinz got a job as the wrestling and football coach at Miami East High in Miami, Ohio. As soon as his

son Matt started to play football, Heinz schooled him on the fundamentals of the sport—emphasizing basics like leverage, tackling, and
blocking. In junior high, Matt was an uncommonly intelligent player,
using guile and savvy as much as strength and quickness. By the time
he attended Piqua High in Piqua, Ohio—a town that was close to
Miami, where by that time Heinz had become a principal at Miami
East—Finkes was a polished player. In his senior year, he was named
USA Today and *Blue Chip Illustrated* All-America as a defensive
end. He wasn't very big—6'2", 215 pounds—but he dominated games
from his position on the line. He also dominated the classroom, graduating seventh in his class of three hundred.

Matt was raised in a house in the country, on a lonely road amid
fields of corn and soybeans north of Piqua. The winters were brutal
there, which was why Matt fantasized about playing college football
in the sun and fun of the University of Hawaii. "He had a rosy plan,"
said Heinz. "He'd lie on the beach and play football under the palm
trees. It was all that honeymoon stuff."

"I wasn't really going to play at Hawaii," said Matt. "But I did at
least want to go on a recruiting trip to Hawaii, so I expressed some
interest. Unfortunately, you have to commit before you go on a
recruiting trip, so I never went."

Finkes opted to attend nearby Ohio State and play for Buckeye
coach John Cooper. Finkes was undersized his freshman year, and, as
a result, got knocked around by heavyweight upper-classmen. But by
the end of his first season in Columbus, Finkes had gained 30
pounds, pushing his weight up to 255. He started every game in his
last three years at Ohio State and finished his career with the second-
most tackles for loss (59) and fourth-most sacks (25) in school history. His senior year he was named All-Big Ten.

Heinz attended every one of his son's games, dating back to eighth
grade. "I missed one of Matt's games when he was in seventh grade,"

said Heinz. "The only reason was that I was being inducted into the Wilmington College Hall of Fame. I was going to skip it, but Matt said, 'If you do that, then I won't play the game.'"

Matt's grandmother, Ottile, didn't miss many games, either. She watched most of them on television, even when it was extremely painful for her to do so. In Matt's senior year, 1996, Ottile had undergone delicate eye surgery in which a gas bubble was placed in a hole near the retina. To help the eye properly heal, Ottile had to lie face down for twenty hours a day for two weeks. "For our Penn State game my senior year, she lay on her stomach in a folding lawn chair in front of her TV and used a mirror to watch us," said Finkes, smiling at the memory. "She called me after the game and told me it was kind of tough to follow. Everything was upside down and backward."

Finkes converted to linebacker in the pros, but because he lacked great straight-line speed, he only lasted one season with the Jets. He was cut in the 1998 preseason and moved back to Columbus to finish his degree in economics. The next year the Redskins cut him in the preseason. But before he was given a pink slip, he caught the watchful eye of Jim Criner, who saw Finkes in that camp. Criner selected Finkes in the NFL Europe free-agent draft in 1999 and then put him on the Claymores' protected list for the 2000 season. "Matt gives us great leadership," said Criner. "He's a solid tackler and anchors our defense. He makes all the calls and gets people in the right position. Every team needs a guy like Matt."

But guys like Finkes are rare. He's the type of person who can stay out all night and perform wonders the next morning at practice. One night in Glasgow during the 2000 season, for example, Finkes wound up at the house of a guy he'd met that evening at a club. Along with others who straggled into the house from the club, Finkes debated the Russian Revolution of 1917, pro and con, until the first light of dawn. Finkes then slept in the stranger's bathtub for a few hours, but he was still able to make it to the team bus by 10 AM before it departed for practice. As Finkes sat on the bus reading the paper, he was as bright-eyed and as sharp as a teacher's pet. Ten minutes before he jogged out onto the practice field on that windy, wet day, Finkes polished off the crossword puzzle, cracking jokes the entire time and dropping the kind of ten-cent words that give most people fits on the SATs. This was an amazing feat of endurance. All of Finkes's friends were routinely shocked that he could have so much late-night fun and still be productive by day.

"Matt has got this unique ability to get the most of out life," said tight end Willy Tate, Finkes's closest friend on the team. "One thing is for sure: If you go out with Matt for dinner or to a bar or wherever, you are going to have an interesting time—and you never know where you're going to end up."

This quality made Finkes popular among both players and coaches. Though his all-or-nothing lifestyle in Scotland was unconventional by the standards of most athletes, Finkes cherished it. And you couldn't blame him. In the world of NFL Europe, his was a life well lived. "Some people take football over here very seriously, which they should," said Finkes. "I take it seriously when I have to. But at all the other times, I'm out to enjoy myself."

9 The Coaching Staff

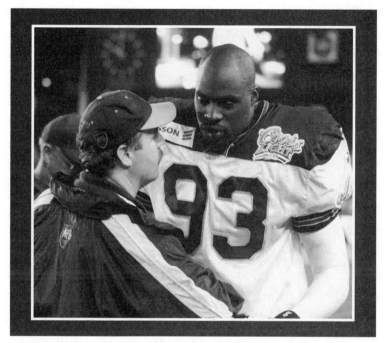

Defensive line coach Jim Tomsula with defensive end Rasheed Simmons.

Frankfurt, Germany. Five Days Before the Claymores' Game in Berlin

THE COACHING STAFF, which didn't take a full day off the entire season, was in a mixed mood on the players' day off. They were relieved to be 2–0 and atop the league standings, but they also shared an unspoken, uneasy feeling that the Claymores were due to play a sloppy game. Neither victory had been artistic; a third poor performance, the staff was convinced, would result in a loss. "It's hard to dominate in this league because of the parity," said Myrel

Moore. "But you can live with that. You can't live with undisciplined play. That reflects poorly on us." And all the coaches were acutely aware that any bad performance negatively impacted their chances of landing that dream job in the NFL.

To prepare for the Berlin Thunder, the coaches piled in a van and traveled to an American sports bar in downtown Frankfurt called Champs to watch the Berlin–Barcelona game, which was on that evening. This is certainly not how NFL teams scout an opponent. NFL teams can rely on a handful of firsthand observers, state-of-the-art video equipment, and computer programs that catalog an opponent's tendencies. But NFL Europe teams operate on shoestring budgets, forcing them to be creative in the way that they scout, and do most things.

Once in the van, the coaches quickly got lost. Criner was riding shotgun and every direction he gave seemed to be a poor one. Sitting in the back, a few of the coaches couldn't help but compare Criner's sense of direction to his sense of coaching. Though Criner didn't know it, there was a quiet rebellion brewing among the assistants. Some of them felt that Criner's unwillingness to take suggestions was undermining the team's effectiveness. Sure, not many people like their boss, but this was serious. Just hours after the Frankfurt win, one coach nearly quit, disgusted with Criner. "I'm at the end of my rope," said this coach. "I get yelled at for things I'm not responsible for and Criner doesn't seem to listen to me. It makes you wonder why you're doing this."

When the coaches finally found Champs, all did not go smoothly at the bar. A squat, swag-bellied German bouncer stopped the coaches at the door. Next to the bouncer were two other large men, grinning at his side like great white sharks. In choppy English, the head bouncer informed three of the coaches that they could not, under any circumstances, enter the establishment because they were wearing shorts. Champs has a dress code, he told them. Criner, who was wearing pants, calmly entered the bar and started to talk to the manager. Though the manager had no idea who the Claymores were— "What zez e Clee-moor?" he asked—he eventually allowed the entire coaching staff to enter.

Only two minutes remained in the first half by the time the coaches slid into their seat at the bar. During stops in the action, FOX, instead of going to commercials, showed highlights from past NFL Europe seasons. One clip, from 1995, featured shots of Scotland taking on Barcelona. A closeup of Criner appeared on the screen. "Damn, Coach," said Kevin O'Neill, the running backs coach, "you sure looked a lot younger back then." Criner half-heartedly smiled, but he wasn't amused. The truth was Criner had aged considerably in the last few years. There were more sprinkles of gray in his hair and more crinkles in his skin. The stress of coaching, with its average eighteen-hour workday, doesn't allow the years to pass gracefully.

Berlin won the game 28–14. Thunder quarterback Eric Kresser was impressive, throwing for four touchdowns. The Claymores' coaches didn't take notes, because the camera angles were poor and little insight was to be gleaned from the game. The best camera angle for scouting a team is from the endzone, which FOX rarely used. "We didn't get much out of this," said Alcalde. "There were only a few times when you could see the whole field. I think it was worth our while, though, because it gave us an idea of what Berlin would do."

On the way back to the Marriott, the coaches passed by the train station in downtown Frankfurt, which prompted Criner to take a trip down memory lane. He told his staff about the time he and his wife took a train to Italy a few years ago after the season had concluded. "We were easily the oldest couple on the train," Criner recalled. "And the young people partied like crazy. It was nuts. When we changed trains, they helped us with our bags and treated us with great respect. When they all got off the train before us, I wanted to go with them. I wanted to go party." Criner then laughed. The moment was sweet with nostalgia—and it was one of the few times in the past three days that the coach had actually smiled.

It is less than five miles from Champs to the Marriott, but it took over an hour—and about twelve U-turns—for the coaches to finally find their way back to the hotel. They were tired and ready to retire for the evening, but as they stood and waited for the elevator that would take them to their rooms, their senses were shocked when three women, presumably ladies of the night, strutted alongside them. The women were decked out in short skirts, tight tops, and loads of pungent perfume. To no one's great surprise, these three women exited the elevator on one of the players' floors. The women didn't have appointments, so to speak; they simply knocked on doors and whispered sweet nothings in limited English. But it took just a few attempts before the women slipped quietly into a room. They wouldn't be seen again until early the next morning, leaving the hotel in the predawn grayness. Since it was midweek and there was no curfew for the players, the coaches just smiled when the ladies left the elevator, as if they all remembered what it was like to be young and footloose.

THERE IS A standard setup of coaching staffs in NFL Europe. The head coach is usually older and well connected with people in the NFL. Normally, the head coach has a confidante who is also older. This coach has no ambition to be a head coach, but typically has NFL experience—for the Claymores, this coach is Myrel Moore. The coordinators are usually younger guys who aspire to be head coaches someday, like Scotland's offensive coordinator Vince Alcalde. The other assistants will come from the lower levels of college football like NAIA. The Claymores' defensive line coach Jim Tomsula and defensive-backs coach Richard Kent fit this mold. When not working for the Claymores, they both coach at Catawba College, a Division II school in Salisbury, North Carolina.

The Claymores' staff has had their problems with each other in the past. One night last season, Vince Alcalde returned to the hotel to perform bedcheck after being out at a pub. Alcalde was a few minutes late for his task, and Criner knew it. That night the two coaches almost came to blows.

"Maybe you don't need to be here," Criner told Vincent.

"Well, Coach, maybe I don't," snapped Alcalde.

The next morning the two met for forty-five minutes in Criner's office. "Can we work this out?" asked Criner.

"I hope so," said Alcalde.

During their chat, Criner emphasized the need for a hierarchy among the coaches and the need for everyone to abide by the rules. If an assistant coach couldn't obey his wishes, Criner said, he would be put on a plane and sent back to the States. Alcalde agreed and the two have been friends ever since.

Not all interactions between the coaches are as serious, however. Last season defensive line coach Jim Tomsula had a little fun with Criner. Even though Tomsula hates mornings the way most people hate cold showers, there was a brief time in spring 1999 when Tomsula voluntarily started his workday at four each morning. He did this not because he wanted to get a jump on analyzing the technique of his players or on scouting the tendencies of an opponent. No, Tomsula was motivated by what he considered a higher virtue: He wanted to play a mind game with Criner.

Criner, like many NFL head coaches, prides himself on being the first one in the office each morning and the last one to leave each night. He believes an hour worked at sunup is worth two hours by sundown. While this is an admirable philosophy, it can also be an annoying one if you're the person who has to face Criner every morning. So Tomsula, an inveterate practical joker, decided to play a little one-on-one with Criner about midway through the '99 season. He knew that Criner came into the office around 5:30, so Tomsula set his alarm clock for 5:00 in order to beat Criner to the large hotel room that served as the coaches' main office. The first time Tomsula showed up before Criner, he leaned far back in his desk chair and waited. And waited. When Criner strolled in at his customary half past five, Tomsula bellowed with a bright smile on his face, "Goooooooooood morning, Coach. How the hell are *you* doing? It's damn great to be alive, isn't it?"

The game didn't end there. After a few more mornings when Tomsula beat Criner into the office, Criner decided he'd had enough. Criner—not one to shy away from a competition—started arriving at the office at 5:00. At first, Tomsula was startled by the sight of the coach sitting at his desk when he rolled in at 5:15. But then he had to laugh. "That's when I knew the heat was on," said Tomsula.

Soon Tomsula was sitting bleary-eyed at his desk at 4:45. Impressed and invigorated, Criner was sitting at his desk the following morning at 4:30. This insanity continued for about two weeks. Eventually, Tomsula was catching shut-eye in his office and praying that Criner wouldn't see him dozing. Criner never did; the coach ended this unspoken battle of wills when he stopped acknowledging Tomsula each morning. He just came in at his usual 5:30 and marched straight to his desk.

"That was a lot of fun," said Tomsula. "The whole thing was asinine, but then again, sometimes asinine things happen in this league."

THE PROVING GROUND

Tomsula's sharp sense of humor, coupled with his impressive sense of compassion, made the defensive line coach a powerful presence in the Claymores' locker room this season. He was the only coach on the staff whom all the players listened to intently when he spoke. Tomsula earned this honor because of various generous deeds he performed throughout the season. In training camp, one of his defensive linemen had a nasty case of the flu. He couldn't sleep and he was considering quitting and going home. Tomsula knew this, so one evening past midnight, Tomsula walked to an all-night drugstore in Orlando and bought some flu medicine. When he returned to the Harley Hotel and handed the medicine over, the sick player was overwhelmed with gratitude. "No one in my entire life has ever done anything like this for me before," the player told Tomsula. This is how Jim Tomsula builds trust and respect.

Defensive line coaches typically have the most difficult job of any coach on a pro staff. By their nature, defensive linemen at the highest levels of football tend to be violent. That's what makes them so good. On every play, they are hitting an offensive lineman as hard as they can. Tomsula frequently implored his players to "bring the violence on every play," which they always tried to do. For some players, however, it is difficult to flip the switch and turn the violence off when they walk off the field. "Defensive line coaches, probably more than any other coach on a staff, have to be baby-sitters," revealed one Claymore coach. "He's usually got a few guys who are out of control and it's his job to control them—both on the field and off."

Tomsula was good at this. A former Mr. Pittsburgh, Tomsula once bench-pressed 560 pounds and squatted 800 pounds. This sort of brute strength gave Tomsula instant credibility among his players. And Tomsula had a razor-sharp focus on football. He only brought one pair of khakis and one blue shirt to Scotland, which is what he wore on every road trip. All the other times he was decked out in Claymore coaching gear, which looked as natural on him as a navy blue suit on a banker. "I'm a very simple guy," explained Tomsula, "who just happens to love the game of football."

10 Road Life

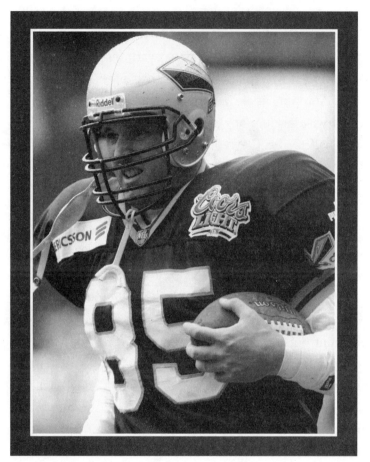

Tight end Willy Tate.

Frankfurt, Germany. Four Days Before Game Three

THERE'S AN OLD joke that's told in locker rooms all across the NFL. *Question:* What's the hardest part about going on the road? *Answer:* Trying not to smile when you kiss your wife goodbye.

Not all athletes cheat on their wives, of course. But in the NFL there's always—always!—women hanging around the team buses after games hoping for that magical meeting with a player. This was also the case in Frankfurt. After the Claymores game with the Galaxy, the area around the team bus was swarming with young, heavily made-up women with misty looks in their eyes. "Let me put it this way," said Antonio Dingle, a defensive tackle who was married. "The opportunity is there for any player who wants it."

About half of the Claymores' players were married. The league didn't cover the cost of spouse travel, so many of the players couldn't afford to fly their wives over for the season. During the early part of the season, only a few of the players' wives and girlfriends made the trip overseas. "It's hard to just stop your life and come to Europe for three months," said Kesa Koide, who was dating Kevin Daft. "It's a big sacrifice."

While the players practiced at Waldstadion four days before they played the Thunder, five of the wives and girlfriends of Claymore players went out for an afternoon on the town. Ann Criner, Sondra Moore, Amy Hesse, Kristine McElmurry, and Kesa Koida arrived in downtown Frankfurt at noon. The women didn't know each very well, so their conversations didn't run too deep. For Moore, however, this was by design. She and Ann were the veterans of the group, having been football wives for over twenty years. "One of the first things that Myrel told me when he got his first job in the pros with the Denver Broncos was that I shouldn't get too attached to the players' wives," said Moore. "He said he might have to cut their husbands at any minute, so I couldn't let myself get too involved. I'd just end up feeling bad. I still abide by that rule."

That philosophy served as a golden rule for most of the season. Kesa and Kristine became close friends, but the rest of the women pretty much kept to themselves, resigned to the fact that when you're with a NFL Europe player or coach, life during the season was no European vacation.

Frankfurt, Germany. Three Days Before Game Three

The team had been in Frankfurt for four days, but for many players it felt more like four months. When not practicing, the players had little to do. The Marriott was eight miles outside of Frankfurt, so if they wanted to go into town the players had to spend the equivalent of about $50 for a round-trip taxi ride. If they stayed in the hotel—which most of them did—they usually watched television in their rooms. The problem was, the only English-speaking channels in Frankfurt were CNN and the BBC. "I've never watched so much news in my life," said tackle Ben Cavil. "I never realized that CNN was such a cool channel."

Being force-fed the news made for some interesting conversations on the bus. The fall of the NASDAQ, the fate of Elian Gonzalez, and whether or not Attorney General Janet Reno was a man were subjects that were debated extensively as the Claymores made their way to and from practice at Waldstadion. While theirs weren't the most cogent analyses of global affairs, the players at least discussed something other than money, women, and sex—the usual topics of discussion.

The travel and the extended time on the road were affecting the Claymores on the practice field. The first two days of practice in Frankfurt, according to Criner, were the worst two of the season. "This is a crucial game for us," Criner explained as he sat on the bus. "If we can go 3–0, it will take us a long way toward the World Bowl. It usually takes seven wins, and to be off to such a good start after two road trips would be huge. But right now the offense still has to catch up with the defense. The key is not to put our defense on the field in a bad position. I think it will be very tough for anyone in this league to drive the length of the field on our defense."

Frankfurt, Germany. Two Days Before Game Three

The start of the final practice in Frankfurt was still ten minutes away, but Jim Tomsula was already out on the field. He walked alone on the thick green grass, deep in thought. Though backup running back Kelvin Eafon was not one of the players he coached, Tomsula was still worried about Eafon. The Claymores had decided to cut Eafon and the coaching staff didn't know how he was going to receive the news. "Right now we're thinking of telling him at the airport when we leave for Berlin," said Tomsula. "That way we can put him on a plane for home and we can just get on another plane. We're really not sure how he's going to take it. It could get ugly."

Eafon was a divine athlete. In 1994, he was the High School Athlete of the Year in Dallas. A standout in both basketball and football, Eafon had to chose one sport before accepting a college scholarship. He opted to play basketball at the University of Arizona, whose team went on to win the NCAA title in 1997. Unfortunately for Eafon, a year earlier he'd decided to switch back to football and play running back for the Wildcats, so he missed out on cutting down the nets the following April. "I have no regrets about that," claimed Eafon. "I wanted to be a football player. I had to sacrifice a few things."

As a senior at Arizona, the 5'11", 218-pound Eafon was named a captain. Though his strength was blocking, Eafon also excelled in short-yardage situations. He scored 16 touchdowns as a senior—all on runs of 10 yards or less. Only six players in PAC-Ten history had scored more touchdowns in a season. "I think Kelvin is an NFL player," said Arizona head coach Dick Tomey after Eafon's senior season. "He's our best blocker and best receiver out of the backfield. He's tough enough for anything thrown at him."

That may have been the case at Arizona, but in Europe Eafon had a difficult time accepting his role as a backup. Nearly every day since training camp, he'd complained that he wasn't getting enough time with the first unit. He also hadn't endeared himself to anyone by telling people that he empathized with Lawrence Phillips, the troubled running back out of Nebraska who'd had numerous run-ins with the law. Most recently, Phillips had been released from the San Francisco 49ers because, much like Eafon, he couldn't accept a backup role and had stopped paying attention to his coaches.

"I understand where Phillips is coming from," Eafon said on the bus to a teammate.

"But all the guy had to do was obey the rules," replied Eafon's teammate, "and at worst he makes league minimum for ten years."

"I couldn't kiss ass like that," snapped Eafon. "Never could I kiss ass like that."

Confidence in one's abilities is a prerequisite for being a successful athlete. But when the line between confidence and arrogance blurs, trouble often starts. It had in Eafon's case, and at this time the Claymores were struggling to handle what had become a delicate situation. But there were still three days to go before the kickoff of the Berlin game, which was the deadline for Eafon's release. When his roster spot became available, Scotland planned to activate linebacker Jon Hesse, who was nursing a broken finger. "It's going to be a long three days," warned Tomsula. "I just hope this doesn't blow up."

The Claymores had made personnel mistakes before. In Week Five of the '99 season, Scotland was short one defensive end because of numerous injuries. Though Tomsula objected, Criner decided to sign Kejaun DuBose, a defensive end who'd attended Northwestern. DuBose arrived in Frankfurt on a Saturday morning after flying all night. The Claymores were playing the Galaxy later that evening. As soon as DuBose got off the plane, he met with Tomsula for several hours, going over line calls and the gameplan. DuBose, who was understandably jet-lagged, had trouble staying awake during this long meeting. For the game he was awake—but barely. When DuBose lined up for the first time on the Claymores' fifth defensive series, he was destroyed, playing like someone who hadn't slept in over thirty hours, which, indeed, he hadn't.

In football, sometimes even legitimate excuses for poor play don't matter. And a few days later, when the Claymores found an available defensive end more to their liking, DuBose was put on a plane and sent home. This was not Criner's finest moment as a talent evaluator. Today, he doesn't like to talk about this incident, as it reflects poorly on the entire Claymore organization. "We fucked up," said one Claymore coach frankly. "I just hope that that never happens again."

AT THE END OF the team's final practice in Frankfurt, Criner asked his players to gather around him. He informed them of a surprise: Tomorrow they were going to go on a sightseeing tour of Berlin, which would include a stop at the Berlin Wall. As Criner looked for a reaction from his players after the news, he saw nothing. Just a bunch of vacant looks. "Obviously, most of these kids didn't know the difference between the Berlin Wall and the wall in their hotel room," Criner said later. "That's why I had to give them a little history lesson about the Wall and its significance. This generation just doesn't know history."

Criner, like all good coaches in NFL Europe, was much more than coach. He slipped into the role of father on many occasions throughout the season. He at times scolded his kids for inappropriate behavior. He praised them for good work. And he frequently tried to teach them a thing or two about the history of the land that they were in. He didn't have to do this—many NFL Europe coaches don't—but to Criner one of the league's best features is that it exposes players to new cultures and new ideas. "They need to get something more out of this than just football," said Criner. "Hopefully they can grow and mature a little as well. And maybe even learn something."

East Berlin, Germany. Thirty Hours Before Kickoff

The plan was to grab a quick lunch and then go on the tour, but things quickly went awry. Criner had arranged to take the team to a Burger King in downtown Berlin—he knew how much his players missed greasy American food. But the bus driver had no idea where this particular Burger King was, even though the Claymores' travel coordinator had told the bus company where they needed to go weeks in advance. After circling the city for forty-five minutes, the driver stopped to confer with another bus driver. Few things in life will cause Criner to become red with anger, but incompetence is one of them. "What the fuck is going on?" he yelled, when the driver stopped the bus. Criner got out, took two steps, and then—with the entire team watching—stepped into a big pile of dog shit. Criner stomped the ground and let the expletives fly fast and furious. "This is as mad as I've ever seen coach Criner," related tight end Willy Tate, who also played for Criner and the Claymores in 1996 and '98. "This is a disaster."

As the drivers and Criner tried to figure out direction to the Burger King, Tate entertained his teammates on the bus with a story. In the first weeks of the 2000 season, Tate had developed a reputation for being a master storyteller. He had a Garrison Keeler–like feel for timing and cadence as he spoke. He used his hands expressively and could flawlessly slip into different, distinctive voices. What he related this afternoon, he said, was a German folktale usually told on a wedding night.

"So, after two Germans get married in winter, they jump into a sleigh," began Tate. "They're having a great time, when suddenly the husband goes quiet. His wife asks what's wrong and starts nagging at him. So he gets out and says to the horse, 'One.' He gets back in the sleigh and the wife starts saying how happy she is. But her husband is still quiet. Again she asks what's wrong. He then gets out again and says to the horse, 'Two.' When he gets back in, his wife starts talking about how beautiful they both looked that night and how perfect everything was. But once again, he grows quiet and she asks why. He gets out once more and says, 'Three,' and then shoots the horse. The wife goes hysterical, she wants to know why he did that and the husband then takes her hand and says, 'One.' "

Everyone erupted in laughter. For a moment, everyone forgot they were on a bus in Berlin. They were all living in Willy Tate's fertile imagination.

TATE LEARNED THE art of storytelling on a ranch in the high desert of Eastern Oregon. For the previous two years, he'd been out of football, working as a cowhand mending fences, tending cattle, and, in his spare time, riding the ranges and hunting pheasant and quail. Tate was content with his simple life on the ranch, but his serenity was shattered by a phone call he received in February 1999. That was the night he found out that his father was dying.

"A neighbor of my dad's in Sacramento called and told me that he hadn't seen him in some time," said Tate. "So I told the neighbor to go into his house and check on him. When he did, he found my father in bad shape. He was jaundiced and had lost a lot of weight. The neighbor took my dad to the hospital where they found his colon had ruptured and that there were a bunch of cancerous tumors on it. At that point, they knew he didn't have long to live."

Tate immediately jumped into his pickup and drove south to California. He was at his father's bedside a day after he received the bad news. For two-and-a-half weeks, Tate's father battled his cancer, then quietly passed away. His son, keeping vigil by his side, was crushed.

Richard Tate had played football at Cal-Polly in the 1960s. He was a slow, undersized cornerback, but he'd overachieved and turned into a fine player, much like his son. Young Willy learned the game at his father's knee. "My dad just loved everything about football," Tate remembered fondly. "Everything." After his father's death, Tate again packed up his pickup and just drove. For an entire month, he traveled across the country, periodically stopping to visit friends and family. He drove down into the red clay country of New Mexico, then through the flatiron plains of Texas, then east to the swamps Florida, then up the Eastern Seaboard to Boston, then across the rust belt of Michigan and Ohio, across the prairie of South Dakota, then back to Oregon. In all, he put 16,000 miles on his old pickup. "I just wanted to think," said Tate. "I was hoping to have that moment of epiphany and, well, I guess it never happened."

But Tate's escape along the long ribbon of America's asphalt did in fact afford him some clarity. When he was on the road, Tate constantly thought of his father, about how much his dad had enjoyed talking football and watching his son become one of the best tight ends ever to play at the University of Oregon. When Tate's odyssey ended, he called Criner. Tate had played for Criner in 1996 and '98 and Tate wanted to let the coach know that, at age twenty-eight, he still thought he had some good football in him. And just like that, Tate's American journey became an international one. He was going back to Scotland.

Along with playing tight end—or H-back, as the Claymores called it—Tate was also the long-snapper on punts and the holder on field goals. It was the little things he did so well that made him such a big-time player for the Claymores. "I had a feeling that Willy would still be a productive player," said Criner, "but I didn't know he'd be so productive. But aside from that, he's one of the true leaders on this team. I really like what he's given us."

"It's such a great feeling just being around the guys and playing again," said Tate. "Nothing beats it."

Players on the team regarded Tate as a guy they could trust. One night during the 2000 season, a player phoned Tate in his room at 5 in the morning. This player had taken six tabs of ecstasy and was on the verge of freaking out. Tate, who doesn't use drugs, tried to calm him down. "First, we got into a discussion as to why he took so many tabs in the first place," said Tate. "Then he said, 'Willy, there are twenty-four panes in my window and they're all moving back and forth. Do you know why that is happening?' I thought about for a moment and then I said, 'The only thing I can tell you is that it's poor craftsmanship.' " The two players had a good laugh over that, then talked until daybreak. By then, things had calmed down significantly.

Tate grew up in Elk Grove, California. He didn't start playing organized football until his freshman year of high school, but he was a natural. With his big, soft hands and broad body—he was 6'4" and 230 pounds—he attracted attention from schools across the country. He visited UCLA, but was turned off by the urban setting. He then traveled to Eugene, Oregon, and toured the sprawling campus of the University of Oregon. This was Tate's kind of place. The school was close to the outdoor activities that Tate enjoyed the most: hiking, rafting, and camping. He was sold right away.

In Eugene, Tate blossomed like an April garden into one of the top tight ends in all of college football. His sophomore year he had 331 yards receiving for Oregon's 1992 bowl team, including catching the only touchdown in a rainstorm as Oregon beat Oregon State in the

THE PROVING GROUND

annual "Civil War." That made Tate an instant hero on the streets of Eugene. His junior year he was voted a team captain—a rare honor for a nonsenior—and he earned All-Pac Ten honors. Heading into his senior season, he was picked by a few publications as a preseason All-American. But when the team met for their first practice of the '94 season, Tate was nowhere to be found. He had disappeared, vanishing as quickly as a breath into cold air.

"Willy just decided he'd had enough," said Steve Greatwood, the Ducks' tight-ends coach. "It was a mystery to us."

But it wasn't a mystery to Tate. During his junior year, Oregon started 3–0 and in the fourth game of the season built a 30–0 lead over Cal. Then everything collapsed. Cal rallied for a 42–41 win, making it the third greatest comeback in Division I-A history. For the rest of the season, Oregon never got off the mat. The team finished 5–6 overall and 2–6 in the PAC Ten. The coaches attributed the meltdown to a lack of leadership, which Tate took personally since he was a captain. A few weeks after the season, Tate withdrew from his classes. He packed his car and, in the dead of winter, left Eugene. He didn't even tell his coaches or his teammates.

"My junior year was really a trying season," said Tate. "And after it was over, I just lost the desire to play. I was sick of school and felt like I needed time away. So I just left."

Tate moved with a friend to Winchester in Southern California and worked for several months at a dairy. As he tended cows, Tate devised a plan to sail around the world with several other people. But it never panned out. "That was a last grasp at childhood," said Tate. "We came close to doing it, but we couldn't pull it all together. It's not something you can do by the seat of your pants."

A few weeks before the 1995 NFL draft, an agent called Tate and told him that a handful of NFL teams were interested in him. Those words left Tate breathless. He had been positive that his football days were over. It was one of the few things in life that he'd ever been sure of. But as he listened to what the agent was saying, Tate realized that he missed those carefree days of playing ball, of being with the guys, of being free from the daily grind. The agent told Tate that a few scouts would be at a workout in Eugene and that he should go. Tate agreed. It turned out that he wasn't drafted, but Tate performed well enough at the tryout to be signed by Kansas City as a free agent. He made the team's practice squad, but never saw much action. The following season he spent some time with Tampa Bay. In his brief NFL career, Tate never landed a full-time job. The 2000 season was his third tour of duty in NFL Europe.

"It seems that every time I'm ready to give up football, something happens and I'm able to keep going," said Tate. "When I'm done playing, I'm hoping to buy some land and start a ranch. My dad always had a dream to do that, and we planned to do it together when he retired. He came from a poor family and he really wanted to do that. He was two years away from retiring when he died. Maybe I can make his dream a reality."

11 Worst Call

Free safety Blaine McElmurry.

East Berlin, Germany. Day Before Game Three

AFTER FINALLY MAKING it to Burger King in Berlin and eating lunch, the team had to cut the tour to thirty minutes because they were running behind schedule. The tour was supposed to last two hours. But time was precious as the Claymores needed to get on with the business of preparing for the game. There were meetings to attend, a walk-through to do, an 11 PM bedcheck to make. Chris Ward, a defensive lineman, bought three rolls of film to document his experience at the Wall. But because everything was rushed, the players only caught a brief glimpse of the crumbling East-West barrier. The bus passed by the Wall, pausing for only five seconds. "Damn," said Ward, who *did* know his history. "I really wanted to see that."

The hotel the Claymores stayed at was located in a tough, hardscrabble section of East Berlin. In 1999, the Thunder had lived in the same Courtyard Marriott. But by the end of the season, the Berlin coaching staff had practically prohibited players from leaving the hotel, afraid for their safety. This caused the morale of the team to nose-dive, and, as a result, word got out that playing in Berlin was about as much fun as playing in Siberia.

After a quick walk-through in the large hotel patio, Criner called a team meeting in a cramped, first-floor room. "Men, this team has a chance to be special," Criner told his players. "And if you've ever been on a football team where you know that every guy is doing everything he can to pull his own weight, then you know it's one of the most enjoyable and most exciting damn things you can ever be involved with. That's how teams win championships. Let's make sure we line up tomorrow and let the damn Thunder know what it's all about."

Criner dismissed his players, but asked his travel staff to stay in the room. The Claymores' point man on all travel matters was the team's assistant video coordinator, Kevin Brown. Because of budgetary constraints, no team in NFL Europe has a full-time travel secretary. Assisting Brown with travel concerns was Stephen McCusker (the national coach) and Darren Becker (the equipment manager). Criner called this impromptu meeting because he was upset over a few travel glitches. Some passports had been misplaced and a few staff members had tried to get their own hotel room, even though league policy mandates that support staff share rooms on the road.

Criner spoke softly at first, like a gentle breeze that foretold the storm. "We've had a lot of travel screw-ups that have caused our franchise a hell of a lot embarrassment," Criner told his staff. "I take damn good care of our football team. I make sure that we eat well, that we stay in the best places that we can, and I fought like hell this offseason so that everyone could have their own room in Scotland. I don't have control over league policy. I don't want you going behind my back and trying to get single rooms on the road, which is against league policy. If you want to get me pissed, goddamn it, that's something that will get me pissed in a hurry. And I'll chew some ass royally if that happens again. You don't ever go behind my back on anything. This deal with the passports has caused a lot of headaches and embarrassment. If I ask you to pick up the passports, you pick them up. Three kids packed their passports in their bags in Frankfurt and they were sent home to Scotland. Luckily, we caught them in time. I know that the players should be more responsible, but we know that they're not. That's why we have to pick up the passports."

But an hour later, Criner called the rooms of several coaches and told them to come over to Ratskeller, a jazz club a few blocks away from the hotel that he and Ann had found on a walk. Criner made a point to invite all of his travel staff, which was his way of saying that travel gaffes were really no big deal.

Located in the basement of an old building that resembled a church, Ratskeller had lots of atmosphere—low ceilings and candlelight. As the musical sounds of Louis Armstrong filled the smoky air, Jim and Ann enjoyed themselves. "Bad leg and all, I can still dance to this," said Criner between sips of red wine. "Hell, I can dance on the tabletops to this."

Suddenly, NFL Europe didn't seem like such a bad gig for the coach. The hours were long and the players were sometimes inept, but nights like this, when you could find a great jazz club, somehow made all the drudgery bearable.

East Berlin, Germany. Game Day

The buses didn't depart for the stadium until 3 PM, so the players had the afternoon to themselves. Many sat in the sunshine along the River Spree, which was directly behind the hotel. Some read books out there, others wrote in their journals. A few gazed at the water for more than an hour, never uttering a word, just listening to the gentle flow of the river. If the Claymores had been 0–2 as opposed to 2–0, it would have been difficult to imagine these scenes of tranquility. Winning has a way of curing all ills—especially cases of severe homesickness.

The players arrived at the stadium in East Berlin at 3:58 PM. By this time, even though kickoff wasn't until seven, most of the Berliners at the pregame party were deep into their first six-pack. The party in Berlin was a slightly more subdued affair than in Frankfurt, but it was still friskier than most tailgating sessions in the States. Behind the stadium, men in full body armor performed mock sword fights. A machine simulated punts, as about ten Germans tried in vain to catch them. A flag football competition took place and, as in Frankfurt, there was a main stage. Here the DJ reviewed the rules of the game and dispensed advice on when to cheer. Before the Wall came down in 1989, most East Berliners had never heard of American football, much less understood it. So these pregame crash courses served an important purpose.

A few hundred yards west of the stadium stood the remains of the Berlin Wall. Years ago, at the soccer matches that were held at Jahn

THE PROVING GROUND

Stadium, guards used to stand on the roof of the stadium and shoot anyone who tried to leap over the Wall to dash to freedom and West Berlin. Before the game, a few of the Claymores' support staff walked over to the Wall and retrieved some historic rubble. Later, they would give it away to the players.

Fifty minutes before kickoff, Kelvin Eafon sat alone on one of the sidelines benches. He hadn't been told of his release yet, but he had been informed that he'd been deactivated for the game. As he sat there, he listened to music on his headphones and watched the sunset. Thirty minutes later, at Criner's pregame speech, Eafon had a towel wrapped around his neck. Then he started to cry. He couldn't bear to have anyone see tears streaming down his cheeks, so he covered his head with the towel. He knew the dream was dying. "Make this the best game you've played all year," Criner told the team. "Play with enthusiasm and play with class. Play our style of football. Have fun and lay it on the line."

As soon as Criner was finished, Eafon ran out of the locker room ahead of his teammates. He jogged the 500 yards to the tunnel that led into the stadium. He then waited for his teammates. As the PA announcer introduced them one-by-one, Eafon hugged each team member before he ran out onto the field. Eafon may have had his problems in NFL Europe, but this was a memorable moment for him. Even players who'd had little tolerance for Eafon's arrogance were touched by his display of emotion.

FOR THE THIRD consecutive week, the game did not start well for the Claymores. The offense went three-and-out on its first possession— the third time that had happened—and then Berlin marched down the field. Kicker Jarret Holmes, allocated to the Thunder by the Chicago Bears, hit a 50-yard field goal to give Berlin and 4–0 lead. (That's not a misprint. In NFL Europe, field goals that are 50 yards or longer are awarded four points.)

On the third play of Berlin's first possession, Claymore linebacker Phil Glover banged his helmet into one of the Thunder's guards. It was a typical football collision, but it left Glover in a fog. During practice that week, Glover, a former standout at the University of Utah who'd been allocated to the Claymores by the Titans, had deflated the padding in his helmet because it was too tight on his head. Unfortunately, he forgot to inflate the padding before the game. So when he got drilled in the head for the first time, everything went black. He staggered off the field and lay down on the sidelines, obviously with a concussion. After a few moments, the black lightened to gray. A few moments after that, he came out of it. "I was thinking of a play from when I was in Pop Warner, like ten years ago," said Glover. "I hadn't thought of that play since it actually happened. That's when I knew something probably wasn't right." Fortunately, Glover only missed a few plays. He returned, but for the rest of the game he occasionally lined up in the wrong position.

Of all the players on the Claymores' roster, Glover probably had overcome the most. When he was in high school in South Central Los Angeles, his mother sent him to live with his father and stepmother in Las Vegas. She didn't want her son to be suckled by the streets and she was fearful of the gangs that swarmed over the neighborhood. She thought young Phil would have better chance of making it in life if he was in Las Vegas. But Glover wasn't in Vegas very long before his father, who had drinking and gambling problems, packed up and left town. "As I started getting older, my stepmom and I started banging heads," Glover remembered. "When I was fourteen, I said forget it. I got tired of being the scapegoat and said I was moving out.

"She said, 'OK, you want to be such a bad ass, leave.' So I moved around from place to place, then moved in with a good friend of mine,

Chance Larsen. His mom, Sheila, ended up taking guardianship of me."

Glover enrolled in Clark High in Las Vegas and was an immediate success on the athletic field. Glover had a squat, compact build with thick, powerful legs. At 6 feet and 170 pounds, he had a 38-inch vertical jump and ran the 40 in 4.48. He was a tireless football player, controlling games from his linebacker position. In his senior year, he led the Cougars to a state football title. That same year Glover won the state wrestling championship in the 171-pound weight class.

Off the field, Glover's life grew more complicated when he and his girlfriend, Carmen, had a son. (They eventually married.) Glover was a seventeen-year-old child with a child. But he didn't want to repeat the sins of his father, so Glover moved in with Carmen's parents and supported his new family, working three different jobs after school. He was an athletic trainer, a pizza delivery guy, and a bus boy at the Sheraton Hotel. Life was a struggle. "A lot of people leave when they are scared," said Glover. "Initially, I guess I was scared. But I sat back and thought about it. What would I be doing to that child if I left? I know how that feels. It's difficult not to have your father around."

Phil completed high school and then accepted a scholarship to Washington State. He lasted two years there before transferring to Utah, where he became one of the top outside linebackers in the country. "Phil was very disciplined," said his wife, Carmen, noting that Phil spent his college summers working as a bouncer at a club and counselor at a youth correctional facility. "He knew exactly what he wanted, no mater what obstacles he encountered. He was determined to succeed."

Glover was selected as the 222nd overall pick by the Tennessee Titans in the 1999 draft. He signed a three-year deal with the Titans and got a $27,000 signing bonus. Glover spent most of the '99 season on the Titans practice squad. He was in Europe to solidify his spot for the 2000 season. "My goals have not been realized," said Glover. "I still got a long ways to go. But I feel like I'm getting closer."

When Glover talked about his future, he got a hard look in his eyes. This was a guy who had seen it all. "The difference between me and those others is that I chose to be responsible," said Glover. "I decided I can't do what's being done to me. Some guys step up to the plate. It hurts me when someone doesn't accept the responsibilities of being a father. It's not fair to the child."

THE CLAYMORES APPEARED to be in control of the game at the beginning of the second half. They led the Berlin Thunder 17–14 and were driving for a score early in the third quarter. Daft was having a nice game, as he threw a pretty ball to Rickey Brady for 16 yards that gave Scotland a first down on the Berlin 23-yard-line. But two plays later, the craziest play of season would turn the game around.

Backup running back Ben Snell took a handoff from Daft and found some room around the left end. Berlin linebacker Richard Hogans closed fast and popped the ball from Snell's hands. The ball bounced straight to Thunder safety Richard Yancy, who recovered it at the 20. Yancy then tripped over Scotland's Tremayne Allen and fell to the ground. As he was on the ground, Claymores' wideout Scott Couper touched him with his right hand. Nonetheless, Yancy jumped up and started jogging toward the Claymores' end zone.

At first, no one paid attention to Yancy. The Claymores' defense was coming on the field and many of the defenders walked right by him. Then, suddenly, one of the referees started running up the sideline, following Yancy. Yancy began sprinting. By the time he crossed the goal line, there were roughly forty-five players on the field. The referee, much to the consternation of the Claymore coaches, signaled for a touchdown. "It was the single worst call I've ever seen,"

THE PROVING GROUND

squawked Criner. "There's no question about it—the guy was tagged and he was *down*."

For the rest of the game, the Claymores were in a daze. They committed stupid penalties on defense—defensive tackle Noel Scarlett was flagged for unsportsmanlike conduct for poking a Thunder player in the eye—and the offense could never regain its rhythm. Despite this, the Claymores still had a chance to win in the last minute of the game.

Trailing 24–17 with 52 seconds left, Scotland started its last drive of the game on its own 38-yard-line. They had no timeouts. On first down, Daft gained 19 yards on a scramble. He then hit Tate for 11 yards and then Couper for another 11 yards, which moved the ball to the Berlin 21. After spiking the ball with 15 seconds remaining, Daft found Stecker out of the backfield. Stecker, who had rushed for 127 yards on the night, caught the ball in the right flat and headed out-of-bounds at the 12-yard-line. But instead of going out and stopping the clock, Stecker inexplicably cut inside. He lost his footing on the cut, and fell down. Stecker tried to hand the ball to the referee, but the official asked for a new ball. The Claymores, who were ready to go at the line of scrimmage, had to wait for the new ball to be set. The referees' blunder cost Scotland any chance at winning, as the clock expired before they could get a snap off.

In the locker room afterward, Criner asked everyone to come into the back room, the one space that was big enough to accommodate the entire team. There were tall windows in this room, and German fans stood on the other side of them, taunting the Claymores by flipping them off and pounding on the windows. When Jon Hesse walked over to them, his towering frame was sufficient to scare the fans off. Criner was too mad even to yell. He looked ashen, expressionless, as if he were wearing a death mask. In a quiet, defeated voice, he spoke:

"Men, we should have won that football game," he said. "We beat ourselves. You know the reason I called everyone in here is because we need to make a decision about what we're going to do about penalties. They are killing us, on both sides of the ball. You know we have a hell of a good football team—potentially. You know, potential is a lot like horseshit. If you don't spread it around and use it to make things grow, it just stinks up the place. And that's what we did tonight. The more critical you are of yourselves and the higher standards you set for yourselves, the better football player you'll be. You'll only be as good as you want to be. Now we have this same team on our home field in a week. Let's show *them* who's boss."

The first person out of the locker room after Criner's speech was Eafon. He walked outside and looked up at the starry night with eyes that were as lifeless as buttons. His emotion was gone, and so was his willingness to ever play for Criner again. "I led the team in rushing in every scrimmage, but Criner never gave me a chance in games," said Eafon. "But I took it in stride. I came over here to prove myself, know what I'm saying? But now I think I shouldn't have even come. I've been wasting my time. I guess I've gotten a chance to play special teams, which I'd never done before because I was too important to the offense. I felt that if I was out there, I could have done some things. This team is good enough to win the whole thing. But I don't know if they will because a lot of these guys don't know how to win. You gotta stay poised. You can't press. You can't get nervous. Do you know what I'm saying? Do you know?"

12 The Blame Game

Andy Colvin (*far left*) with some of the local press corps.

East Berlin, Germany. Three Hours After Game Three

EVERY KID WHO dreams of playing professional football should spend some time with players right after a game. It is the little things you see that are revealing. A limp. A stiff neck. A tender knee. A bandaged head. And a tiny white pill.

As the Claymores ate their postgame meal in the main conference room in the Marriott, the pills were popped as if they were Tic-Tacs. The Berlin game was one of the dirtiest showdowns in NFL Europe history, according to many Claymore staffers. Late hits flew on almost every play. Punches were frequently thrown in the pile. And players from both teams made deliberate attempts to take out knees. Now several of the Claymore players were in serious pain, as if they'd just been in a car accident. To the rescue came a doctor, passing by each table and dispensing his magic potion of a prescription pill similar to Vicodin—an addictive, codeine-laced painkiller that had once gripped Brett Favre—as nonchalantly as a dentist gives away a toothbrush at the end of an appointment. There was something disturbing about the ease with which the doctor doled out the drugs. It fueled the notion that the players were being used—a view that many of the players would articulate in the coming weeks.

"Without the painkillers, I'd never make it," confessed Finkes, who after the game felt pain in nearly every bone in his body. "The pain is too great after games. I don't think people can really appreciate how hard football can be on your body."

On two occasions Finkes got intentionally stepped on and kicked as he was lying on the ground at the end of plays. Late in the second quarter, Jon Hesse had one knee on the ground after a play as he tried to catch his breath when a wide receiver from the Thunder took a 15-yard running start and drilled him in the head with his helmet— a roguish maneuver known as "ear-holing." "That cheap shot," said Myrel Moore, "was about the dirtiest thing I've ever seen in all my years of coaching."

The Claymores were just as guilty. The worst offender was defensive tackle Noel Scarlett, who poked a player in the eye while standing two yards from an official. Scarlett was in a pushing match with two other players when he resorted to the poke, which among players is generally considered the most repellent of all dirty tactics. "That was some Moe and Curley shit," said safety Chris Bayne. "It was just stupid."

Scarlett's cheap shot was one of the few in the game that triggered a flag from the referees. In NFL Europe the quality of officiating is like the quality of air in Los Angeles: Some days it's good, most days it's bad. Like the players, the referees in Europe were trying to catch the eye of the NFL. Most of the refs came from the college ranks and they journeyed to Europe to gain experience and further their chances of landing a job in the NFL. But because most of them hadn't refereed at the professional level before—where, even in NFL Europe, the pace of the game is noticeably quicker than big-time college ball—the referees seemed to get more calls wrong than right.

But what upset the Scotland coaches more than the incompetent refs and the dirty play was the fact that the Thunder and their wily ways baited some of their players into making silly mistakes. For example, before a Claymores' punt late in the fourth quarter, Kevin Peoples, a safety for Berlin, taunted linebacker Ryan Taylor, who was on the line of scrimmage preparing to block. The two had tussled all day long on special teams, and Peoples wanted one more shot at Taylor. Before the snap, Peoples pushed one of his teammates, who was lined up across from Taylor, out of the way and took his place. "I'm going to give it to you real good, mother-fucker," Peoples told Taylor. Just then, Peoples lifted his right arm up in a quick movement. Taylor reacted and moved his feet. He was called for an illegal-motion penalty. After the punt, Scotland safety Marcus Ray approached Taylor. "Don't let that mother-fucker beat your ass," said Ray. "Think next time."

In the next few days, a hot topic of discussion among players was why there was so much dirty play on the field in NFL Europe. A few white players privately blamed it on black players and the environment in which they grew up, as the racial divide on the team deepened. "One of the best things about football is being forced to spend time with guys you wouldn't normally be around," said a white player, who spoke frankly on the condition of anonymity. "I feel like

I've learned a lot about black guys and how they act and sometimes I just don't understand it. Some of them will do things like intentionally poke somebody in the face and not care about whether they get caught by the refs. To them, it's okay to get flagged for a personal foul and hurt the team, as long as that guy on the other team knows that he's going to get fucked with if he fucks with that player. You see the same shit in poor neighborhoods. One black guy will kill another black guy just so everyone in the neighborhood knows that you can't fuck with him. He doesn't care that he's in jail; all that matters to him is that he got back at the guy who messed with him in the first place. Some of these guys just have no discipline."

A black player on the team, who was in on the discussion and also requested anonymity, responded: "There may be some truth to that, but you can't generalize, just like I can't generalize and make a blanket statement about all whites." He went on: "I don't think not having discipline is a black thing or a white thing. I think a lot just goes back to how you grew up and how you were raised. There certainly are a lot of white guys who don't have any discipline. Just look at the game film. I've seen undisciplined white guys on basically every team I've ever played on, including this one."

Glasgow, Scotland. Six Days Before Game Four

Kelvin Eafon was in his room at the Central, talking on the phone, when Scotland's running-backs coach Josh Brannen knocked on his door. The Claymores had only been back in Glasgow a few hours when Criner dispatched Brannen to fetch Eafon. It was time to send Eafon home.

"You're just a play away from getting a phone call and us wanting you back," Criner told Eafon. "If one of our running backs gets hurt, we're going to call you because you know our system and we like your effort." Eafon knew that he would never be back, but, like Criner, he pretended that it was a possibility. He said all the right things and the two parted amicably. The next morning Eafon was on a 5 AM flight to the States. "I'm not getting anything out of this anyway," said Eafon before he left, glad to be going home.

Eafon left Scotland on the first day of May, which was a day off for the players. Myrel Moore spent that afternoon writing a long letter to the league about both the inept officiating in the Berlin game and the dirty play of the Thunder. Nothing would ever come of this letter, but it gave Moore a chance to vent. "It was something I needed to do," said Moore. "If this league is ever going to get better, the officiating has got to improve. That was embarrassing. Really, even the NFL should be embarrassed."

Moore is the only Claymore coach who has NFL experience. In the 2000 season only five of the forty-one coaches in NFL Europe had ever coached a down of football in the NFL. "That's a problem," said Moore. "If an NFL Europe coach's job is to prepare players for the NFL, then it would make sense that they be coached by men who have NFL experience. There simply needs to be more coaches here who have the NFL on their résumés."

Based on what he'd seen so far this season, Moore thought that the Claymores would beat most of the top college teams. "We'd have trouble with teams that are real quick, like Florida State," reasoned Moore. "But we wouldn't have trouble with big, plodding teams like Ohio State or Nebraska. I think we have six guys on defense that have the potential to be on NFL rosters next season and maybe three guys on offense. A lot of others guys will have a chance to make it, but they'll need luck. Lots of it."

Criner spent part of the afternoon preparing a speech. Most of it had nothing to do with football but with travel in Europe. Numerous problems had popped up at the tail end of the latest trip. For example, when checking out of the hotel in Berlin three players claimed they hadn't taken anything from the hotel minibar—when in fact they had and had refused to pay for it. When a small blond woman behind the reception desk demanded that they pay, the players grew agitated and tried to intimidate the woman. Eventually they paid, but it was an ugly scene that did nothing for the team's reputation.

There were other blunders. Three players—Damon Gibson, Hurley Tarver, and Kory Blackwell—strayed from the group in the Frankfurt airport. If a coach hadn't had them paged at the last second, they would have missed their connecting flight to Scotland. Then on the plane back to Glasgow, when a stewardess asked the players to remove their headphones for takeoff and landing, many of the players refused.

Criner hated it when his players behaved like this. He could tolerate losing—he coached at Iowa State, after all. But when his players acted thoughtlessly and without class, he felt like he had somehow failed. Criner believed in using football and the experience of NFL Europe as a means to build character, to forge a player's mettle. Yet character flaws were the reason why many of these young men were here—whether such flaws were a lack of discipline, a lack of focus, or a lack of commitment, and Criner knew it. So whenever the opportunity arose to talk about issues such as responsibility and integrity, Criner seized it.

"Don't be the Ugly American," said Criner the following morning at a team meeting. "If we're not a classy outfit, if we don't have pride in who we are and who our teammates are, it will hurt us in the run for a championship. I've never been around a renegade outfit that has won. Class shows through. If you've got class, it will pay off in the way you handle stress, pressure, everything. Don't be the Ugly American when we travel. Now, let's act with class off the field and play with class on the field. Let's have a good week of practice and get those SOBs on Saturday."

The speech worked. The Claymore had their best three consecutive practices of the season in the days leading up to their rematch with the Thunder. In particular, the offensive line looked more fortified, largely because of the addition of offensive tackle Scott Curry. For the first three weeks of the season, Curry was in Montana waiting for his wife to give birth. Allocated to the Claymores by the Packers, Curry was one of the top offensive linemen in the league during training camp. But as the birth of his child neared, Curry got permission from Criner to leave the team and be with his wife. In Curry's absence, Jason Tenner assumed his spot in the lineup. Tenner, who had just switched from defensive tackle to offensive tackle at training camp, struggled mightily in Berlin. He gave up four sacks to defensive end Jonathan Brown and was overmatched on nearly every play. Hours after the game, as Tenner was eating his postgame meal, he asked one of the assistants for a play-by-play stat sheet of the game. When he saw that he had surrendered four sacks, he nearly fell off his chair. For the rest of the night the gregarious, easygoing Tenner barely uttered a word.

Curry, who was selected in the sixth round by the Packers in 1999 out of Montana University, arrived in Glasgow when the team was still in Berlin. He moved into his room in the Central and made frequent phone calls to his wife Shawna to check on Colton, their healthy baby boy. When the team returned to the Central from Berlin, Curry wandered down from his room and greeted the team in the lobby. As soon as the players saw the 6'4", 290-pound Curry, he was given a messiah's welcome. There were hugs and handshakes—and a feeling that the team's biggest problem had just been solved. "As soon as I saw Scott," said Willy Tate, "the bags that I was carrying sure got a lot lighter."

Curry was just glad to be playing again, to be one of the boys again. "It was frustrating trying to follow the team when I was at home," he said. "I checked on the Internet, but it's hard to find scores. I'm a little out of shape, but I don't think I'll be that rusty. I just hope I can remember all the plays."

Glasgow, Scotland. Three Days Before Game Four

Thursday was media day for the Claymores. Even though practices were open to the press all week, it was rare for more than two reporters to come to practice on days other than Thursday, when six to eight writers would show up. This suggested two things: American football was still a minor sport in Scotland, and the local reporters who covered the sport weren't that interested in thoroughly researching their stories. With the exception of the *Sun*'s Andy Colvin, the writers who covered the Claymores conducted very few independent interviews. Instead, they fed off the Claymores public relations director, Steve Livingston, writing entire stories from his press release and e-mails.

At the end of each Thursday practice, the eight or so writers who regularly attended media day could speak one-on-one with any player or coach on the team. Unfortunately, they didn't take advantage of this almost-unlimited access. They worked en masse, asking every player virtually the same questions. "It's pathetic," admitted Andy Colvin. "There just isn't a lot of motivation here to go out and really find a story."

Scottish reporters worked this way because that's how they typically covered soccer, the main sport in their country. Access to soccer players was normally very restricted, so reporters would pool their information at the end of each day. Now the same principle applied to their coverage of the Claymores. The result of this could be seen in the local papers throughout the season. With a few exceptions, every time one paper ran a feature story on a player, you could find almost the exact same story in the other papers.

At the end of their Thursday practice, Criner called his team to the center of the field. "This was another outstanding workout, men," Criner said, pumping them up before they faced the press. "Now the news media may be looking to ask you something to create controversy. Just ignore it. We don't want to add anything to the Thunder's bulletin board. Let's just go about our business and act in a professional manner. If a question comes up and you don't want to answer it, then don't answer it. Remember, act with class."

Criner always met with the press in a small, second-floor room at the team's practice facility, which was at a local college about a fifteen-minute bus ride away from the Central. There were only eight chairs in the room, lined up next to each other in two rows of four. The ringleader of the local press corp was the *Sun*'s Andy Colvin, who always asked the first question. He was also the man the other reporters looked to when there was an awkward silence in the room.

When Criner entered, he wanted to talk first about the Berlin Thunder, the team Scotland would play in three days. "One of the hardest things you have to do in this league is play opponents in back-to-back weeks," Criner said. "But I can honestly say that I'm excited about that opportunity this week. I want to get the bad taste of that defeat out of my mouth. And the *way* we ended up losing that game—the damn officials gave them a touchdown. Then the league turns around and gives the guy who scored the touchdown an award for being National Player of the Week. That really burns me up! That's totally ridiculous—for both the referees and the league officials to do what they did."

After the press conference, the reporters were invited to eat lunch with the team in a dining room located down the hall. When the reporters entered the cafeteria, it was almost empty, as most of the players were still showering. After getting his food from the buffet, one rookie reporter walked to a table in the back and sat down by himself. Minutes later a few players—all black—joined the reporter, who was white. As they chatted about life in Scotland, defensive back Kory Blackwell approached the reporter, who was attending his first Claymores' practice of the season and was therefore not aware that he was sitting at a table where only black players sat.

"Yo, mother-fucker, you're in my seat," Blackwell said to the reporter.

"There's plenty of available seats," the reporter replied.

"I said you're in my seat," Blackwell repeated. "Get the fuck up, motherfucker!"

At this point, the reporter didn't know if Blackwell was joking or not. Aaron Stecker, who was sitting nearby, told Blackwell that it was no big deal. But Blackwell just stood there stone-faced and unblinking. Not wanting to see where this was going, the reporter rose from his seat and moved to a different table, his pride splattered all over the floor. Blackwell laughed as the reporter sat down at another table, but no one else in the room thought it was funny. Criner's lecture about handling reporters with class had apparently not sunk in with every player.

Edinburgh, Scotland. Game Day

Two hours before kickoff, Claymore coaches Jim Tomsula and Vince Alcalde strolled across the grass field at Murrayfield Stadium. As the springtime sunlight washed over them, they began talking to Mickey Mays, Berlin's defensive-line coach. "Boy, you got yourselves a real running back in Stecker," Mays said. "I don't know how we're going to stop him today. We're just going to have to do everything possible to stop the run."

Alcalde and Tomsula nodded their heads and smiled slyly. Alcalde had spent all week preparing to face nine-man fronts designed to shut-down Stecker. He'd added a shovel pass to Stecker and few other plays that he believed would beat those stacked fronts. As Mays left, Alcalde and Tomsula gave each other a discreet high-five and giggled like little kids sharing a funny secret.

Before the game, Criner also spent time walking around the stadium. He talked to opposing players and coaches, then ducked into the Claymores' locker room. A few minutes later he walked out of the stadium and paid £2 ($3.50) for a hamburger sold to him by a vendor. "I bet NFL coaches don't have to do this," he said with a laugh. He then signed some autographs for fans who were attending the pregame party—which was a calm affair compared to the raging celebrations in Germany—and spent time talking to a few of the most devout fans, a menagerie of regulars that Criner knew on a first-name basis. Criner is that rarest of coaches, the kind who talks to fans as if they are equals. This was why the 10,000 or so faithful Claymore fans adored Criner. Before and after every game, he would chat with them, always being sure to thank them for their support.

TEN MINUTES BEFORE kickoff, silence filled the Claymores' locker room. No one moved. Players sat in front of their lockers, their heads cast downward, their eyes on the tile floor. The coaches stood as still as statues. No one looked at each other. One minute passed, then two. Still no movement, no noise. The room was charged with intensity as everyone meditated on two questions: Am I good enough? Am I strong enough?

Such reflection was something that the coaches hadn't seen all season. Normally, in the tense moments between warmups and kick-off, the locker room fell into a fearful silence. But this was different. This was what a focused, determined, and unafraid team looked like. "We've got this thing won," Tomsula said as he walked out of the locker room. "You could feel it in there and you could see it in there. It was in their eyes. I'd bet my life that we win this game."

Tomsula then wobbled out onto the field. Clearly this was a man who knew his football. Because, in a few minutes, Jim Tomsula would witness something that in the NFL Europe was as rare as the Spotted Owl: the perfect game.

13 Dirty Day

Running back Aaron Stecker.

Edinburgh, Scotland. Game Day

IT ONLY TOOK three plays for the savagery to begin. Scotland had the ball on its 31-yard-line and Daft dropped back to pass. He threw downfield to Scott Couper, but the pass fell incomplete. What most the of the 9,542 fans at Murrayfield didn't see was that, just as Daft flung the pass, Stecker was blindsided by Berlin linebacker Lamont Green. He was hit so hard that the Claymores initially feared that their star's season was over.

During the play, Stecker was a secondary receiver. He ran a little screen pattern toward the Berlin sideline. As he was finishing his route, he was looking back at Daft, so he never saw Green coming. At full speed, Green hit Stecker in the head with both his helmet and right fist. As soon as Green administered the blow, the entire Thunder bench erupted in cheers. Because the bench's attention was on Stecker, rather than on the ball, it was clear that the attack was premeditated.

Stecker lay on the ground for nearly three minutes, motionless, as if he was about to become past tense. Blood seeped from his mouth. When he got up, he walked by Green and gave him a hard, hateful look. After Stecker gathered his wits for a few minutes on the sideline, he jogged back onto the field. The first person he sought out was Green, whose jersey number was 55. "All right, 55, I got your number," yelled Stecker as he made his way to the huddle. "Now I know who you are. I don't know when, it could be today or it could be a few years from now, but I'm getting you back. You better be watching your knees."

"Yo, man, be cool," responded Green. "I'm from the ghetto. Be cool."

"I don't care where you're from," said Stecker. "Whatever it takes, I'm going to get you."

When Stecker arrived at the huddle, the taste of blood was still in his mouth. Now he put the smell of money in front of his teammates, pledging to give £5 ($7.50) to anyone who took out Green. Guard Jason Gamble then added another £5 to the bounty. Green was never injured in the game, but it was not for a lack of effort on the part of the Claymores. "That guy [Green] has to be the dirtiest player I've ever seen," said the Claymores' Gamble. "Stecker is our meal ticket, and we're going to protect him."

THE PROVING GROUND

Once Stecker reentered the game, it was over. He rushed for 81 yards and scored three touchdowns as the Claymores annihilated the Thunder, 42–3. It was by far the Claymores most complete game of the season. The offense rolled to a season-high 325 yards and the defense was dominating, holding Berlin to just 12 first downs. The only drama of the game—aside from all the dirty play—occurred late in the fourth quarter on the Claymores' last series of the day, when Takayuki Sunaga of Tokyo, Japan, entered the game at quarterback.

Known simply as "Tak" by his teammates, Sunaga played for a club team in Tokyo. At 6'2", 211 pounds, he was the biggest player in his Japanese league—bigger, even, than all of his offensive linemen. For someone who'd only started playing football a few years before, Sunaga threw a pretty ball. He wasn't the most accurate of passers but, in an emergency, he could be a servicable NFL Europe quarterback. Sunaga certainly didn't have the arm strength of John Elway, but he was better than even Elway at drawing the opposing team offside with his cadence, according to Myrel Moore. "Elway was the master of getting defenders to jump," said Moore, who was on the Broncos' coaching staff from 1972–80. "But Tak is better. I guess it's because he's calling the signals in what to him is a foreign language. In practice we'll tell our guys what the count is going to be, and, amazingly, Tak still draws them off about half the time. It's really incredible."

As Sunaga jogged onto the field at the two-minute warning against Berlin, every Claymore player rose from the bench. They all wanted Sunaga to attempt a pass. Sunaga's family had flown twenty-three hours from the Land of the Rising Sun earlier in the week to watch this game. And now, it looked like they were going to see a first, as no Japanese quarterback had ever attempted a pass in a professional football game. For the first two plays, Criner called for running-back dives into the line of scrimmage. On the third play—which would be the last play of the game—Criner again called for a run. In the huddle, though, the players wanted Sunaga to pass. They begged him to overrule Criner and do it—which no doubt would make big news back in Japan. But Sunaga dutifully obeyed his coach. After the game, even though the Claymores just destroyed the Thunder, Sunaga's head sagged as he walked off the field.

In the locker room, Sunaga was the only player who wasn't feeling good. Everyone else was giddy—especially the coach. "Right now you have everybody in this dadgum league sitting up and paying attention to us," said Criner. "I'll tell you something else. That's the kind of football we're capable of playing week in and week out. You can do anything, as long as you focus and concentrate during practice. I'll be honest with you, men, I don't think I've ever seen a better Claymore performance than the one we had today, even during our championship season. But I'm going to tell you guys something"—at this point, tears were trailing down Criner's sunburned cheeks and his voice cracked—"you should feel damn proud of what you did today. You laid it on the line and you kicked the shit out of them. Great job."

When Criner walked into the press room to offer comments and answer questions, a handful of Scottish reporters gave him a thunderous round of applause—something that is frowned on in every NFL press room. "I'm obviously very pleased," said Criner, "but I was also disappointed with what I thought was a lot of dirty football on the part of the Berlin Thunder. We kept our composure, played football, and let all that other crap just go over our heads. A week or two weeks ago, we might have retaliated, and all that does is hurt you. Today, we got a couple of players seriously hurt and almost got some others seriously hurt on shots that I thought were totally uncalled for."

After every home game, the Claymores threw a postgame party in one of Murrayfield's banquet rooms. This gave the front office a chance to wine and dine its sponsors and other VIPs. Also, from time to time, the Claymores would invite a few devout fans to these festivities, giving them a chance to get up close and personal with the players, like groupies with backstage passes to a rock concert.

The Claymores had played a near-flawless game, but the coaching staff, though pleased, wasn't in the mood to celebrate. As they stood together in a corner of the banquet room, eating hot dogs and hamburgers and nursing bottles of Coors Light, they were all concerned for Myrel Moore. Early in the second quarter, as Moore stood on the sideline, a running play came right at him. As was the case with Criner in Frankfurt, Moore got pinned by two offensive linemen standing behind him who weren't watching the action on the field. Hit hard in the ribs, Moore fell fast and violently to the ground. He struggled back to his feet, but he had trouble breathing for the rest of the game. After the final whistle blew, he walked gingerly off the field, hopped in a car, and was driven to the hospital. He would later discover that his ribs, while not broken, were severely bruised.

"I can't believe that same shit happened again," said Tomsula on the 45-minute bus ride from Murrayfield Stadium in Edinburgh back to the team hotel in Glasgow. "I tell the guys over and over to protect their coaches on the sidelines, and they just don't get it."

Glasgow, Scotland. Four Hours After the Game

That night nearly every player on the team hit the town. About twenty Claymores—both black and white—went to an Irish pub called O'Neill's, located in the West End of Glasgow. "The amazing thing about football is that when you're doing good, all the players seem to get along," said Tate, as he sat at a table in O'Neill's. "Usually not many black guys will come and hang out at O'Neill's, but once we start winning, you'll have defensive backs and wide receivers coming out with us. If we're losing, no way do they come. But when we're winning, they'll definitely come just because they want to be around their teammates. I remember after we won the World Bowl back in 1996, everyone went to the same bar. That was probably the only time that happened during the entire season."

At the table, Tate entertained several players with a story. One day during practice at the University of Oregon, Tate said that he saw a few students passed out on the lawn by the practice field. The previous night there had been a Grateful Dead Show at the University, whose school colors are green and yellow. Tate noticed one of the students stand up and rub his eyes. "He just looked around for about a minute and then he said, 'Wow, man, it's the lemon wedges taking on the lime wedges.' " The table cracked up, and the evening of fun was on.

During the early part of the season, Tate and a few other players had befriended a local singer and guitar player named Karl Byrne. Every Sunday night Byrne played Irish folk songs and any other song the crowd at O'Neill's requested. The Claymores sat in wooden chairs in a semicircle at the front of the bar, five feet away from Byrne. For the first two hours everyone was having a grand time. Then, around 10:30 PM, the mood abruptly changed. About a dozen players from the Thunder, who had been watching the Claymores though the front window, entered the establishment. None of them was smiling.

When Byrne saw the Thunder players, he announced to the crowd, "And I'd like to congratulate the Scottish Claymores on destroying the Berlin Thunder this afternoon." The crowd of fifty-five went wild. But the Berlin players' faces still bore the look of an agitated bear. "There's going to be a fight here tonight," Finkes predicted. "The bad blood is about to boil over."

As the Berlin players made their way into the bar, the Claymores were closer as a team than they had been all season. They had only been together for two months, but now they were willing to use their fists to defend each other. This meant something, because there's nothing that forges friendships faster than the shared experience of a great battle. That's why the bond between football players is a transcendent phenomenon. You may have known the left tackle on your team for only a few months, for example, but if you ever needed a helping hand years later, asking him for a favor would be like asking a priest for forgiveness; it would be a done deal the moment the words flowed from your lips. Once formed, football bonds are virtually unbreakable.

But as ready as both teams were to let the fists fly, it never came to that. A few Claymore players, wanting to defuse the situation, bought some drinks for the Berlin players. As soon the guys from the Thunder got a few beers in them, the tension let up and their anger evaporated. Luckily, Stecker didn't show up at the bar, because there were several Berlin players who still wanted a piece of him. The Thunder players sat at the back of the bar and took in the scene. They watched as the Claymores sang songs together such as "American Pie" and "Piano Man." They watched as the Claymores slapped hands, bought each other drinks, and acted as if they genuinely liked each other. "This is what NFL Europe should be about, having a good time with your teammates," said Eric Kresser, Berlin's quarterback. "We don't have a place like this in Berlin, that's for sure. This must make them a better team because it looks like these guys really like each other. That's a huge advantage, especially in this league."

Thunder linebacker Sedric Clark was still upset, however. "The Claymores are known as the dirtiest team in the league and we made a decision as a team that we weren't going to take it," he said. "That's why we went after them. We committed some stupid fouls, but they know that we're not going to take their shit. If we see them again, it will be very interesting. But I knew we weren't going to play well today. I mean, when we flew out we had to fly through Frankfurt.

There was a strike going on there, so the players had to get on three separate planes. Some guys didn't get into town until two in the morning. The next day, the bus didn't show up at our hotel to take us to practice. So we had to take taxis, but the problem was that nobody knew where the practice field was. Then the taxi driver got lost. When we finally got there, our equipment wasn't there. So it was just a mess, man, a total mess."

As Clark stood in the back of the bar, he did admit that he was jealous of Claymores in one regard: he'd rather live in Glasgow than in Berlin. "Our hotel is in East Berlin and the black players have been told not to go out alone; there are gangs of skinheads around our hotel," he said. "So we always go out in large groups. There is a great nightlife in Berlin, but it's about a thirty-minute cab ride away."

Even though Clark and his teammates had a 4:30 AM wake-up call the next morning to begin their journey back to Berlin, the Thunder players stayed out late buying drinks for each other. Eventually, most of the Claymore and Thunder players talked and shook hands. Outside a pub in the West End of Glasgow, at about 3 AM, they said their goodbyes. Under the soft light of the moon, the animosity had melted away. At least for now.

14 The Ziggy Story

The Claymores' introduction before their game at the Rhein Fire.

Düsseldorf, Germany, Four Hours Before the Claymores' Game at Rhein in 1996

ANYONE WHO'S BEEN with NFL Europe for a few years has a good bus story: How one huffed and puffed and then broke down, how one got hopelessly lost down a dark alley in Amsterdam, or how one nearly got into a catastrophic accident on a narrow street in Barcelona. But of all the bus stories that Ann Criner has heard—and endured—over the years, none brings a sweeter smile to her face than the one that happened in Düsseldorf in 1996. That was when the

Claymores came to town to take on the Rhein Fire and had the unfortunate experience of crossing paths with a bus driver named Ziggy. "Over the years it's just become known as the Ziggy story," said Ann with a laugh. "And we've tried—boy, have we tried—to forget it."

Four hours before the game against the Rhein Fire in 1996, the Claymores boarded an idling bus outside of their team hotel in Düsseldorf. As each player climbed aboard, the driver said, "Ah-lo. Me name is Ziggy and I am from Frankfurt." Everyone thought this was strange. Why would a Frankfurt native be driving their bus in Düsseldorf?

Soon it was apparent that Ziggy wasn't their intended driver. The Claymores didn't know it, but a wedding reception was taking place at the hotel and the wedding party had chartered their own bus—*this* bus—to ferry guests to Frankfurt. The problem was, Criner and his staff didn't figure this out until Ziggy zoomed past the stadium and just kept on going. Criner tried to talk to the driver, but Ziggy only knew a few words of English. So as the team rolled southward to Frankfurt, with the stadium growing smaller and smaller in the rearview mirror, panic swept through the bus. No one knew what to do.

A few miles outside Düsseldorf, Vince Alcalde finally remembered that one of the Claymore kickers spoke German. Alcalde called the player, who was asleep in the back of the bus, to the front and had him tell Ziggy to turn around and follow the signs that had footballs on them. It took a few more miles for Ziggy to grasp the gravity of the situation, but he finally got the Claymores going in the right direction. By the time the Claymores' chariot arrived at Rheinstadion, kickoff was only twenty minutes away. The players didn't even get a chance to stretch and wound up losing the game, 15–14.

"Championships are won on the road in this league," said Criner a few days before the Claymores traveled to Düsseldorf to take on the

Rhein Fire in 2000. "It's hard for a team to stay focused when they go on the road. But I have a good feeling right now about our players. They seem to be ready for the Rhein Fire challenge."

Glasgow, Scotland. Four Days Before the Claymores' Game at Rhein

Before the players left the United States for Scotland, Criner told them to bring warm clothing. He also told them that springtime in Scotland is nothing like springtime in the States. As the players soon discovered, Criner was dead-on right. The first days of May 2000 were cruel. It was cold and damp, as the clouds hung low over Glasgow. Some players never felt like they could get warm, as if they lived and slept in an icebox. "I never knew the weather was so bad in Scotland," said Antonio Dingle. "It's rotten all the time."

Many players got sick. The flu bug jumped back and forth among the players all season long. At one point in the season, nearly half the team was feeling under the weather. "Not many of us brought the right clothes," said safety Blaine McElmurry. "That's why you have guys who aren't feeling well. And once you get a cold here, it's tough to shake it, because our immune systems are so beat up."

At yet another dreary day of practice, a cornerback named Central McClellion limped around the field, swaddled in three layers of sweats. Midway through the third quarter against Berlin, McClellion was blocking on a punt return. After the whistle sounded and the play was over, Scotland's Marcus Ray got clipped by a Thunder player and was pushed into McClellion, landing on the back of his right knee. Just like that, McClellion's season—and likely his career—was over.

After a few laps around the practice field at a glacial pace, he walked over to the team trainer, who informed McClellion he was being sent back to the States to rehabilitate the partially torn ligament in his knee. McClellion was devastated. When he returned to the hotel to pack, he bumped into safety Blaine McElmurry in an elevator.

"What's wrong, buddy, you look like you've seen a ghost," McElmurry asked.

"They're sending me home," replied McClellion. "Man, I really don't want to go. I was just starting to enjoy this place. Some guys want to go home. They cry themselves to sleep, but not me. I needed this time to impress the NFL scouts, damn it."

"I'm sorry, buddy," said McElmurry as he stepped off the elevator. "You just gotta believe that it will all work out in the end."

Three months earlier McClellion had been working with at-risk youths in Columbus, Ohio. Cut on the last day of training camp by Cleveland in 1999, McClellion thought his football days were over. Then that magical phone call came—even though McClellion at first didn't pick up the receiver. When Claymore coach Richard Kent called McClellion, the cornerback didn't bother answering because, when he read Kent's name on his caller ID, he didn't know who he was. But the Claymore coach persisted and eventually got in touch with McClellion. He told him that the Claymores wanted him and his 40 in 4.41 speed to play cornerback. "I thought, This is my chance to get back to the NFL," recalled McClellion.

When he arrived in Scotland, McClellion experienced culture shock. But like many of his teammates, McClellion grew to love life in Scotland because people would stop him when they saw him for the first time since his playing days at Ohio State. "There are hardly any black guys here and people will the do the craziest things when they see me," said McClellion. "Some people will come up and ask me if they can just touch my skin. It's weird, but I let them. Then sometimes we'll be in a club and a woman will just walk straight up to me and put her tongue in my mouth. She'll say, 'I've never kissed a black guy before and I want to kiss you.' The club scene is crazy."

As soon as McClellion stepped onto the plane, he knew that the little fame he had won here was gone. He was just another player whose career appeared to have ended, quietly, in Europe.

IN 1999, CRINER and the Claymores were 3–1 when they traveled to Düsseldorf to take on the Fire. The trip was a calamity; Scotland lost 37–6. After that demoralizing defeat, the Claymores went 1–4 for the rest of the season. So Criner viewed this season's matchup as a watershed game. "The two teams that are lining up this weekend are the two teams that are 3–1 and at the top of the league standings," Criner told his team during a meeting at the Central. "Last week, we played a better game than anyone else. But that's history. Now we have to start playing like champions. We need to focus on our opponent and on our gameplan. They're anticipating 43,000 for this game, but we can neutralize the crowd if we're ready to play. Let's do it."

In the days before the Claymores flew to Germany for their game against the Fire, members of the coaching staff spent a few hours calling the States trying to track down Donald Sellers, one of the top players on the '99 Claymores' team. Sellers led the league in receiving yards in 1999 with 931 and was second in catches with 58. This season's Claymores team was lacking a big-play receiving threat, and Criner believed that Sellers could be the solution to that problem. But Criner's offensive coordinator didn't want Sellers to come within a country mile of the Claymores. "I don't want him," said Alcalde. "He's got great talent, but he's got a terrible attitude."

This is a dilemma facing coaches in every league in every sport: Is it worth taking a chance on a gifted player who has potentially serious problems? At the beginning of the season, Criner didn't think so; he put as much importance on a player's timber as his talent when he assembled his roster. But now that the season was progressing so well, with a championship in reach, the coach's view on the matter of player character appeared to shift. You could almost chart it on a line graph: The coach's tolerance for bad apples grew proportionately with how much he thought that apple could help the team win a championship.

"Every day Donald would say, 'I don't want to be here,' " recalled Darren Becker, the Claymores' equipment manager. "Nobody on the team is like that this year, so I'd be really surprised if they asked Donald to come back. I mean, his attitude really sucks. And it affects the other guys."

That may have been so, but it didn't keep the coaches from burning up the phone lines and trying to locate Sellers. They had a few things they wanted to discuss with their former star player.

IN THE OFFSEASON, the Central Hotel management informed the Claymores that for the week of May 14 to 21 (which started when the Claymores returned from Düsseldorf), the hotel was fully booked. A teachers' convention was scheduled to take place at the Central, so the hotel didn't have enough rooms to accommodate both them and the Claymores. Scotland's general manager Will Wilson hunted around town for an alternative place for the team to stay and chose the Westerwood Hotel, which is located twenty minutes outside Glasgow on a golf course. Later, Wilson discovered that the teachers had cancelled their convention and that the rooms were once again available at the Central. But the Claymores had signed a contract with the Westerwood and the hotel wasn't about to let them out of it. "It's a mess," conceded Wilson, "but there just wasn't much we could do about it. We're just trying to make this go as smoothly as possible."

Which was not going to happen, given the fact that Criner decided to split up the team. Married players and players with girlfriends would stay at the Central along with a few coaches; everyone else would be shipped to the Westerwood. During this fractured week, all the team meetings—even those in the early morning—would take place at the Central. This meant that players at the Westerwood would have to rise at 6 AM, eat breakfast, ride the bus to the Central, attend a team meeting, take the bus to practice, get through practice, hop a bus back to the Central, sit through more meetings, then ride a bus back to the Westerwood. The travel time alone would fill up about two hours, making for long days and short tempers. Even though the move to the Westerwood was still a few days away, it had already become a sensitive subject among the players.

"This is not the way a professional team, even a NFL Europe team, should treat their players," griped guard Jason Gamble, who had to bunk at the Westerwood. "Maybe I should just go out on the street, pick up a girl and say she's my girlfriend. Then I could stay at the Central. We should all be treated the same. You can't give special privileges to certain players. It upsets team chemistry."

Glasgow, Scotland. Three Days Before Game Five

Every Thursday Criner and his staff chose the captains for the upcoming game. As the team stretched before practice, Criner would call out a few names and explain why a certain player deserved to be captain. It was a clever coaching stratagem. Even though these players were professionals, they still needed the occasional ego stroke.

On May 11, Criner named Noel Scarlett a captain, telling his team that Noel played an almost-perfect game last week. Scarlett's chest swelled a little when he heard the news, and then after practice Scarlett decided to hit the blocking sled for ten extra minutes for the first time all season. "Make a guy a captain for a game and this is what he does," said Antonio Dingle, as he walked off the practice field and saw the silhouette of Scarlett attacking the sled.

At the end of practice, Criner gathered his team around him at midfield. He was in a lighthearted mood, but he turned sober when he started talking about the upcoming game. "Don't let the travel destroy our focus," he said. "Let nothing distract us from whipping the shit out of the damn Rhein Fire. There's been a lot of stuff in the papers down there about guys saying this and that, but let's make sure we do our talking with our shoulderpads."

Criner was referring to a few comments made by the Fire's Kevin Drake on the nfleurope.com website. In an interview with Rhein's PR director, Drake had apparently made disparaging remarks about Criner and his staff. "I'm so happy to play for the Rhein Fire right now," Drake was quoted as saying. "Here, you find a lot more discipline compared to the Claymores. None of the Scottish coaches paid attention to that when I played there in 1999. That's probably one of the reasons that the Claymores, after a winning start, finished last season at 1–5. The Claymores didn't want me for the 2000 season, so my biggest wish for this game is to score three touchdowns, like I did against Barcelona."

When Vince Alcalde heard about Drake's comments, he was miffed. It was Alcalde who had called Drake four days before the free-agent draft and asked him if he'd submitted the proper paper work to the league's New York office. Drake hadn't, so he spent the next few days exchanging faxes with the league. Alcalde told Drake, who was the Claymores' fourth wideout in 1999, that Scotland planned to select him in one of the latter rounds of the draft. Alcalde believed that since Drake was a late addition to the draft, no team would pick Drake. So Alcalde was surprised when the Fire drafted Drake in the 19th round, one pick before the Claymores had determined to select Drake. "If it wasn't for me, Kevin wouldn't be in this league and he wouldn't playing right now," said Alcalde. "For him to bad-mouth us, who really got him where he is today, is a little hard to swallow."

Criner was upset that the league's website would publish such a slam on his coaching. Criner had long suspected that the league didn't give a whiff about the Claymores because they drew such low numbers at the gate, and this incident only confirmed that in his mind. "Criner is just a whiner," one league official answered. "He thinks we're all out to get him when, in fact, that whole Kevin Drake thing was about the league just trying to stir up a little controversy to spice up the game. It was all for the fans and all for publicity. But Criner obviously didn't see it that way."

The only person more stunned by the web posting than Criner and Alcalde was Drake himself. He claimed he had never said anything remotely close to what was published and that he was just a pawn in the larger game of the league trying to sell tickets. "I was just talking to our German PR guy and we were discussing what I saw on film," said Drake. "What appeared on the website wasn't what I said at all. Maybe something was lost in translation, I don't know. But I'm friends with a lot of the guys on the Claymores and I owe Vince Alcalde a lot for him helping me get signed up for the draft. It was just a major, major miscommunication."

So in the days after the website posting, there was Drake denying it, Criner exploiting it, and the league defending it. If nothing else, it made for a fun subplot for the fans—which, of course, was exactly what the league wanted.

AT LUNCH ON the Thursday before the Rhein Fire game, Criner and Coach Kent frantically made calls on their cell phones, trying to find a defensive back to take McClellion's roster spot. They called NFL scouts, CFL teams, and every other football contact they had in their address books. It is never easy to convince a free agent to come to Europe in the middle of a season. Not only are most players wary of NFL Europe in general, but they also have to deal with the fact that they're the new guy on a team where everybody else knows each other. That's why Criner always told the players he cuts in camp that they're just an injury away from being asked to return to the team. But this doesn't always work. Last year, one player whom Criner had cut, flat out told a Claymore coach to go jump in a lake when he called midseason to see if he was interested in returning to Scotland.

"What we're really trying to do is get a team in the NFL to sign a guy and then have that team allocate that player to us," said Kent. "There are guys who were eligible for the NFL Europe free-agent draft who weren't drafted. But, you know, there was a reason they weren't drafted. So we're calling our friends in the NFL and just hoping that there's somebody out there who can adequately fill Central's shoes. But it's complicated. We have to find the right player, see if he's interested. Then we have to find an NFL team that's interested in that player, have that team sign the player, then have that team allocate the player to us. I get tired just trying to explain it."

Kent then polished off his turkey sandwich. He then retreated to his office where he would spend five more hours on the phone, trying to make all the pieces fit into in the jigsaw puzzle that his search had become.

15 The Songs

Quarterback Marcus Crandell.

Düsseldorf, Germany. Eve of Game Five

THE LIGHTS IN the conference room dimmed, and the film started to roll. Myrle Moore had called a special teams meeting twenty hours before the Claymores kicked off against the Fire. Held in a first-floor room at the Düsseldrof Marriott, the meeting was a special one for Moore, who became as animated as be would be all season long when he started to speak. "We all know the crap that Kevin Drake has been talking this week," Moore said. "I think there's a way we can shut him up."

In film study, Moore had noticed that Drake was the team's long-snapper on punts. All season long, Drake hadn't been hit as he ran down the field. Teams were content with letting him get off the line of scrimmage with little more than a bump. When Moore realized this, his eyes lit up like a man who had just discovered the path to Nirvana. At the meeting Moore instructed safety Chris Bayne, who lined up just off the line of scrimmage on punt returns, to "ear-hole" Drake as soon as he started running downfield. "You can't line up over the long-snapper, but once he leaves the line of scrimmage he's open game," said Moore to Bayne. "If you get a good lick on him, there will be a little extra something in your paycheck. You understand me?"

As Bayne nodded his head, he smiled luminously, as if the money had talked.

Düsseldorf, Germany. Game Five

Three hours before kickoff, 30,000 fans were in full throat. They were standing in front of Rheinstadion and singing and dancing as if they were attending the hottest New Year's Eve party this side of the millennium. A band played on a stage and everyone seemed to have a German flag in one hand and a beer in the other. The crowd in Düsseldorf was older—and decidedly less female—than the one in Frankfurt, and there weren't as many whistles. But the folks in Düsseldorf still made an ungodly amount of noise. It was a wild scene with a good vibe. Where else in the world could you jam 30,000 beer-swilling folks into a ten-block radius and have only eighteen police-men to control them?

Meanwhile, another kind of party was going on inside the press-room, which was unlike any other in NFL Europe. The buffet was extensive and the Schlosser Alt beer flowed from several kegs. A few German attendees—presumably reporters, even though their faces were painted in Rhein Fire burgundy and yellow—devoured a mound of raw beef, a.k.a. steak tartar. The Scottish reporters cringed when they saw this. "There's a reason why every reporter in Scotland hates the German media," said one Scottish writer with a laugh. "They're pigs."

AS THE CLAYMORES stood in the tunnel waiting to run out onto the field, third-string tight end Nachi Abe experienced the highlight of his season. A tight end from Tokyo, Abe hadn't seen much action all season. His main duty was to block on kickoff returns, though he missed many more blocks than he made. Two weeks earlier, when Scotland played at Berlin, Abe's teammates watched in both amuse-ment and horror as the Thunder's Vershan Jackson butchered Abe every time Berlin kicked-off. Abe, who'd played on a company team in Japan, was no match for Jackson, a tight end on Nebraska's 1997 national championship team. From the bench, the Claymore players at first got a kick out of seeing Abe get steamrolled. But it was less funny after each kickoff. Toward the end of the game, Jon Hesse, who played with Jackson at Nebraska, called out to Vershan as he was lin-ing up for yet another kickoff, pleading for mercy.

"Vershan, you gotta take it easy on my man," yelled Hesse.

"I'm just taking pride in my job," replied Jackson. "It's nothing personal."

Hesse and his teammates then watched Jackson flatten Abe again.

But, as always, when Abe got up, he jogged off the field with a megawatt grin on his face. He was happy just to be there.

As Abe waited in the tunnel in Düsseldorf for yet another round of punishment, an Asian boy in the stands with a bandana bearing the Japanese flag peeked into the tunnel. The boy's head hung upside down in front of Abe. As their eyes met, the little boy flashed an excited grin, thrilled to see an Asian hero football player. The boy stuck out his hand, and Abe gave him a high-five. Abe would freeze this moment in his mind, its details burned into his memory like an exquisite piece of art. Because he knew that he had just made it as a professional football player. "That was nice," Abe said later. "My first fan."

Such an experience seemed to make up for the hardship Abe endured during the season. Not only did his body get abused, but so did his mind. Abe struggled with the English language, and he often had trouble understanding Criner at practice. One time Criner asked Abe why he went left when he was supposed to go right. Abe's simply replied, "Yes." Criner didn't see the humor in this, but this struck Abe's teammates as divine comedy, as they struggled to keep straight faces.

"Everyone on the team loves Nachi," said Willy Tate. "He's certainly not the best player in the world, but he's always got this great smile on his face. Just looking at him lightens your mood."

THE FIRST HALF of the game was Daft's worst thirty minutes of the season. He seemed in a hurry on every play, which is a common mistake for novice quarterbacks in big games. He overthrew nearly every pass, completing just four of nine attempts in the first half. Stecker was typically brilliant at the start of the game, as he ripped off a 59-yard touchdown run around the left end to give the Clay-

THE PROVING GROUND

mores an early 7–0 lead. But Rhein Fire quarterback Danny Wuerffel hit wide receiver Jeff Ogdon for a 30-yard touchdown pass in the final moments of the half. On the extra point, holder Rodney Williams bobbled the snap. When it became apparent that he wouldn't be able to set the ball in time, he took off around the right end. Matt Finkes was there waiting for him, but Finkes bit on a fake to the inside. Williams then beat him to the corner pylon for the two-point conversion.

Trailing 8–7, the Claymores jogged to the locker room. Once they got there, it seemed as if they were facing an insurmountable deficit. Coaches Kent and McCusker engaged in a heated argument in front of the players; eventually, they had to be separated. In another corner of the locker room, Criner and Alcalde huddled together and spoke quietly, which was a good thing. They were arguing over play selection and what would and wouldn't work. After a few minutes, Alcalde walked out of the locker room shaking his head and cursing.

The players could see the panic in the coaches' eyes. "You don't win championships by yelling at each other," said Finkes later. "It's as if the coaches had never been in a pressure situation before and didn't know how to react. I mean, we're only down a point. Don't freak out. But when we saw that, we quit believing we could get the job done."

On their opening drive of the second half, the Fire marched quickly down the field, scoring on an 8-yard pass from Wuerffel to Drake. Scotland came back with a 29-yard field goal from Rob Hart, but the Fire put the game away with 11:09 remaining in the fourth quarter when Wuerffel hit Drake for a 55-yard touchdown completion. Rhein won 22–10.

Daft's struggles had continued in the second half. In a little more than three quarters of action, he was just 7 of 14 for 45 yards. Because he had trouble seeing and hitting downfield receivers, the Fire were able to put eight men near the line of scrimmage to shut down Stecker. Midway through the fourth quarter, Criner sent backup quarterback Marcus Crandell into the game. He gave the Claymores a much-needed spark, completing 14 of 23 passes for 131 yards, but he also tossed two interceptions.

The defeat was especially bitter for the Claymores' coaches because they knew that a precious opportunity had slipped through their hands: No team in the history of NFL Europe had ever started the season 4–1 and not made it to the World Bowl. To make matters worse, it was Drake who'd led the Fire to victory. Not only did he score two touchdowns, but he also eluded Chris Bayne every time he entered the game as Rhein's long-snapper. Bayne just wasn't quick enough to deliver the consciousness-rattling hit that Coach Moore had craved. "That dude was just too fast," said Bayne after the game. "He had some serious wheels."

"Men, it just wasn't our day," Criner said in the locker room. "We had our opportunities, but we just didn't capitalize on them. We're number two now and they are number one. We play them again, so we'll get an opportunity to do something about that. Our next two games are at home so let's just put them in the win column and put our mistakes behind us. Remember, the more critical you are of yourself, the better football player you'll become."

Five minutes later, Criner stepped into the pressroom. As he sat down, he asked Andy Colvin to bring him a dark beer from the media bar. Colvin did, and just as Criner took a swig, a traveling party of German revelers stopped outside the pressroom. They were blowing whistles and singing "Oh Baby," the 1962 chart-topper that had become the unofficial anthem of NFL Europe in the 2000 season. Fans had picked up this song in Orlando, when four dozen vacationing Germans stopped by training camp to check out the Galaxy and the Fire. Criner, as he sat at his press conference, listened for a few moments as the fans crooned:

THE PROVING GROUND

Hey, HAAY-aay BAY-beh!
Oooh! Ahh! I vant to know-oh-oh-WHOAH-oh
IFF yull bee my gull

After one refrain, Criner decided he'd heard enough and began his postgame comments. "We should have brought Marcus in a little bit earlier and given him a shot, since Kevin was ineffective," Criner said. "But I don't want to get into a quarterback controversy. I'm just happy that we're still alive in the championship race."

That night was a quiet one for the Claymores. Most of the players were in bed early, eager to make the game yesterday's news. At the hotel the next afternoon the coaches broke down the game-film with the players in a downstairs ballroom. After viewing the video, the coaches' initial suspicions were confirmed: Something needed to be done at quarterback. Daft just wasn't effective enough. He wasn't seeing open receivers—and they *were* open—down the field. This is a career-killing type of problem, and not one that Alcalde and Criner would likely be able to solve in practice. "I don't know what we're going to do," said Alcalde, "but clearly the issue of Kevin needs to be looked at."

Edinburgh, Scotland. Night After Game Five

That evening the team flew back to Edinburgh. From there, they took two buses to Glasgow. The players didn't chat it up on the lead bus; most of the players just gazed out the window at the passing scene. But then, halfway to Edinburgh, a soft, lilting melody rose from the back of the bus. At first, only a few players paid attention. But when the sweet sound grew louder, then louder still, more players turned their heads. What they heard was cornerback Hurley Tarver, one of the quietest players on the team, singing "Amazing Grace." After a few refrains, Tarver stood up. With the reddish light of the setting sun framing his outline, Tarver tugged on the heartstrings of every player as he continued to sing.

"That was out of this world," said Kory Blackwell. "If that can't bring this team together, I don't know what will."

Tarver then sang a few more songs as the bus forged through the twilight. The Claymores were 3–2 and struggling. The season seemed to be falling apart.

16 The Cut

Coach Criner.

Glasgow, Scotland. Three Days before Game Six

CHAD ABERNATHY DARTED through the cold rain, heading swiftly toward the idling bus after the Claymores' practice. He walked smoothly and confidently, and when he sat down in his seat he never complained about any ailments during his talk with safety Blaine McElmurry. Abernathy was a perfectly healthy football player, even by his own account. Yet for the last two weeks the reserve offensive lineman had been exiled to the injured reserve list with what the Claymores' trainer had labeled—dubiously—a lower back strain. "If Abernathy's hurt," said Willy Tate, "then I must be dead."

It's simple to hoodwink the league when it comes to injuries, because they are highly subjective and hard to pinpoint—even by physicians. This kind of deception has been going on since the days of Vince Lombardi and is standard practice in NFL Europe and its mother league, as it gives teams roster flexibility. "A lot of guys get hurt at very convenient times," said one Claymore player. "A minor injury can become something major in a heartbeat, especially if it serves the best interests of the team."

This week the Claymores' roster was in flux. Cornerback Kordell Taylor was coming over from the States to replace injured corner-back Central McClellion. Taylor, who had just been signed by Chicago, roomed with safety Blaine McElmurry when the two were at the Jacksonville Jaguars training camp in 1998, so Criner expected him to fit in well. Criner also decided to cut offensive lineman Rome Douglas because of his inept play. The last straw for Douglas came against Rhein on a field goal attempt when Rome was bull-rushed and knocked back three yards. The only reason the kick wasn't blocked was because the ball somehow flew between the hands of the defender who had blown past Douglas.

In the last three weeks, Criner had had numerous private chats with Douglas. They'd watched hours of film together and had dissected all of Douglas's techniques, both in games and in practice. A longtime offensive line coach, Criner knows the intricacies of line play the same way a good accountant knows the nuances of the tax code. In each of his sessions with Douglas, Criner went over with his offensive tackle everything he needed to improve upon in extensive detail. This was why NFL coaches like to send Criner offensive line-men. He's one of the best teachers a player can have. When Criner and Douglas conferenced, the coach would be disgusted by what he saw on the video screen. Nearly 50 percent of the time, Douglas either flubbed his assignment or got beat. Criner warned Douglas that he needed to start playing significantly better if he wanted to remain a Claymore. "If I cut you loose, that's probably going to be it for your career," Criner warned Douglas. "You understand?"

Douglas nodded his head, but the message never got through.

"I've coached eight guys since I've been with the Claymores who are now starting offensive lineman in the NFL, and Rome Douglas is a better athlete than all of them," said Criner. "But he's got no heart compared to the rest. None. Unless he can turn that around, and I don't see how he will, he's done."

During practices, defensive linemen taunted Douglas mercilessly. They called him everything from a wussy to a pussy, but the words never even dented the wall that Douglas had erected around himself. Even the team's public relations director, Steve Livingstone, didn't care for Douglas, who snapped his fingers to get Livingstone's attention whenever he wanted something from him. "I'm really not having a good time over here," said Douglas, a few days before he was let go. "The food is terrible. The weather is terrible. And our team is starting to play terrible. I don't know if we can turn it around or not."

Whatever the solution to the team's problems was, Rome Douglas would be part of it.

SINCE TRAINING CAMP, the players had talked about playing golf at the Westerwood Resort. Golfer Seve Ballesteros designed the course, which is spread over rolling hills and is one of the finest links in the Glasgow area. On the players' day off following the Rhein game, the Claymores' front office organized a free group outing to the course. But on the appointed day, rain poured down, scaring almost everybody away. Only two Claymores—Matt Finkes and Willy Tate—finished all 18 holes.

"It's going to be real interesting to see what happens this week," Tate said to Finkes as they walked up the eighteenth fairway. "For the first time all season, you now see guys starting to go their own way and do their own thing. Guys are starting to get selfish. This could be the beginning of the end."

The selfishness Tate spoke about had been obvious two nights earlier. Even though Criner told the majority of the team to stay at the Westerwood Hotel when the Claymores returned from Düsseldorf, about twenty-five nonetheless checked into rooms at the Central. They did this late in the evening when no coaches were around. The hotel manager told the players they weren't supposed to stay there, that they were supposed to be bussed out to the countryside hotel, but a few of them got in his face and dared him to disobey their demands. "I ain't going to spend all that time busing into Glasgow everyday," defensive end Rasheed Simmons told the manager. "That will take my mind off football. I just ain't going to do it."

So that night more than a few Claymores blatantly—brazenly— ignored the wishes of their coach. But Criner sensed he was losing his team, so he did nothing about it. All season long Criner could perceive the subtlest shifts of mood on his team, and he knew that his players were on the verge of losing hope. The next day, instead of lighting into his team, Criner simply told the players again that they must stay at the Westerwood. This time the players fell in line and followed Criner's orders, accepting the fact that they'd have to spend about two hours a day on the bus. The players' brief mutiny died then and there.

The goal of the week for the Claymores was to get back to the basics. At practice they worked on the fundamentals of football: tackling and blocking. While most of the players found these tasks to be

THE PROVING GROUND

as invigorating as watching paint dry, Criner loved the exercise. He enjoys teaching the rudiments of the sport. It is his favorite part of being a football coach. Which explained why he was upbeat all week, even though his team was 3–2 and seemingly coming apart at the seams.

Before practice on Thursday, Criner stood alone as the players stretched 40 yards away. The rain came down at a 45-degree angle, in sheets. It was cold. It was windy. The players complained about the elements. Even the assistants complained. Yet, as Criner stood there under the bleak sky, staring directly at the rain, he was grinning. This was his idea of fun.

17 The Gamble

Wide receiver Donald Sellers.

Glasgow, Scotland. Two Days Before Game Six

THE DOORS OF the hotel flew open and out Donald Sellers stepped into the cool morning. With headphones the size of coconuts on his head, he was the last player to exit the Central and get on the bus that would take the team to Friday's practice. As soon as he appeared, he became a sore subject among the players already on the bus. "D. Sellers is back," said Finkes. "I don't fucking believe it."

When Criner called him two days earlier, Sellers was hanging out at his girlfriend's house in South Phoenix, wondering what he should do with his life. It wasn't easy for the coach to find Sellers, and when he finally did, Criner insisted on an answer right away: Did Sellers want to come back to Scotland and help the Claymores win a championship? Sellers was unsure. Last season he loathed living in Scotland. He didn't think he belonged in the backwaters of professional football, and before he even went to Scotland for the 1999 season, he told Rams coach Dick Vermeil as much. At the time, Sellers was on the Rams' practice squad and in February 1999 Vermeil asked Sellers if he'd go to Europe to improve his route-running skills. Sellers didn't want to go, but he knew that if he wanted to remain a member of the Rams, he had no choice. "The Rams were putting in a new offense and I thought it would have been better for me to stay in the States and learn it," Sellers said. "But the coach didn't really ask me to go. He told me."

So Sellers went to Scotland and—no surprise to him—had a spectacular season. But he also had a spectacular attitude problem. He fought his teammates in practice. He told the coaches to fuck off. And, sometimes, he dogged it in games when he felt he wasn't getting thrown the ball enough.

None of this, of course, was lost on the Claymores' coaching staff. Each week NFL Europe coaches send a report to the parent team of every player who is allocated from the NFL. According to several sources, Criner and his staff eviscerated Sellers in these reports, detailing how his noxious attitude had poisoned the team. While the reports didn't pin the team's 1999 collapse on Sellers, they came close to it. "When I came back from Europe last year I was tired and beat up," said Sellers. "I got hurt right away in training camp and I was released. That just proved to me that coming to Europe was a bad thing for me."

Sellers's mind changed in the coming months, however. Sellers was out of football for the 1999 NFL season. The Rams cut him in preseason and he never made it onto another roster. For the five months of the NFL season and for the first three months of the off-season, he sat around and contemplated what went wrong, how he could have done better. He put a spotlight on his soul and realized that he had taken the game for granted. He was good, yes, but he never lifted weights. He never ran extra laps. And he didn't spend enough time studying the playbook, which was his downfall, given the fact that he never played wide receiver until he got to the pros. At the University of New Mexico, Sellers was a dynamic run-pass quarterback. But he only possessed a mediocre arm. He wasn't selected in the 1998 NFL draft, but the Rams invited him to camp as a free-agent wide receiver. "I really thought I was going to stick with the Rams last season," said Sellers. "I should have a Super Bowl ring right now."

Winning a ring was the crux of Criner's sales pitch when he phoned Sellers after the Claymores lost to the Rhein Fire. Criner also emphasized to Sellers that he would only have to spend a little more than a month in Scotland and that things would go so quickly that he wouldn't have time to get homesick. "None of our wideouts are stepping up and making the big plays," Criner told Sellers. "If we can get somebody who can make the plays, then I think everyone will raise their game to a higher level. You're that guy, Donald. You can get everybody on track."

After considering the offer for a few minutes, Sellers agreed to come to Scotland. Those eight months out of football had done something to him: the time away had made him realize how lucky he was to be able to play a sport for a living.

The next morning Donald Sellers was on a plane destined for Glasgow. As soon as he touched down, the Claymores had a lot more sugar and spice—though not necessarily somebody nice—on their roster.

THE PROVING GROUND

"THE THING ABOUT Donald is that he's not a speed guy," said Criner, excited, as he walked to practice on the day of Sellers's return. "He runs the 40 in the 4.6 range. But, boy, can he go and get the football. When we had him and Yo Murphy last year, shit, you couldn't stop us. Both of those guys went up and got the ball. We could have passed for 500 yards in every game. The problem we have now is that our receivers are small and either they aren't getting open or the quarterback can't find them. Kevin, our quarterback, who I think is our biggest problem right now, does not read coverage well and he doesn't know where to go with the football. We've spent a lot of time trying to teach him that, we've simplified our gameplan so he doesn't have to make as many reads, but it's just not working. We've cut back, cut back, cut back, and we're trying to make it so he can read defenses better, but there just hasn't been any improvement. We're trying to get him to look deep and then throw underneath, but for whatever reason, that's not happening. But the thing about Marcus, our other QB, is that he throws interceptions. He's not as careful with the ball as Kevin is. So we're caught in a catch-22—one guy protects the ball but can't move the offense, and the guy who *can* move the offense doesn't protect the ball. Well, maybe Donald can open things up a bit and make life a little easier for both quarterbacks."

At practice before the Claymores' game against Frankfurt, Sellers was spectacular. He made both the simple and the difficult catch with an elegance that surpassed that of many NFL receivers. He ran hard and—though he was jet-lagged—his stamina appeared strong. But there was a minor problem. Last year Sellers wore the jersey number 4. This year wide receiver Damon Gibson, who wore 84 in games, donned the 4 jersey in practice. But because Sellers was friends with the equipment manager, who also was with the team last season, the manager gave Sellers the 4 practice jersey. Gibson, who is only 5'9", was given 78—Rome Douglas's old practice jersey. That jersey hung down to Gibson's knees. Sure, football isn't a hotbed of fashion, but

Gibson still felt slighted. Gibson had been with the team since the first day of camp; Sellers had been in Scotland for a few hours.

"Sellers is pissing people off already and he hasn't been here but for a few hours," said one Claymore staffer. "I can't believe Criner brought him back. He must be desperate."

Indeed, this reeked of desperation. But Criner knew the rhythms of NFL Europe life as if it was an old 45 record from that he still played over and over. Maybe, there was magic—and a melody—in this move.

18　The Pass

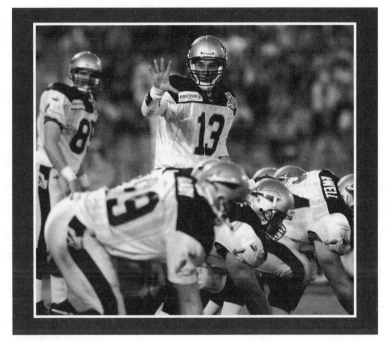

Quarterback Kevin Daft.

Glasgow, Scotland. Eve of Game Six

THE FRANKFURT GALAXY were 1–4 and struggling. When a team gets off to a slow start in NFL Europe, it rarely recovers. An early season swoon is a mortal wound because players lose interest, coaches then respond by pushing them harder, which only causes further disillusionment and despair. "It looks like they're packing it in," said Criner privately. That was true. Many of the players on the Galaxy were already looking homeward when they came to Glasgow to face the Claymores. "Our team is in trouble right now," agreed

Frankfurt quarterback Pat Barnes. "When we eat our meals at our hotel, guys don't even sit together. It's bad. I don't know how we're going to get through this. We basically have to win the rest of our games to have a chance, and no one really thinks we can do that. All I know is that these next five weeks may end up being the longest of my life."

The night before the game, offensive coordinator Vince Alcalde had a meeting with his quarterbacks, Daft and Crandell. For over an hour, they broke down film. But Alcalde lingered over one play longer then the rest—a play that perfectly illustrated the Claymores' offensive problems. It was from the first series of the Claymores' game at Berlin. Though the game took place nearly three weeks before, Alcalde reviewed it with his quarterbacks this week because it pinpointed their main weakness.

Scotland's offense was facing a third and two on the Thunder's 34-yard-line. As Alcalde held a laser-pointer in his right hand and the remote control in his left, he constantly pushed play and rewind. "Okay, fellas, we run 74 Z Curl," said Alcalde. "Seven defensive players are in the box. Our tight end rolls right. The linebacker tries to hold up the tight end. When the linebacker does this, we know that right away we get the ball to the running back flaring out of the backfield. It's third and two. He's going to get that first down because the linebacker is held up and he's not going to get to Stecker on time. But the quarterback doesn't make the right read and holds the ball. The curl route isn't there because of good coverage. But then the quarterback never looks to the tight end, who is wide open the second that the linebacker rolls off him. So we throw to the running back late, and by that time everyone on the defense is looking that way. The tight end, by the way, is so wide open that if you get him the ball, he'll run for 50 yards. But we throw late to the running back and Stecker gets tackled a yard short of the first down. We're just not thinking,

fellas. Gotta understand what the situation is. We're just not execut-
ing on third downs."

In his defense, Daft said that he was trying to act as if he was
going to throw to the curl route on the right side of the field,
thereby drawing the defense that way, and then come back and hit
Stecker on the left side of the field. But if he had read the linebacker
correctly, his response should have been: Throw right away to the
running back; if that was covered (which it wasn't), then throw the
curl; if that was covered (which it was), then throw to the tight end
dragging across the field. Instead of doing any of this, Daft held
onto the ball too long. The defense, which keyed on Stecker to
begin with, pursued in Stecker's direction. But even though Daft
made the incorrect read and threw the ball late to Stecker, Scotland
still should have gotten the first down. The problem was that
Stecker didn't realize that the Claymores only needed two yards for
a first down. So when he caught the ball, he came to a stop, tried to
juke a defender by stutter-stepping, and then got tackled a yard short
of the first down. If he had just put his head down and bulled forward, he would have made it to the yardage marker and the Claymores' drive would have continued. In one play, the key players
failed to think, forgot their gameplan, and hurt their chance to win
the game. These are the type of basic skills that players come to
Europe to perfect.

AT PRECISELY 3:11 AM, on the morning of game day, a fire alarm
sounded at the Central Hotel. That afternoon all of the Claymores
had moved back into the Central from the Westerwood. At first,
many of the players ignored the alarm and slept through it. But by
3:55, nearly every player stood outside the hotel shivering in the
chilly night air. Three fire trucks had arrived, sirens wailing. It was

clear that this was no prank, as smoke wafted through the hotel's hallways.

Criner didn't utter a word. He just walked around as if in a fog, not talking to anyone, not even his wife. Many players eventually drifted back into the lobby of the hotel and tried to sleep on the carpeted floor. Then at 4:35, the source of the smoke was found: It was coming into the hotel through an underground vent that ran from the Central to a nightclub called Bonkers across the street. The fire had started in the club's basement. "You know what the moral of this story is," said Tate to Finkes with a sly grin, "there's a secret passageway to Bonkers."

At 4:48, the Claymores were allowed to go back to their rooms. Some players fell asleep right away. Some in an hour. Some not at all. "This is absolutely the worst thing that could happen the night before a game," said Myrel Moore. "You really need two good nights' rest in a row to feel your best at game time. Now we won't even have one. Will this affect us? You bet it will."

Edinburgh, Scotland. Game Six

When Criner gathered his players around him in the locker room five minutes before they were to take the field against the Galaxy, he saw yawns and tired eyes everywhere. Criner himself looked sleep-deprived. "If you play the way you practiced this week, we will win this dadgum football game," said Criner to his players. "Go out and have fun and lay it on the line. Take it to them. This is our home field. Make sure we let them know how we handle teams when they come into our own backyard." It wasn't exactly a win-one-for-the-Gipper kind of speech, but Criner's tank was running on fumes. It's tough to inspire on two hours of sleep.

THE PROVING GROUND

On the first snap of the game, Galaxy quarterback Pat Barnes tried to hit a receiver on a crossing route but Finkes read the play and stepped in front of the sideout. The ball hit Finkes square in the chest. He dropped it, the ball slipping through his fingers as if covered in grease. "Goddamn it," yelled defensive back coach Richard Kent from the coaches' box. "That's exactly what we needed to start this game."

Though they didn't get the turnover, the Claymores' defense held the Galaxy without a first down. Scotland's offense then drove the length of the field and scored on a 4-yard pass from Daft to wide receiver Selucio Sanford, marking the first time this season that the Claymores had hit paydirt on their initial offensive possession. But instead of savoring the score, Alcalde merely groaned. From his seat in the coaches' box he could see that Stecker was getting shut down, as the Galaxy were putting nine men in the box. "Jesus," said Alcalde to himself. "This is not good. If they stop Aaron, they stop us."

As if on cue, the offensive machine of the Claymores began to sputter. In the span of three minutes they lost three fumbles, which enabled the Galaxy to build a 21–7 lead at the end of the first quarter. One of the fumbles was caused when Daft dropped back to pass, scanned the field for a full four seconds, then was hit on his blindside, knocking the ball loose. That play marked the seventeenth time this season that Daft had been sacked, which was the most in the league. In recent days, many of the offensive linemen had voiced the opinion that Daft held onto the ball too long. Two of the lineman actually suggested that Daft was more concerned about his statistics than winning, because he rarely threw the ball away when facing pressure.

Earlier in the week, Criner and Alcalde informed Daft and Crandell that each would play two quarters against Frankfurt. Crandell was elated, naturally. Though Crandell was an atrocious practice player, he somehow found a way to make plays in games—his hallmark when he was at East Carolina. When Daft was given the news, he was crest-fallen. He had come to Europe to play, not to sit on the bench for half the game. When Alcalde saw the look of disbelief on Daft's face, he was more than a little surprised. It was as if Daft had no idea that he wasn't playing well.

When Crandell entered the game in the second quarter, the offense was revitalized. He moved the team down the field with crisp, quick passes. Stecker scored on a 2-yard run to make it 24–14 late in the quarter, which was the count at halftime.

"We get the ball to begin the second half," said Criner in the locker room. "If we go down and score, we're right back in the game. Shit, if we get two scores we're in the lead. We can't control what has happened, but we can control what we do about it. Let's go."

The Claymores didn't score on their first drive, but after Frankfurt's Ralf Kleinman missed a 49-yard field-goal attempt, Draft drove the offense deep into Galaxy territory. Facing a fourth and one at the 14-yard-line, Criner decided to go for it instead of kicking the easy field goal, which would have cut the lead to a touchdown. "We can get this," Criner told Alcalde over the headset. "I've got a good feeling about this."

But the gamble failed when Daft was tackled for a 3-yard loss on a quarterback sweep. It was the first time all season that the Claymores had run this play and they were hoping it would surprise the Galaxy defense. But the play was stuffed because of a missed block by an offensive lineman. On the Claymores' next possession, Daft once again orchestrated a nice drive, culminating with an 11-yard touchdown pass to Sellers, which made the score 24–21 early in the fourth quarter. It was a beautiful catch, as the ball was overthrown. But Sellers managed to free himself from gravity and was fully extended when he snatched the ball out of the air. As soon as he caught the ball, he was crushed by Frankfurt safety Marcus Washington. The helmet-to-helmet hit broke Sellers' nose. This was precisely the kind of tough, gritty play Criner had envisioned Sellers making when he extended him the offer to come over.

Late in the fourth quarter, the Claymores had one final chance to either tie the game or take the lead. Crandell, who was back in, began the drive by throwing his best pass of the season, as he connected with Sellers over the middle for 34 yards to the Galaxy's 19-yard-line. Two minutes remained. Six plays then produced 12 yards, but the Claymores were unable to push the ball into the endzone. Rob Hart then came on and hit a 24-yard field goal, sending the game into overtime.

In NFL Europe, the format of overtime is a little different than that of the NFL. In Europe, if one team receives the kickoff and marches down the field and scores a field goal, the other team then has one possession to either tie that score or beat it. If their possession ends on downs or a turnover, then the game is over. If they kick a field goal, it continues. If the two teams are tied at the end of fifteen minutes, then the game ends in a tie.

Frankfurt won the toss and elected to receive. It took seven plays for Barnes to guide the Galaxy down the field for a touchdown, as he hit Mario Bailey for a 4-yard score. The Claymores' defense, which didn't surrender a point the entire second half, was dragging, as if running through water. Frankfurt had worn them down, and Myrel Moore knew it. "We just can't stop them," he told Kent over the headphones. "We just have to hope that they make a mistake."

When Scotland got the ball, Criner decided to reinsert Daft into the game, even though he'd been sitting on the sidelines for the past forty minutes. At first this seemed like an inspired move. Aided by a 34-yard pass-interference call on Sellers, Scotland reached the Galaxy's 9-yard-line in just three plays. Two plays later, Daft hit Sellers on a slant route for a touchdown.

Hart once again trotted out onto the field for the extra point. But as the teams were lining up, Alcalde instructed Criner to take a time-out. "We gotta think about this, Coach," said Alcalde. "We can end the game on this play with whatever we want to call, or we can try to win it with our defense. But to me, our defense looks tired. I think we should go for it. Let's ask Myrel." Criner summoned Moore, and the defensive coordinator had three words for the coach: "Go for it."

The play Alcalde called was "Shift Amsterdam." The formation started with three tight ends and two running backs. When the quarterback came to the line and everyone was set, he yelled "Amsterdam." At that point, all three tight ends shifted into different positions. Two lined up as wideouts and one lined up in the slot position. One running back then moved into a tight-end position. The idea behind the play was to create mismatches, for instance, having a big, strong tight end covered by a smaller free safety.

Every day in practice before the game, the Claymores had worked on this play. The primary receiver was tight end Rickey Brady, who shifted to a standing position in the slot. What Brady did was run four yards upfield, hit his defender as hard as he could backward, then spin around for the ball. Even when the Claymores' defense knew that the offense would run "Shift Amsterdam" in practice, they couldn't stop it. "It had been our best play in practice all week," said Brady after the game. "I'm a big guy, about 6'4" and 240 pounds, and no small free safety is going to be able to stop me from getting the ball."

It just so happened the smallest free safety in the league lined up to cover Brady on the 2-point conversion. The Galaxy's Jim Cantelupe was listed at 6 feet, but he was closer to 5'9". When Brady saw that Cantelupe was covering him, he knew that he'd be open. "My eyes lit up," said Brady. "I was sure that the game was won."

As Daft walked up to the line of scrimmage, Alcalde thought the same thing. On seeing the undersized Cantelupe on Brady, he quietly said, "Okay, Kev, just do it like we practiced. We got this thing."

Daft yelled "Amsterdam." The players shifted. Daft called his signals, then was centered the ball. He took three steps back and planted his back foot. Brady ran off the line and gave Cantelupe a solid chuck. Brady turned. He was open but Cantelupe, who attended Navy and possibly loves playing football more than anybody in the Free World, was close behind him. Nonetheless, Daft threw the ball. As it floated through the air, Cantelupe, as furtively as possible, slid his hands on top of Brady's shoulder pads to prevent him from jumping. Meanwhile, both Ben Snell and Willy Tate were wide open in either corner of the endzone. There wasn't a Frankfurt player within four yards of Snell and seven yards of Tate.

Daft desperately wished he could pull the ball back. It sailed about five yards over Brady's head. Even if Cantelupe hadn't been hanging on his shoulderpads, Brady couldn't have caught the ball. But Brady was open. All Daft had to do was drill the ball into his body, because Cantelupe was behind him, boxed out like a basketball player who has no chance at the rebound.

After the ball fell incomplete, Daft put his hands on his hips. Tate's hands flew up in the air in exasperation. Snell stomped his foot to the ground. Brady fell to the ground and lay as motionless as road kill. In the coaches' box, Alcalde buried his head in his hands. "Why did Kevin throw the ball 10 yards over Rickey's head?" Alcalde yelled. "Rickey was wide open. He was *wide fucking open*. You work your ass off and then he makes a throw like that." Then his eyes puddled up. It was too tough to take.

"We had too many early errors and too many late mistakes, men," said Criner in the locker room. "The situation right now is that there are three teams tied for second place. Nothing has changed. We were in second place before the game and we're still in second place. But we know that Frankfurt doesn't beat us if we don't give them all those opportunities early. We need to be critical of ourselves. The race is still ahead of us. Make sure that next week we play a better football game early. We can be a hell of a lot better and we can still be champions. Does anybody have anything to add to that, coaches or players? This isn't my team; it's *our* team so say what needs to be said to make us better."

For a few moments, nobody said anything. The players just looked at each other. Then Sellers, who had been in Scotland for a mere sixty-four hours, flexed his vocal muscles. "We eliminate those early turnovers and we win. It's as simple as that," said Sellers. "Come out next week and kick some ass. Put this game behind us and let's get back on track."

"Well said," added Criner. "We don't need any dissenters. Anybody dissents and I'll send his ass home."

With that, Criner exited the locker room. For a few minutes, he stood alone, drawing deep breaths. He was cooling down, trying to get himself back to a state of emotional equilibrium. When he walked down the narrow hallway and entered the press room, he was remarkably calm. "That was a tough one," Criner told reporters. "I'm proud of the way we came back. The thing I regret the most is not kicking the field goal when I went for it on fourth down. I thought we could make the yard, especially with the quarterback sweep, which we had put in just for these guys. We just didn't block it as well as I thought we would. In terms of our position, we're no worse off than we were at the beginning of the ballgame. The race is still ahead of all of us. Now, it's just who can be the better second-half team. We went for two because I was concerned with how well they were moving the ball. Our receiver was open, but we just didn't throw the ball well."

Colvin asked the first question of the press conference, as usual. "Did Sellers's performance surprise you?" Criner cut right to the point. "Ever since Donnie got cut from the NFL, we've wanted to get him in here," the coach said. "He has very good route-running ability, he can catch the football, can take a hit, and he gives us a big receiver that we haven't had. This means our passing game will get consistently better."

A few minutes later, Sellers limped into the pressroom. He couldn't breathe out of his nose because it was broken. He hadn't slept in thirty-six hours. And he could barely lift his right arm because his shoulder was so sore. With all that, he had still caught eight balls for 113 yards. "One of the reasons I came back was because I knew this team had a chance to win," Sellers said. "We've got a good defense, a nice running game, and a nice little passing game. I really feel like we have a chance to go to the World Bowl. I was disappointed with how things went last year, and that's why I wanted to come back. But right now I'm hurting. My nose is broken. My tailbone is hurting. My shoulder is aching. I'm out of shape. So right now I just want to get something to eat and go to bed."

While Sellers called it an early night, most of his teammates did not. About thirty Claymore players and about twenty Galaxy players went to the Velvet Room and stayed at the club until it shut down at 4 AM. Frankfurt quarterback Pat Barnes, who in NFL Europe has developed a well-cultivated reputation as a barfly, lived up to the hype. He bought shots by the trayfull for Matt Finkes, Willy Tate, Rob Hart, and a dozen other Claymores. For hours, the players swapped stories about life in NFL Europe. Everyone was having a fine time.

But as the evening wore on, it was clear that many on the Claymores were tired. They were tired of football, tired of Scotland, tired of losing, and, most of all, tired of getting yelled at by their coaches. "We just don't have the players to get the job done on offense," said Finkes. "Then Criner has the audacity to say that we lost as a team. Bullshit. The offense lost the game for us. They lost all the fumbles in the first half and they didn't get the job done in the endzone. We worked our asses off just to keep the game close. The least that Criner could do is acknowledge that the defense is what's carrying this team."

With four games left in the regular season, things had soured in Scotland.

19 The Leader

Offensive tackle Ben Cavil.

Glasgow, Scotland. Five Days Before Game Seven

THE MEETING TOOK place in the middle of the field, two minutes after practice was over. Despite a hard, frosty wind blowing from the west, the players stayed on the field to talk as Criner and the rest of the coaching staff trudged toward the showers. The players stood in a tight circle and tried to figure out how they could save their season.

"We need to stay together," said offensive tackle Ben Cavil, the first player to voice his thoughts. "In everything we do, we have to do it together. I've noticed some guys are starting to do their own thing. That's fine if you want to lose, but if you feel that way, you should just go home. We've been busting our butts for too long and traveled too far to let the season go to waste. Just stick together."

Over the past few weeks, Cavil had quietly emerged as the leader of the team, as the one player whom both the white players and the black players respected. At twenty-eight Cavil was the oldest American player on the team. He was also one of the few players who had been a starter in the NFL. In 1995, Cavil had signed with the Chargers as a free agent out of the University of Oklahoma and had begun the life of a journeyman. He spent that season on the injured reserve and the following season on the practice squad of the Philadelphia Eagles. Then in 1997, he was traded to the Baltimore Ravens for a seventh-round pick. The following two seasons he started 14 games—a span of time that Cavil said marked the best period of his young life. "There's nothing better than just balling and being with the guys," he said. Cavil was released in the '99 preseason by the Ravens and spent all of that year out of football. He moved back home to League City, Texas, and began selling cars at a GMC Pontiac dealership. He was a natural at hawking. Blessed with a quick wit and a wide, winsome smile, Cavil could sell automobiles almost as soon as they were unloaded off the trucks.

"It wasn't something that I thought I'd be good at, but I was," said Cavil. "And it's fun. Because there's nothing I like doing more than just talking to people, and that's really what selling cars is all about."

Cavil was perfectly content with his post-football life when Criner called him in March 2000. Criner needed help on his offensive line because of injuries and failed physicals, and he'd heard through the coaching grapevine that Cavil was out of football but still had some miles left in his big body. After receiving word that he was wanted in Scotland, Cavil told his boss at the car lot that he needed to take a leave of absence. The seduction of playing football—even in Europe—was too powerful to resist. "They didn't even throw me a going-away party," said Cavil. "I guess they figured I'd be back."

In Scotland, Cavil spent most of his free time in his room, which he kept immaculate. Everyone called him Big Ben for the obvious reason: Cavil, at 6'4", 320 pounds, is a mountain of a man. "I've been big my entire life," he said. "And I've always had big feet. When I was twelve, I wore size 12. Every year it went up until I was fifteen. When I turned fifteen I wore 15. I was praying that my feet would quit growing, because my friends gave me such a hard time."

For a man so large, Cavil was extremely nimble and light on his feet. He felt he still possessed the talent to play in the NFL, but his biggest problem in getting back to the league was the fact that he would be a fourth-year player in 2000. "If you're just an average NFL player, then it's hard to stay long because the minimum salary they have to pay you increases each year that you're in the league," said Cavil. "For me, next year my minimum will be, like, $400,000. I'll probably be battling for a roster spot with a rookie whose minimum salary will be around $100,000. That makes it hard for older guys who aren't exceptional to stay in the league."

This season Cavil was comfortable with his life in Glasgow. But many players were not. Homesickness and a lack of team harmony, among other things, had infected the Claymores. These are two issues that Donald Sellers understood intimately, and after Cavil was done speaking to the team in the huddle, he turned things over to Sellers. "I just got a few things to say," said Sellers. "I was over here last year. I'll be the first to admit that I had a bad attitude. I didn't think that I belonged over here. A lot of guys had that attitude last year and that's why we lost. Well, listen. We're stuck over here and we might as well get through it and play the games like we're capable of playing them. We only got a month to go. It's only a month out of our lives. Let's dedicate ourselves to football and to winning games and we can win this whole damn thing."

For Criner and his staff, the problems of the 2000 season were eerily reminiscent of the problems of 1999. In week seven of the '99 season, according to many players who were on that team, the Claymores gave up. Players started hitting the bottle hard—and more than a few players were seen by the coaching staff smoking marijuana on numerous occasions. The team fell swiftly into decay. "You reach week seven and you just want to go home," said Finkes. "That's the biggest problem with having the league over in Europe. Guys just get sick of it. They miss their families. They miss America. The coaches' response to this problem, both this year and last year, is to give the players a little more free time and cut back on some meetings. Thing is, I'm sick of seeing guys on the team and I don't want anything to do with them. I see the same guys, day in and day out. We're paid shit money and now playing football just for the sake of playing football doesn't seem that great anymore. Guys are at their breaking point. This happens every year and it probably happens to each team."

Aside from the Week-Seven Blues, as this phenomenon is known throughout the league, Criner faced another problem that was threatening to destroy the Claymores' season: racial tension. Over the past few weeks, the racial divide on the team had grown deeper. Off the field, there was virtually no interaction between the white players and the black players. They sat segregated by race on the bus, in the locker room, and in the dining hall. Criner believed that this unspoken hostility was undercutting team morale. "We're on the verge of having a real race problem on this team," said Criner privately. Criner would never address the issue with the team, even though he knew it was wreaking havoc on the Claymores' run to a championship. "This could ruin our season," said Criner, "but I'm going to do my damnedest to make sure that that doesn't happen."

To focus the team back on football, Criner and his staff emphasized the importance of the Claymores' next game, which was at home against Barcelona. All week during practice, the coaches stressed that this game would make or break the season. "If we win, guys will get into the season again and it will pick up everyone's morale a little bit," said Finkes. "But if we lose this game, it's over. Our season will go right into the shithouse. I guarantee you, guys will stop caring. But if we can pull out a win, guys will hop on the bandwagon and they'll try and they'll think we can do something. Last year during our losing streak, the coaches tried to talk us into doing something. They were like, 'Win this and if a couple of breaks go our way and three other teams lose, we'll be right back in it.' And guys were like, 'Whatever. Don't lie to me. I know we've got a one-in-fifty-million chance to make it to the World Bowl.' But now we're still enough in the hunt that if we win this game, our season could be saved. And I think everyone actually believes that."

Cornerback Duane Hawthorne.

Glasgow, Scotland, Four Days Before Game Seven

IT WAS AN eternal flame, a fluorescent light that was never extinguished. Players could walk by the coaches' main office in the dead of night, in the middle of the afternoon, or early in the morning, and they would always see a glint of light coming from the underneath the door. Inside the office, there would be at least one Claymore coach trying to figure out a competitive edge. The workday sometimes wouldn't end until the sun had risen over Glasgow. "I've heard that young doctors put in a lot of hours, but I think we put in more," said Myrel Moore. "It's nuts."

At this point in the season, the Claymores needed to win three of their last four games to ensure a berth in the World Bowl. Ever since training camp, the general feeling among league officials had been that the Claymores and the Rhein Fire were the class teams of the league. This belief was also shared by NFL executives. The feeling among the Scotland coaches was that if they didn't at least advance to the championship game, it would reflect poorly on their ability to coach and nurture talent. The gold standard at all levels of football is winning. But nothing that the coaches were doing—changing gameplans, changing starters, changing practice routines—was working. No matter how hard the coaches tried to push the boulder up the hill, it kept rolling back down.

"There is a ton of stress on the coaches," said free safety Blaine McElmurry. "One day a coach is mellow and everything is cool, and the next day he can be a totally different person. It's very hard to deal with that. I know that they don't sleep very much. And eight weeks of little sleep is bound to affect your body. Losing makes it worse. They know that the NFL is watching and they know it won't do them any good if we don't win it all. Right now, I wouldn't want to be in their position."

McElmurry, who is white, also had a unique perspective on the issue of race. When he played high-school football for his father at Missula High in Missula, Montana, there were no black players on the team. When he played safety at the University of Montana, there were a few black players on the roster, but none were safeties. When he signed as an undrafted free agent with the Green Bay Packers in

1997, he and fellow safety Mike Prior were the only white defensive backs on the team. Ever since then, in his stints with the Titans, Jaguars, and Claymores, McElmurry has been the only white defensive back on each of these teams.

"I remember the first time I walked into the Titans locker room and saw Eddie George standing there without his shirt on," recalled McElmurry. "I almost fainted. The guy was huge, he had muscles everywhere, and he was only a running back. I didn't think I belonged. But the more I played, the more I realized I *did* belong. It's kind of the same thing when it comes to race. At first when I go to a team, the black defensive backs will look at me in this really weird way as if they can't believe what they're seeing. But once they realize I can play, they accept me. Even at training camp with the Claymores this season, all the black defensive backs didn't treat me with any respect until they saw I could play.

"Outside of football, though, I don't hang out with the black defensive backs. It's not a black and white thing, but it's more of me hanging out with people who are more like me. That's why you don't see us sitting around being all friendly to one another on the bus and at lunch and dinner. The two groups just seem to do their own thing. But I don't see it as a big problem."

"It *is* a problem," disagreed cornerback Duane Hawthorne, who is black. "The coaches like to say that we're all one big happy team, but we're not. First of all, the black guys and the white guys just don't hit it off, so that makes it tough for us to be a unified team. Second, there's been a lot of shit happening lately that proves to me that we're not a close team. Like the other day, one of our players pulled a knife on one of his teammates. Now that's not something you'll see on a championship team. In fact, every time we go out something like that happens. Guys will fight over the stupidest things. I think we're just sick of each other."

THE PROVING GROUND

Indeed, during this two-game losing streak the players seemed to have especially short fuses. Players threatened each other almost on a daily basis, as if the word "teammate" had disappeared from everyone's vocabulary. No one was ever hurt—not even the player who had the knife pulled on him—but the collective morale of the team was plummeting. And no one seemed to know how to fix everything that was going wrong.

There was yet another problem blowing in the stiff Scottish wind that week, which was also dividing the team. At the Claymores first meeting in training camp, the coaches had promised the players that they would treat the allocated and nonallocated players the same. But they didn't keep their word, according to numerous players. "Allocated guys are treated differently, no doubt about that," said McElmurry, who was allocated to the Claymores by the Jacksonville Jaguars. "It's just the little things, like coaches not riding you as hard about certain things and just being more forgiving in general. But you know what? The little things add up after awhile and the nonallocated guys start to get pissed. That's what's happening right now. Plus, there's pressure from NFL teams to play allocated players. That's the whole idea of the league. If you've got two guys who are even and one guy is allocated and there other one isn't, you're going to play the allocated guy. Think about it. It's stupid for the coaches *not* to play the allocated players, because if they don't, it will damage their future relationships with coaches in the NFL."

The net result of all these problems: the Claymores weren't performing as well as they could on the field. They were just going through the motions—playing undisciplined, unemotional, unfocused football. One example: When Myrel Moore reviewed the film of last week's loss, he saw that safety Marcus Ray drew a personal foul for a late hit that occurred about three seconds after the whistle blew. A practice the next day, Moore approached Ray. "What the hell was that personal foul all about?" he asked Marcus. "We can't do that shit and expect to win."

"I'm really tired of all this, Coach," said Ray to a confounded Moore. "I just want out."

"I can arrange that for you," snapped Moore, who then walked away. Wisely, Moore didn't push Ray too far. If he had, Ray would have gladly accepted a ticket home.

Two years ago, Ray never thought his route to the NFL would take him through Europe. In his junior year at Michigan, in 1997, Ray was second on the Wolverines in interceptions with five, and third in tackles, with 66. He was a first team All-Big Ten and was a leader on a team that split the national title with Nebraska. He seemed to be on a path to the pros.

At the beginning of Michigan's championship season, in August, Ray acquired a tattoo. After suffering through what he still says was the most painful ninety minutes of his life, Ray walked out of a tattoo parlor in Ypslianti, Michigan, with the detailed likeness of Pamela Simmons, his mother and best friend, on his right forearm. Today she smiles up softly from Ray's arm.

Simmons was seventeen when she gave birth to Ray. A month away from starting her senior year at Linden McKinley High in Columbus, Ohio, Simmons got no help from the biological father in raising Marcus, but she did get assistance from her own mother, Mary Ray. After giving birth, Pamela stayed in school and was, to a small degree, able to live a normal life. She went to parties. She kept statistics for the boys' basketball team. And she spent time with her girlfriends. Still, she always had a baby to think about. "Having Marcus made me grow up fast," said Simmons. "I had to graduate from high school, get a job, and take care of my son."

In August 1993, when Marcus was seven, his mother took him on a city bus to sign him up for little league football. "There were no male role models in his life, no father figures," said Simmons. "I wasn't sure how to go about it, but I wanted to give him that." Football provided young Marcus with the support network he'd never had. Coaches treated him like a son, and Ray responded well. By the time he was senior linebacker at Eastmoor High in Columbus, he was coveted by college coaches all across the country. But his mother told him to attend a school that stressed academics as much as football. So Ray chose Michigan.

Before his senior season, Ray was voted a team captain. "I was riding high going into the season," said Ray. "I was rated high." Yet it all ended for Ray before the 1998 season even started when he was suspended for six games for having improper dealings with an agent. Over the summer Ray had attended a concert in Cincinnati with some pals. Two of his friends were unable to pay their hotel bill and Ray allegedly called agent James Gould, who put the tab on his credit card. When it was discovered, Ray's season, not to mention his reputation, was tarnished.

"The whole experience was devastating," said Ray. "I had just been voted team captain and that title got stripped. We started out 0–2 and I was the scapegoat for that. It was very difficult."

Ray returned to the Wolverines lineup after serving his suspension, but he wasn't the same player. He didn't get drafted—most teams weren't sold on his speed, as he runs the 40 in the 4.7 to 4.8 range—but was signed by the Raiders as a free agent. They had sent him to Europe. Now Ray hoped a strong season with the Claymores would help him land a full-time job with Oakland, where he would play alongside his former college roommate, cornerback and Heisman Trophy winner, Charles Woodson.

St. Andrews, Scotland. Five Days Before Game Seven

To escape from everything that was going wrong the Claymores, quarterback Kevin Daft and his girlfriend Kesa Koida took a train north to St. Andrews, home of one of the world's premier golf courses. They walked around the quaint town, finally visiting St. Andrews Cathedral, where they climbed the church tower. While they stood there in the mist, looking at the spectacular vistas, Daft dropped to his knee and asked for Kesa's hand in marriage. She accepted. "It was perfect," said Kesa. "Just perfect." It was, in fact, one of the few completely perfect moments in the Claymores' season so far.

Glasgow, Scotland. Three days Before Game Seven

At practice, the Claymores were surprised to see a new face in uniform: Siran Stacy. The players had heard of him, but none of them knew quite know to greet Stacy, who'd played for the Claymores from 1995–97. In his first and third seasons in Scotland, Stacy rushed for 758 yards—the third-best single seasons in NFL Europe history—and in 1996 he'd led the Claymores to a World League title. Criner told the local press that Stacy was brought over to Scotland to be inducted into the Claymores' Hall of Fame at halftime of the Barcelona game. While this was true, it was only partially true. Stacy didn't know it, but he was actually in Scotland for a tryout. The entire Claymore organization wanted to see if his 32-year-old body was in football shape. Stecker was getting beat up in games, and Criner wanted an insurance policy—especially one that was an old hero who could spur ticket sales.

When Stacy worked out with the scout team, he showed surprising quickness, reminding Criner of those halcyon days of the mid-90s when Stacy dominated the league. Stacy starred at Alabama from 1989 to '91, but was a step slow for the NFL. In his NFL Europe career, however, he established himself as one of the two best running backs to ever play in the league—along with NFL exile Lawrence Phillips, who played for the Barcelona Dragons in 1999. Stacy was a graceful and complete runner, quick enough to reach the corner on a sweep, strong enough to the push the pile up the middle. "Siran was about as talented of a back as I've ever had," said Criner. "Plus, he was a great leader. When he spoke, everybody listened."

While Stacy was unquestionably a leader in the past, he was also a lot younger then and prone to making youthful mistakes. One such indiscretion occurred in the aftermath of the Claymores' 1996 World Bowl victory played on Scotland's home turf at Murrayfield. The team was celebrating their championship in the locker room, and the World Bowl trophy—a volleyball-sized crystal orb—was being passed around to each player. Many of the players kissed the trophy, others hugged it, some just touched it. But no player was more enchanted by its glistening beauty than Stacy. As the celebration continued and then spilled over into a VIP room at Murrayfield, Stacy conceived a bold and not-so-bright idea: He was going to steal the World Bowl trophy and take it home with him to Alabama.

According to many of Stacy's 1996 teammates and coaches, this is what transpired: At the party in the VIP room, when no one was looking, Stacy put the crystal orb into his gym bag. He then boarded the team bus, eventually sharing his scam with a few players. At the time everyone thought of it as nothing more than a practical joke. The players were in high spirits and not too concerned. They had just been crowned champions, a celebration was awaiting them at their favorite pub, and tomorrow the team would return to the States as victors.

Two busses carried the Claymores from Murrayfield back to the

Central Hotel. Stacy sat in the back of the second bus. The lead bus broke down with an engine problem about five minutes after leaving the stadium. For two hours, the bus sat on the shoulder of a highway while mechanics tried to fix it. Instead of celebrating with their team-mates and fans back in Glasgow, the players wandered around in the darkness of the Scottish countryside. They drank a few beers that the players had smuggled onto the bus and they ate a few dry turkey sandwiches the bus driver had stored in a cooler. "Talk about anticli-mactic," said wide receiver Scott Couper, who was on that 1996 championship team. "We worked our tails off all season and we won; then we had to celebrate by ourselves in the middle of nowhere. Only in NFL Europe."

When the bus that Stacy was on reached Central Station, the run-ning back quietly slipped out, then walked into the train station, which is a connected to the Central Hotel. Stacy found a trashcan with some newspapers in it and buried the trophy there. His plan was to retrieve it out of the trash before he headed to the Glasgow airport early the next morning. It almost worked.

"He came close to pulling it off," said Vince Alcalde. "But someone saw him put the trophy in a trashcan, and the coaching staff was alerted. It was a stupid, immature thing to do, but we had just won so it really didn't seem like that big of a deal."

His plan was foiled, but even his teammates who thought Stacy was irresponsible were impressed that he'd attempted to pull off such a ambitious heist. "I just had to laugh at the whole deal," said Willy Tate, who was also on that championship team. "And I laugh even harder whenever I hear Coach Criner call Siran a responsible team leader. I guess time has a way of changing how one remembers people."

As the thirty-one-year-old Stacy ran with the scout team, Tate and his teammates had no idea that this was an audition. They thought it was just Criner letting his former superstar relive the glory days of his past. And judging by the smile on the coach's face as he watched Stacy run, Criner liked what he saw. In fact, it wouldn't be long before the newest member of the Scottish Claymores would also be their oldest member.

21 Streaker

Diehard Claymore fans in action.

Glasgow, Scotland. Two Days Before Game Seven

THE PLAN HAD crystallized. It would be the Mona Lisa of streaks—beautiful and with attitude. After a week of phone calls, Matt Finkes and Rob Hart had most of the details of the streak worked out. Gillian Stevenson, a waitress at one of the team's favorite pubs in Glasgow, accepted a payment of $450 to run. She was more than happy to cover her body with notes and numbers in magic marker that, Finkes and Hart hoped, would be broadcast around the globe. Stevenson was an eager participant because she wanted the fame—or, perhaps, the infamy—that would result from the raunchy run. "I've always had a wild side," she said, "so when we started talking about it I figured why not. You only live once."

The key to making it work, according to Finkes, was getting people in place so the streaker wouldn't have to bare all to the police after she ran across the field. "We have to make sure that she doesn't get arrested," said Finkes. "We have to have people in the stands who can hide her and help her avoid the police. And right now I have a feeling that Criner knows what we're up to and he certainly doesn't approve, but at this point I'm all about pissing Criner off. Every player on this team shares that sentiment."

But then two days before the Barcelona game, the plan hit a snag: It turned out that the day after the game was a bank holiday in Scotland. This meant that if the streaker got swept up in a security dragnet, she'd likely have to spend all day Sunday and all day Monday in the slammer. She couldn't be bailed out of jail until Tuesday morning. "This is a problem," said Hart. "The last thing we wanted for her to have to sit in a jail for more than a few hours."

The grand plan was in jeopardy, but the excitement continued to build. Every player was curious to see how it would play out—one of the few things all season that united the team.

Glasgow, Scotland. Game Seven

"Despite everything that's been going on this week, I think our team will play well against Barcelona," insisted linebacker Jon Hesse a few hours before kickoff. "It's been my experience that when a team faces a little adversity, guys start taking their jobs a little more seriously and come out a little sharper, a little more focused. And who knows? If we could have gotten a few breaks, we could easily be 6–0 right now instead of 3–3."

The Barcelona Dragons had won three out of their last four games.

Their record was 3–3, which tied them with the Claymores and Amsterdam Admirals for second place in the league standings. This game was as important to the Dragons as it was to the Claymores. Unlike the Scotland team, though, Barcelona was just starting to peak. "We really feel like right now we've got the best team in the league," said Dragons' safety Brad Trout. "We got off to a slow start, but now we feel like we've hit our groove. The guys on the team seem to really like each other and we're playing solid football."

Neither team scored in the first quarter. Barcelona threatened early in the second when quarterback Corey Sauter ran for a first down and then threw for one. But the drive stalled when Phil Glover sacked Sauter. The Dragons' kicker, Jesus Angoy, then missed a 49-yard field goal.

Rob Hart was especially glad to see that kick fall short. At the end of the season, the kicker in NFL Europe with the most points is awarded a $1,000 bonus. As it stood, Hart and Angoy were tied for the scoring lead with 33 points each. Hart needed this money; he was getting married the following fall and had zero dollars in his bank account. When Angoy's kick fell short, the first person out on the field to congratulate the Scotland defense was Hart. "There's only one way that I'll be able to have a halfway decent wedding," said Hart, "and that's if I get that bonus."

On the Claymores' next drive, Marcus Crandell led at quarterback. As in practice all week, he performed at the top of his game. He fired an 18-yard completion to wide receiver Selucio Sanford, then he hit Stecker for a 13-yard gain down to the Barcelona 12-yard-line. Two plays later, Crandell tossed a 15-yard touchdown pass to Sanford, who made a beautiful diving catch in the endzone. As soon as Sanford reeled in the ball, the Claymores' sideline erupted. It was by far the biggest display of emotion by Scotland all season—everyone sensed the magnitude of the moment. With momentum now on their

THE PROVING GROUND

side, linebacker Jon Hesse made the game-clinching play late in the second quarter. Dropping back into coverage, Hesse read the eyes of quarterback Tony Graziani and hauled in a one-handed interception at the Dragons' 43-yard-line. Making a few smooth moves and patiently waiting for his blocks, Hesse returned the ball to the 11-yard-line. On the next play, Crandell drilled an 11-yard touchdown pass to Sellers, who reached up high to snag the ball. The score was now 14–0.

At halftime, the coaching staff had little to say to the players. Not much needed correcting. The Claymores were playing a complete game, as the offense, defense, and special teams had clicked together for just the second time all season. The second half brought more of the same. The defense dominated and the offense continued to move the ball at will. Scotland defeated Barcelona 28–0. It was the Claymores' first shutout since 1996.

"That was about as good a football game as we've played," said Criner to the press afterward. "I'm tickled to death and pleased for the players because they are the ones who had to recover from a tough loss last week and then come out and play a game like they did today to put us back in contention for a championship."

No streaker show was the biggest disappointment of the game. But in the end, the players just didn't have the heart. "We had the money" said Hart. "We had it all planned: what time she would get to the stadium, how she would get on the field, and when she would run. Then Steve Livingstone [the team's PR director] found out and he tried to arrange the girl's escape. He called an official at the stadium and told him that the players and even some of the Claymores' staff wanted to do it because it would have been great publicity for our team and the league. But apparently this official was very pissy about the whole idea. He said they'd arrest her the moment she tried to run out on the field. So I guess I never should have said anything to Steve in the first place. Then it might have happened. But we had to cancel it once we knew that she was going to get arrested. That just wouldn't have been right."

So their plan to rivet the eyes of the world on NFL Europe was temporarily postponed. Now the only way to get the attention of hard-core football fans back in the United States would be to win the World Bowl.

22 The Fragility of Football

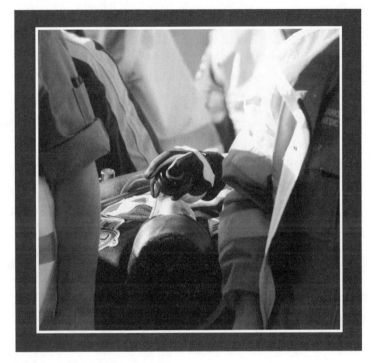

Linebacker Brian Smith.

Edinburgh, Scotland. Late in the
Third Quarter of Game Seven

IT WAS OH-SO gruesome. When Tony Graziani saw it happen, he yelled at the top of his lungs for the trainer to hurry. When Blaine McElmurry witnessed the catastrophic injury, he thought he was seeing the end of many things—a career, perhaps the ability to run, maybe even the ability to walk. When Matt Finkes looked down on

Brian Smith, he couldn't believe that Smith wasn't howling in agony. "It was the single worst injury I've ever seen," said Finkes. "How Brian maintained his composure, I'll never know."

With less than five minutes remaining in the fourth quarter against Barcelona, the Claymores' Myrel Moore instructed his defense to run a stunt blitz. The Dragons had the ball on their 46-yard-line and faced second and ten, trailing the Claymores 28–0. When Smith, an outside linebacker, heard the play call, he knew that he was supposed to wait for the right defensive end to engage the offensive tackle and push him inside. After standing his ground for about a second, Smith then would go on a delayed blitz around the right end. "It was a pretty simple blitz," said Smith, "and we'd been killing them with it all afternoon."

When the ball was snapped, Smith read the end, saw that it was a pass play, then came flying around the corner. When he was three yards away from quarterback Tony Graziani, Smith saw that Graziani was cocking his arm and preparing to unleash the ball. Smith knew Graziani's game well, as the two had played together on the Atlanta Falcons in the 1999 season. Smith was bound for Atlanta after the NFL Europe season, and it seemed likely that he would make the team.

With Graziani about to throw, Smith leaped as high into the air as he could. But just as his feet left the ground, he was blocked by Dragon running back Jesse Haynes, knocking Smith off-balance. When Smith hit the ground, his left foot planted and stuck, but the rest of his body twisted awkwardly. By the time he came to a stop on the grass, his left knee had twisted around nearly 180 degrees. Suddenly, as Smith grabbed his knee and looked up into the over-cast sky, the dangers of football were made clear to everyone on the field.

When Smith peered down at his knee, it looked as if it was dangling by a thread, as if his kneecap was being held in place by fishing line. "The first thing I tried to do was push everything back into place," said Smith afterwards. "But when I put my hand on my knee, I experienced the worst pain I've ever felt in my life."

At first, the players thought Smith might lose his lower leg. This had happened before. In fall 1999, Sam Paneno, a running back for Division II UC-Davis, took a handoff against Western Oregon and ran off tackle. As he pushed forward for an extra yard, he went down awkwardly, because a defender had barreled in from the side and hit his legs while they were extended. When the pile cleared, Paneno still lay on the ground. The trainer came out and he saw that Paneno's lower right leg, which was displaced by an inch or two, was pointed in a different direction than the rest of his leg. But what really concerned the trainer was something that he couldn't see. When a player dislocates a knee, the artery behind the knee can get damaged and disrupt blood flow to the lower leg and foot.

In Paneno's case, the artery behind his right knee was severed. Doctors tried to repair the artery six hours later, but it was too late. Tests after the surgery revealed that 90 percent of the muscles in his lower leg were dead. Advised that he could keep the leg and live with a foot that barely functioned or choose amputation, Paneno chose to cut the leg off. "The amputation was kind of a relief, like, 'Yes, that will solve my problem. Just cut it off," said Paneno later. "It was the beginning and the end at the same time. It was the end of my leg, but the beginning of my getting better."

The Sam Paneno story is still told in football locker rooms as a worst-case scenario. Many of the Claymores were familiar with Paneno's tale, which was why they knew that Smith could be in big trouble. Nearly every player on the field screamed for the trainers to run—not jog, run—to Smith. They knew that time was critical.

The first thing the Claymores' trainer and doctor did was put an inflatable cast around Smith's knee to stabilize it. They wanted to transport Smith to the hospital immediately, but first they decided to hook up an IV to his arm right there on the field. Smith needed to be sedated because he was in excruciating pain. "I wish I had the words to describe how bad it hurt," said Smith later. "It was just an unimaginable kind of pain."

But the painkillers didn't do the trick. Smith was still suffering. So the team doctor then gave Smith some gas. The sight of this caused a few people in the stadium to start crying. From the stands, with all the equipment and doctors surrounding Smith, it appeared that his life was in jeopardy.

An ambulance drove out onto the field to fetch Smith. He was hoisted onto a stretcher—with his pads still on. The Claymores' minister, Steve Connor, jumped into the ambulance along with assistant trainer Brain McGuire. The first thing Smith asked Conner was if his belongings in his locker would be safe. "They'll be fine," replied Connor in his soothing voice. "I'll take care of everything. You just concentrate on yourself right now."

As the ambulance sped to the hospital, Smith and Connor prayed together. They prayed for health, happiness, and a normal life, which was a lot to wish for. Smith's leg was being held together by one artery, one nerve, and one ligament. Three of the four knee ligaments were torn.

After what seemed like an interminable ride, Smith was finally wheeled into St. Victoria Hospital in Glasgow. A team of doctors examined him for about than hour. During the exam, Smith was as scared as he'd ever been in his entire life. His future was about to be determined. Luckily, the doctors had good news for the Claymores' linebacker: His leg was not in jeopardy of being amputated. But, his football career was likely over. There was no damage to the major artery behind the knee, so chances were, Smith would someday be able to once again lead a normal life. His rehabilitation would take at least a year, though.

THE PROVING GROUND

"That was great news, no question," said Smith. "But it meant that my journey was just beginning."

FOR THE NEXT four days, Smith stayed in Victoria Hospital. He was put in a bleak infirmary that housed twenty other patients. They were all in one big, dilapidated room that looked more like a place that made you sick, not well. Smith was the only patient under forty, the only one with a full set of teeth, and the only African-American. He had no phone, no television, no radio, no books, no magazines, and no money. He did have a Walkman, but after one day his batteries died. As he lay there with a deadness in his eyes that you couldn't miss, Smith wondered just how the hell he'd gotten into this.

"I guess it was a decision I made long ago that led me to this point," Smith would say later. "But I don't have any regrets. None."

Back in the late 1990s, Smith was the lone star at the University of Alabama-Birmingham. In his first three years at UAB, Smith started every game at linebacker. At 6'3" and 243 pounds, Smith was quick, agile, and delivered bruising hits. But perhaps his best attribute was that he always played his best games against the toughest competition. In 1999, his junior year, he made 10 tackles against Nebraska and then, three weeks later against Tennessee, he recorded a season-high 14 tackles. After three years of college ball, Smith decided he was ready for the next level. He declared himself eligible for the NFL draft.

Scouts and NFL personnel advised him against turning pro at that point. They told Smith he might be picked late in the draft or that he might not be selected at all. Nonetheless, Smith decided to roll the dice. He hated school and—drafted or as a free agent—he wanted to give the NFL a chance. He felt he was ready.

He watched the draft from his mother's home in Rome, Georgia.

The hours crawled by, minute by excruciating minute, and Smith never heard his name called. But as soon as the draft was over, his phone started ringing off the hook. Several teams wanted to sign him as a free agent. "I was incredibly disappointed not to get drafted," said Smith. "But I still felt like I'd make it once I got to a camp. All I wanted was a chance."

Smith got his chance but he didn't make it. The 49ers released him before the end of the preseason. Much to his surprise and delight, though, Atlanta then signed him for their practice squad for the 1999 season. He came to Europe to solidify his spot on the Falcons' roster for the 2000 season.

But now here he was, scared, confused, and seriously injured—physically and mentally. When Myrel Moore visited Smith a few days after the Barcelona game, he was appalled by the hospital's conditions. "That's maybe the worst place I've ever been to in my entire life," said Moore. "Hospitals in Scotland just aren't the same as hospitals in the United States."

Moore thought Smith's emotional condition was just as disturbing. Smith was deeply depressed, as his football career lay in smoldering ruins. Yet, oddly, Smith's injury had a galvanizing effect on the Claymores. For the few days that Smith was in the hospital waiting for his leg to get strong enough for him to be able to fly back to the States for surgery, a steady stream of players came to visit him. They gave him money so he could call his mother back in Rome, Georgia, from a pay phone to let her know what had happened. They brought him magazines and books. They purchased batteries for him and gave him CDs for his Walkman. Basically, they did everything they could to make life a little easier for their fallen teammate. These small acts of kindness and selflessness brought the team closer together in a way that Criner and his staff never could have.

"It's strange how this whole thing has shaken out," said tight end

Rickey Brady. "Once we saw Brian go down and have to go to that awful place for a few days, it was like all of a sudden guys remembered they were playing on a team. Nothing was ever said, but you could just tell at practice, in the locker room, and even at the hotel, that Brian's injury brought us together."

Two days before the Claymores jetted to the Netherlands, Smith caught a plane destined for Birmingham, Alabama, where he would have major surgery on his knee. The last thing he told his teammates, on the eve of his departure, was that his dream was still alive.

"I'll play again," was what he said.

23 The Kurt Warner Fairy Tale

Kurt Warner with the Amsterdam Admirals.
Photo courtesy of the Amsterdam Admirals

Glasgow, Scotland. A Few Hours After the Barcelona Game

AFTER THE BARCELONA game, Criner approached Siran Stacy. He wanted to know if he'd still like to play a little football. Thirty-six hours earlier, Stacy had no desire to ever strap on a helmet again. He just thought he was just getting a free vacation from his job in sales back in Birmingham, Alabama. "When they called and asked me to come over, I was thrilled," said Stacy. "To me it simply meant a few days away from the daily grind."

Stacy hadn't played a down of football in three years and he'd rarely worked-out since hanging up his cleats. Unlike many former professional players, he was comfortable with his post athletic life. He was a minor celebrity in Birmingham and there were always people who seemed to want to be around Stacy and help him in any way they could.

Even though Stacy had led the Claymores to a World Bowl title in 1996, not all of his memories of Scotland were fond. When he was with the Claymores in 1995, the team lived in the Commodore Hotel, which is located twenty minutes from downtown Edinburgh. "We had roommates that year and there was nothing to do," recalled Stacy. "The rooms were small and the beds were small. Guys got tired of each other by the second week and there were a lot of fights. The biggest problem was that we didn't have anything to do. It was, like, £20 ($35) to take a cab into Edinburgh. So we all just lay around the hotel and did nothing but argue. Consequently, we were a terrible team."

Life during his next year in Scotland was markedly better. The Claymores moved into the Central Hotel in Glasgow and each player got his own room. "The little things mean so much in this league," said Stacy. "Having single rooms and being in an urban area were the differences between having a team that wanted to win and having a team that didn't care."

As Stacy considered Criner's offer, his mind kept flashing back to how the crowd reacted to him earlier that afternoon when he was announced on the field and inducted into the Claymore Hall of Fame. The place went absolutely crazy, giving the returning Stacy a hero's welcome. This did something to Stacy: It made him remember how good it feels to be a player. "I think it was all a setup," said Stacy. "If I hadn't felt that feeling, I wouldn't have come back. But once that happened—man, I knew that if they asked, I'd have to stay. It was almost like I had no control over the situation."

Stacy had only brought a few changes of clothes with him to Scotland, but he didn't need to go on a shopping spree. Three years before he had accidentally left a suitcase full of shirts, pants, socks, and underwear in the flat of an acquaintance who lived in Glasgow— amazingly, his friend still had his stuff. And when Stacy put on some of his old clothes and walked through the long, familiar halls of the Central Hotel, it was as if he had traveled back in time, back to a place where everything was grand. Once again, Siran Stacy was a professional football player.

Amsterdam, Netherlands. One Day Before Game Eight

"This is one of the most disgusting stories I know," said Andy Colvin, recalling one of his all-time favorite NFL Europe tales. "It was 1995 in Amsterdam. The Claymores had just lost yet another game [they would only win two that season] and I went out with a few players and few team employees. We proceeded to get absolutely shitfaced. That's what everybody does when they go to Amsterdam. Anyway, we then got back to the hotel and everyone went to their room, around five in the morning. About twenty minutes later I hear a knock on my door. It was—well, let's just say it was a prominent team employee. He was naked, covered in vomit from shoulder to foot. I cleaned him up. Then, when my back was turned, he bolted out the door. For some reason, he went to the stairwell. There he proceeded to fall down four flights all the way to the bottom. That was where he slept—naked—for the rest of the night. At around seven the next morning, I heard a pounding on my door. It was that same team employee, still naked, only now he's covered in bruises. He asked me to help him get back to his room, which I did. But perhaps I shouldn't have, just to teach the bloke a lesson."

Every year, the game at Amsterdam is a treasured trip not only for the visiting players but also for the visiting press. It's an open city that's alive at all hours of the day and night. Marijuana is available at nearly every corner café and the red-light district is a twenty-four-hour source of temptation. Not surprisingly, each year the Admirals have more problems with drug use than any other NFL Europe team. Even though Admirals coach Al Luginbill vigorously tested his players for drugs during the 2000 season—Luginbill tested his players more frequently than every other NFL Europe coach—it didn't deter players from indulging. Nor did it keep team employees from having a good time once in a awhile.

Last year, an Amsterdam staff member went to downtown Amsterdam one night and dropped acid, according to two sources. At about one in the morning he decided to return to the team hotel. On his way there, though, he noticed an elaborate window display of Smurfs, the little blue troll-like cartoon characters. The next thing he knew, someone was tapping him on the shoulder. It was one of the coaches saying hello. After rubbing his eyes, the team employee realized it was daylight. He had spent all night and most of the morning staring at the Smurfs. Talk about a bad trip.

At an Admirals' staff meeting in '99, according to these same two sources, a team employee attended who had eaten some mushrooms, another hallucinogenic drug. In the middle of the meeting, the drug-addled employee stood up and yelled, "I want to know what the fuck we're going to do about the dancing celery!"

Such extreme stories of drug abuse are rare, no question. But it was common for players to have dalliances with certain substances during their stay in Amsterdam. "When I was with the Jets, I constantly ran into guys who played for the Admirals," said Finkes. "They obviously loved the city and loved the night life—and virtually everyone I've spoken with indulged in some fashion—but Luginbill runs a tight ship."

Luginbill enforced a curfew a few nights a week and he housed his team in a countryside hotel that was about forty-five minutes away from the city center and all its vices, making it an expensive and time-consuming task to travel into Amsterdam. But some players visited the city of Amsterdam for other reasons, like to go to church. In 1998, Kurt Warner was one of those players.

Amsterdam, Netherlands. 1998

Once upon time, there was a football player on his honeymoon. It was October 1997, and Kurt Warner's football career was going nowhere. Sure, he'd played some Arena League ball, but he hadn't registered a blip on the radar screen of any NFL general manager.

On his honeymoon in Jamaica, Warner and his wife Brenda stayed at a resort in Ocho Rios and were having the time of their lives. They danced the nights away and soaked up the sun during the days. Warner was trying to relax and prepare for a workout with the Chicago Bears he was to have a few days after he returned to the States. Then, on the second-to-last night on the island, Warner's right elbow ballooned into the size of a baseball. He had been bitten by something, probably a centipede or a scorpion, and he couldn't bend his arm. He also had a fever and was extremely nauseated.

When Warner returned to the States, his elbow was still swollen. So he called the Bears—he didn't even have an agent at the time— and asked them if they could postpone the workout. "I'm really sorry," Warner told Bears pro personnel director Rick Spielman. "I'm not trying to put off the workout. I really, really want to do this when my arm is OK." Spielman said he understood and the workout would be rescheduled. Alas, Warner never heard from Spielman again. He feared that his NFL opportunity had been lost.

A month passed and there was still no word from the Bears. Then a call came from an unlikely party: Amsterdam coach Al Luginbill, who had been interested in Warner ever since he saw him play in the Arena League from 1995–97. Luginbill wanted Warner to play for him in Amsterdam, but Warner was reluctant. The money was better in the Arena League and now he had a family in the Des Moines area, where Brenda was from and where his Arena team, the Iowa Barnstormers, was based. Warner wanted security, so he told Luginbill, "I don't want to just drop everything and hope an NFL team notices me. If an NFL team will work me out and sign me, then allocate me to NFL Europe, I'll go."

Luginbill told Warner that this wouldn't be a problem, that he knew of several teams that were interested in finding a quarterback and giving him a chance. Luginbill proceeded to contact twelve different teams. To each one, he loudly sung Warner's praises. Yet eleven teams politely replied that they weren't interested. Only the St. Louis Rams were willing to give Warner a tryout. This was Warner's chance—and possibly his last.

In December 1997, Warner boarded a plane from Des Moines and flew to St. Louis for his workout. He felt good and ready to put forth the passing performance of a lifetime. Instead, he was awful. During the 1997 Arena season, Warner had broken his right thumb and it still hadn't completely healed. Warner always believed his accuracy was his strongest attribute as a quarterback, but on this morning he missed everything. He was high, low, or wide on nearly every throw. Warner did show impressive footwork and adequate arm strength, but overall he believed his workout grade was barely passing. He expected the worst.

Rams coach Dick Vermeil and offensive coordinator Jerry Rhome were not present at the workout. Instead, Warner tossed balls to some assistants and front-office personnel. "Look, that's just not me out there," Warner told John Becker, the Rams' director of college scouting. "I'd love to come back again after my thumb heals and show you what I can really do."

Becker smiled and said a few cordial words, but Warner believed he would never be a Ram after such an atrocious display. When he went to home to Brenda, he told her, "Nothing is going to come of this." But he was wrong. A few days later, Luginbill called and said he'd just heard from the Rams. They wanted to sign him. For the first time in several years, Warner hired an agent. On December 23, he signed a no-frills contract that featured no bonus and no guaranteed money.

Warner went to Amsterdam and beat out Jake Delhomme, who was allocated from the Saints, for the Admirals' starting quarterback position. Then, for virtually the entire season, Warner operated at the full height of his powers. His thumb was healed and his performance was jaw-dropping. He lead the league in passing yards (2,101), attempts (326), completions (165), and touchdowns (15).

But perhaps his most important growth took place off the field. Every Sunday in spring 1998, Warner would leave the team hotel, get on a ferryboat, cross the Noordzeekanall, and then weed through the red-light district to get to his place of worship. On his journey, Warner walked past hash bars and clubs with naked women dancing in the windows. Men loitering outside the entrances to these establishments would try to convince Warner to enter, but he always smiled politely and just moved on. "I may have been the least adventurous guy in the city," said Warner.

What Warner lacked in adventurousness, he made up for in leadership. For the first time in his life, Warner inspired his teammates. They knew about his lengthy pilgrimage every week and soon Luginbill was asking Warner to guide prayer sessions. Many players also asked Warner if they could accompany him to church. For the first time in his football career, Warner was the leader of the team. Soon Warner's confidence asserted itself, and there is no commodity more precious to a quarterback than his belief in himself.

One week during the 1998 season, the Rams' vice president of player personnel, Charley Armey, came over to Amsterdam to check out Warner. Armey was blown away. He took Warner out to dinner one evening and told him, "Kurt, you're doing things better than any of the guys we've got back in St. Louis." For the first time in his life, Warner had folks in the NFL noticing his talent. A few months later, when he assumed the starting quarterback position of the Rams, Warner's confidence was at its peak because of his experience in Europe. He was ready to shock the football world—and he did. It's been happiness ever after for Kurt Warner since.

24 City of Sin

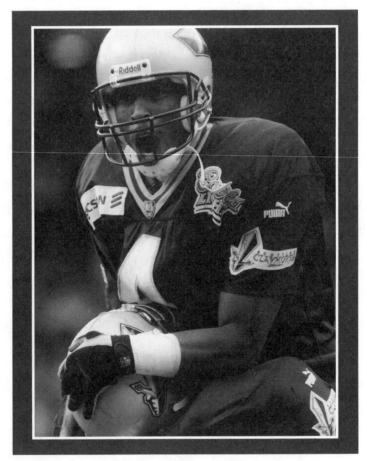

Wide receiver Donald Sellers.

Amsterdam, Netherlands. Eve of Game Eight

THE TRIP TO Amsterdam from Glasgow was a quick, ninety-minute plane ride. On the plane the players were quietly confident that they would win this game. By embarrassing Barcelona last week,

the Claymores had finally tapped their potential. They had eliminated the penalties and played an artful, all-around game. It was the
team's first masterpiece. If they could paint a couple more, then a
championship could be won. For these players, that would be almost
as valuable as a Picasso.

When the Claymores arrived at their hotel, Finkes asked Criner
for permission to buy a soccer ball. Since the third week of the season, Finkes and about a dozen other players had been playing a game
called keep-ee-up-ee every day before practice. The game was simple: Five to ten players stood in a circle and tried to keep the soccer
ball in the air without using their hands. Finkes had left his soccer
ball in Glasgow, and a few of the players wanted to play the game
before the Claymores took on the Admirals. Criner gave Finkes the
okay. The coach believed the game would help keep the team loose
before kickoff.

Amsterdam, Netherlands. Game Eight

The Admirals entered the game with a 4–3 record—the same as the
Claymores. Amsterdam normally played their home games at Amsterdam ArenA, a 51,328-capacity stadium located in the southeast
part of the city. But this weekend, the Euro 2000 soccer tournament
was being played at ArenA, so the Admirals' game against the Claymores had been moved to old Olympic Stadium, a smaller building
(capacity 21,000) that was woefully inadequate for football. The stadium wasn't even long enough to hold a regulation-sized football
field. To compensate, one of the endzones was made to partially
encroch on the track that encircled the field. Officials at the stadium
merely threw a tarp over one end of the track and hoped that that
would solve the problem.

It didn't. When Criner and Luginbill noticed that a portion of end-zone was on the running track, they complained that it was a danger to the players. Even though the game was one of the few all season that was scheduled to be televised live in the United States—making it an extremely important contest—Criner and Luginbill decided to go one way for the entire game. This meant that every offensive series started off north to south. The teams had to switch sides after every punt.

"This is a disgrace to the league and I'm sure everyone is embarrassed," said Willy Tate. "We were all excited because this was our one game that was televised back in the States, and then for something like this to happen, it really takes away from the excitement. I mean, we really look like we are playing for a minor-league outfit."

As Luginbill and Criner conferred, the Claymores enjoyed a game of keep-ee-up-ee. They played for twenty minutes. Kickoff was still more than two hours away, and instead of sitting around in the stands under the cloud-dappled sky, they kicked the ball, laughed, and generally tried to keep their mood as light as possible.

After Luginbill and Criner reached their agreement, Luginbill walked alone along the stadium sidelines and watched the game of keep-ee-up-ee. Later, when Luginbill chatted with game officials, he told them, "These guys aren't focused. I like our chances."

When Criner learned that Luginbill had said this, he grinned like a man who had a poker hand so good it almost hurt. Because this was precisely what he wanted Luginbill to think when he saw the carefree game going on. Luginbill had just fallen right into the teeth of Criner's trap.

IT ONLY TOOK three plays for the Claymores to exert their dominance over the Admirals. That was when Amsterdam quarterback

THE PROVING GROUND

Ron Powlus, a former Notre Dame golden boy, threw the ball directly into the hands of linebacker Jon Hesse, who had floated back into pass coverage. Hesse intercepted the ball at the Admiral's 48-yard-line and returned it to the five. This set up a 5-yard scoring pass from Daft to Scott Couper, who was left uncovered. After Hart kicked the extra point, the Claymores had a 7–0 lead with just two-and-a-half minutes gone.

Scotland didn't let up. After stopping the Admirals' next drive, the Claymores marched effortlessly down the field, concluding with a 15-yard touchdown pass from Daft to Donald Sellers, which was Sellers's fourth touchdown of his short season. "Donald Sellers has made all the difference in our offense," said Tate. "He's given us a wide receiver who can make plays. None of the other wideouts were making plays, so basically, defenses just keyed on Stecker. They can't do that anymore with Donald around."

At the beginning of the second quarter, Powlus was picked again, this time by Blaine McElmurry at the Admirals 21-yard-line. Three plays later, Crandell, who was again rotating quarters with Daft, ran the ball into the endzone on a 5-yard scramble. After another Hart extra point, the score was 21–0.

The Claymores continued to trounce the Admirals in the first half; they entered the locker room with a 35–3 lead. The lopsided margin was the largest halftime points differential in NFL Europe history. Criner didn't say much in the locker room. He simply implored his players not to let up and warned them that the Admirals wouldn't give up. The most dangerous animal is a wounded one, Criner reminded his team.

In the second half, Scotland continued their disciplined gameplan. The Admirals never got close; the Claymores destroyed Amsterdam 42–10. "We're taking care of business," Criner praised his players in the locker room after the game. "We're still in the hunt for the World

Bowl. Today is the way we can always play. Their defense had only given up one touchdown in their last eleven quarters and we lit them up. Let's stay focused and next week let's let the Rhein Fire know what kind of team we are."

It was a short victory speech, but Criner didn't want to jinx the team's success. The Claymores were playing their best football of the season. They were now 5–3 and alone in second place. Rhein was 6–2 and had sole grasp on first place. If Scotland was to advance to the World Bowl, they would need to topple the Fire next week in Glasgow.

The most valuable player of the game was Hesse (pronounced Hess) and the European football weekly *First Down* agreed. Their postgame headline: THE LOCH HESSE MONSTER.

THAT NIGHT IN Amsterdam, Finkes took quarterback Kevin Daft, free safety Blaine McElmurry, tight end Nachi Abe, backup quarterback Tak Sunaga, and cornerback Kordell Taylor out to explore the town. It was Finkes' chance to show the goody-goodies on the team, as he liked to call them, what the city of Amsterdam could offer. As Finkes led the guys around the redlight district and other sections of the city, Daft didn't utter a word. What he saw rendered him speechless. There were prostitutes dancing in windows, tempting men on the streets to come hither into their pleasure palaces. There were winos passed out in the gutters, sleeping the evening's indulgences away. There were street urchins standing in the shadows, waiting for the chance to pick a pocket. There were bars and cafes selling hash and marijuana on nearly every corner, many of which spilled over with people. There were trolleys that zipped up and down the streets, at one point nearly hitting one drugged up traveler. And there were con artists everywhere, trying to scam suckers with games like three-card monte.

THE PROVING GROUND

"It was time for a few of the guys on the team to see what life had to offer," said Finkes. "Amsterdam can be a little too much even for a guy like me, but in small doses the city is great."

After wandering the streets for an hour, the goody-goodies trekked back to the hotel. They had the spirit to stay out longer, but the flesh didn't allow it. Finkes, however, was invigorated by the sights and sounds of Amsterdam. He stayed and walked aimlessly deep into the night. He checked out the action at a few hotspots, and loved every second of it. Since the beginning of the season, Finkes said he was in Europe more for the experience than for the football. And now here he was, reveling in that experience, in the excitement of being in a dynamic and dangerous place. Yes, as he meandered through this city of sin, Matt Finkes was in heaven.

25 Espionage Game

Defensive tackle Antonio Dingle.

Glasgow, Scotland. Four Days Before Game Nine

BEFORE THE SEASON, defensive line coach Jim Tomsula phoned the families of all of his defensive linemen. These were purpose calls, as he was trying to get information about each player. Specifically, he wanted to find out about them personally—their likes and dislikes, their hopes and dreams. What Tomsula learned from these conversations was how to motivate his players, what buttons he needed to push and how hard, which was clear after Scotland's Week One victory over Amsterdam. In that game, the Claymores' defensive line was ruthless in its domination, totaling five sacks and eight tackles for losses. At a position meeting three days after the game, many of the defensive linemen complained that they weren't credited with the right amount of tackles and sacks—the stats they needed to pad their football résumés. As they sat in a semicircle in the defensive line's meeting room, Tomsula told his players to listen to him very closely. He had something to say, and he was only going to say it once.

"Don't worry about that shit," Tomsula began in his tent-revival speaking style. "Do you guys understand that you have a chance to be the best damn defensive line in the history of this league? You can. And next year, when I'm busting my ass over here again and all you guys are counting your paychecks from the NFL, I want to be able to tell my players, 'Hey, that chair you're in right now is where Antonio Dingle once sat. Hey, that chair there is where Chris Ward sat. And this chair here, this is where Noel Scarlett sat. And here's where Michael Mason sat.' I want to be able to say that and I want it to mean something." At the end of his speech, two players left the room wiping tears from their eyes.

Tomsula's rawest—and biggest—talent was defensive tackle Antonio Dingle. Allocated to the Claymores by the Carolina Panthers, Dingle had been the top interior defensive lineman in the league so far this season. Through eight games, he had 19 tackles, 6 sacks, and 3 forced fumbles. When his agent first told Dingle that the Panthers wanted to send him overseas, Dingle requested to play for Frankfurt. Dingle's father was in the military, and he had lived in Germany for five years while growing up so he knew a fair amount of German. When the league allocated him to Scotland, Dingle's first impulse was not to go. Then Tomsula called him.

"He knew everything about me and everything about my game,"

recalled Dingle. "I was blown away. That changed my mind instantly about wanting to come."

Dingle's success in football can be traced back to his experience at Fork Union Military Academy in central Virginia. Over the years, Fork Union has saved such players as Vinny Testaverde, Eddie George, and Daunte Culpepper. In 1994, it was Dingle's football life that was resuscitated on the school's lush hills. This was where he learned how to live a disciplined life. "Before Fork Union, I had no idea what discipline even was," said Dingle. "After I left there, I was a changed man."

As one of Fork Union's 640 cadets, who range in age from eleven to nineteen, Dingle rose at six each school morning and then spent eight hours in class or studying. He attended chapel three times a week, performed military drills twice a week, and lined up in formation each morning and evening. Parties were forbidden at the school, girls weren't allowed on campus without a chaperone; and when Dingle had nothing to do (which was rare), a faculty member would find a task for him, usually something like shining shoes or waxing bathroom floors.

Before he got to Fork Union, Dingle's grades were in the gutter. He had graduated from high school in Fayetteville, North Carolina, but didn't qualify academically at any of the twenty or so colleges that offered him a scholarship. So he went to military school. "Fork Union taught me how to organize my life and balance football with school," said Dingle. "I had trouble doing that before."

After spending a year at Fork Union, both Dingle's game and grades rebounded to playing condition. Schools across the nation tried to recruit him, but he wanted to stay close to his home in Fayetteville, where his mother still lives in a small trailer. So Dingle accepted a scholarship to Virginia. In his junior year as a Cavalier, he was named to the All-Atlantic Coast Conference team. He led all Cavalier defensive linemen with 48 tackles and it was an article of faith around Charlottesville that Dingle would be a top NFL pick. But in his senior season, he seemed to vanish, registering only 34 tackles. He wasn't even the best defensive tackle on his team. "Things were said between myself and the coaches and a bad situation just turned ugly," explained Dingle. "It was like they quit believing in me."

Because of his invisible senior season, Dingle wasn't drafted until the seventh round by the Pittsburgh Steelers. He was cut in the pre-season and then picked up by the Green Bay Packers. Dingle spent 12 games with the Packers, playing in eight, and then was released. The Carolina Panthers quickly snatched him up, though their reason for doing so was more than just wanting Dingle's talent. The week following Dingle's signing with the Panthers, the team was scheduled to play Green Bay. Dingle spent numerous hours in the days leading up to their game against the Packers schooling his new coaches on everything he knew about Green Bay's gameplan. "I told Carolina everything," said Dingle. "I told them how their offensive line set up, what their weaknesses were, what their calls were. And I gave them some of the defensive plays I still had in my notebook. I think it helped. We had an inferior team, but we won the game 33–31."

This espionage pales in comparison with what took place at Super Bowl XXVII. That was when a never-used linebacker for the Denver Broncos played a role in helping Denver win the game. For the first fifteen weeks of the 1998 season, the Claymores' Jon Hesse was on the Packers' practice squad. Then one week before the playoffs, Denver—perhaps sensing that they would meet the Packers in the Super Bowl—signed Hesse to its active roster. (Practice squad players are free to negotiate with other teams and can sign at any time.)

In the week before the Super Bowl, both the offensive and defensive coaches for the Broncos held meetings with Hesse to pour over everything he knew about the Packers. Fritz Shumer, Green Bay's defensive coordinator, was so concerned about Hesse's intimate knowledge of the Packers that Shumer changed all the defensive signals the week before the game. Part of the reason why Shumer was panicked was that he believed Hesse to be one of the smartest players in the entire NFL. The Packers wanted Hesse in the first place largely because he'd scored an astounding 46 on the 50-question Wonderlic intelligence test, the standard test given to NFL draft prospects. Hesse took the test at the 1997 scouting combine workouts two months before the NFL draft. Of the 322 players that took the test that year, Hesse's score of 46 was the best. The next-highest was a 41. Some players scored in single digits.

Hesse supplied the Broncos with everything he could remember about the Packers' gameplan—the team's formation, plays, and tendencies. Based on Hesse's information and suggestions, Denver subtly altered both their offensive and defensive strategies. Part of Denver's offensive gameplan, for example, was based on the fact that Green Bay defensive tackle Gilbert Brown had a bum knee. This injury wasn't reported, but Hesse knew about it and he knew that Brown hadn't done a good job of rehabbing the injury. Hesse told his coaches that Brown would likely get fatigued if Denver repeatedly ran directly at him, which was exactly what the Broncos did.

After the Broncos 31–24 victory, Hesse wasn't asked a single question in the locker room by any member of the media. His role that evening, like his time in Scotland, remained well outside the limelight.

Offensive lineman Jason Tenner.

Glasgow, Scotland. Four Days Before Game Nine

A LITTLE MORE than a week after Siran Stacy decided to accept Criner's offer to play in Scotland, Stacy was full of regret. He loved the football and being a member of a team again, but he despised what a member of the Scottish press had done to him. In an article published in the *Scottish Sunday Mail*, writer Brian Lironi detailed all of Stacy's past brushes with the law, including a 1995 incident in which he was deemed guilty of battery after a jury found that he had punched his girlfriend in the face. This was all old news to Glasgow readers, of course, as it had been reported in the Scottish press during Stacy's first stint with the Claymores. But Lironi's article tried to give the story a new twist by comparing Stacy to boxer Mike Tyson— a convicted rapist—who was scheduled to fight in Glasgow two days after the World Bowl.

On a bus ride to practice, Stacy was horrified to see the story in the paper. Players usually passed around the paper on the bus, and when it got to Stacy he ripped out the article. "You have to feel sorry for the guy," said kicker Rob Hart. "This article just digs up stuff from his past and puts it out there for everyone to see."

Criner and Public Relations Director Steve Livingstone informed Stacy that they were considering filing a lawsuit against the *Mail*, even though they would have little legal ground to stand on. (The facts, after all, were not in dispute.) This show of support took a bit of the sting away for Stacy. Still, he had a terrible week of practice after the story broke.

Glasgow, Scotland. Four Days Before Game Nine

The end was near. When the Claymores returned to Glasgow from Amsterdam, they had only twelve nights left in the Central Hotel. Two games remained on the schedule—at home against the Rhein Fire, then at Barcelona. If Scotland qualified for the World Bowl, they would fly straight from Barcelona to Frankfurt, where the championship game would be played.

THE PROVING GROUND

To guarantee a spot in the World Bowl, the Claymores needed to beat the Fire that week. If they lost, Scotland would still have a mathematical chance of making it to the World Bowl, but it would be longer than a long shot. "Everybody on this team is realizing that winning the World Bowl can really help our careers," said Tate. "Winning programs—be it college or here—send more guys to the pros. No matter what the level, being on a championship team helps you out. It boosts your résumé."

To advance to the championship game, the Claymores needed to shut down the Fire's high-powered offense, led by former Heisman Trophy winner Danny Weurffel, who had haunted the sleep of Claymore defensive coordinator Moore ever since their first matchup. The Claymores had had a chance to acquire Weurffel during the preseason allocation, but offensive coordinator Vince Alcalde, like most of the football world, didn't think Weurffel had enough arm strength to be an effective quarterback. That was the knock on Weurffel coming out of Florida and that was the reason the New Orleans Saints had dumped him after he struggled there for three seasons. But in NFL Europe, Weurffel displayed a feathery touch and prospered in the West-Coast style offense that the Fire ran, which placed a premium on timing routes and short, quick passes.

"I really never expected to be playing in Europe," said Weurffel. "I wasn't allocated and I was just sitting at home one day when the phone rang. It was Fire coach Galen Hall and he told me that a few of their quarterbacks had gone down in training camp and he wanted to know if I'd be interested in coming to the team. At first I didn't know, and I really hesitated, but I hadn't signed with an NFL team yet and I thought this would be a good chance to play."

NFL Europe has not been kind to past Heisman winners. Andre Ware and Gino Toretta bombed in the Old World, and they haven't been heard from in the New World since. But Wuerffel was different. For starters, he was focused. He is deeply religious and never stepped into a single pub while living in the beer-drenched city of Düsseldorf. Through eight weeks, Wuerffel had led NFL Europe in every major passing category save one: the overall passer rating, which Kevin Daft and his conservative approach owned. Behind Weurffel, the Fire had complied a 6–2 record and was alone in first place.

In their preparation for the Rhein, the Claymores' practices were spirited all week. There were more fights than usual, which was a good sign, according to defensive coordinator Myrel Moore. It meant that the players were passionate and ready to play the game of their lives. "They want it, you can see it in their eyes," said Moore. "We're ready."

Criner couldn't sleep the nights leading up to the big game. He realized that the season had come down to this one contest. Hundreds of hours spent scouting players, putting together his roster, devising gameplans and teaching his players how to execute them—it all came together in just a single chance to achieve success. It is precisely because of these moments, these games, that Criner still coaches. This is what gives him his fix, the same kind of feeling that a junkie gets when he puts the needle to his arm.

"There was a time in my life when my son was going to college and I took some time off from coaching," said Criner two days before the game. "On Saturday afternoons, when my son's football team would be playing in an away game, my wife would kick me out of the house. Even though I wasn't coaching, I was a lousy husband because I would be going crazy not being able to watch my son's game and not being around football. So she would make me get out my fly rod and I'd go fishing.

"There is just no excitement like game day. I can't imagine anyone being more excited than me when we kick off with the Rhein Fire. That's what it's all about. You can't find a bigger high."

As Criner reflected on the season, he felt that the turning point was the players-only meeting after game six with Frankfurt. "When I put together my team last year, one of the things I didn't do well was pack the roster with leaders," said Criner. "But now we have that. When the players got together by themselves, they said that they'd lost to a Frankfurt team that they were better than. They beat themselves because of mistakes. That day they decided that they wouldn't allow that to happen again. It hasn't and it's all because we have great leadership in this locker room."

TACKLE JASON TENNER has never been one to keep a close eye on his waistline. At 300-plus pounds, he's a big man and proud of it. But even he was surprised to discover that he'd lost 25 pounds since he arrived in Glasgow. "There are no scales in the hotel or our practice facility," said Tenner, who at training camp had weighed 310. "When I finally weighed myself at a different hotel, I couldn't believe it. I knew I'd lost some weight, but this is ridiculous."

There was a simple reason why many players were shedding pounds. The food at the Central was, in a word, godawful. For the past three weeks, the quality of the food had gotten progressively worse. The players were served three standard meals: cold hot dogs; dry, gray chicken; and greasy, indeterminate meat. Prison food probably would have tasted better and Criner finally did something about it on the day that the Claymores returned to Glasgow from Amsterdam. The team arrived at the hotel a little past noon and none of the rooms were ready yet. So Criner ordered his players to go to the team's dining room. The kitchen staff wasn't prepared to feed them, but Criner demanded they be served something. So the staff wheeled out some hot dogs that were so overcooked it was difficult to bite through them. Even though most of the players were jet-lagged and on the verge of starvation, none ate.

Criner went off. "Goddamn it," he yelled at the hotel chef. "If you don't improve the quality of food starting with our next meal, we're done eating here and done paying you. I'll just give my players money to go out."

Though the quality of food picked up in the next few days, most of the players quit eating at the Central anyhow. Some went to McDonalds three times a day; others patroned a pizza joint just around the corner from the hotel. "I just can't take it anymore," said tight end Rickey Brady. "This has got to be the worst food in the world. How can we be expected to play well and burn tons of calories when they feed us this garbage? It's a joke."

But even though the food was lousy, the collective spirit of the team nonetheless beamed as brightly as a neon sign during this week. The Claymores were winning and the players were happy. In this small universe, that was all that mattered.

27 The Reason Why

Antonio Dingle's sack of Rhein quarterback Danny Wuerffel.

Glasgow, Scotland. Game Nine

AT 5:30 AM, CRINER was walking the hilly streets of Glasgow. He marched at a brisk pace as the sun slowly rose into the blue-gray sky. He hadn't said it outright, but many people associated with the Claymores believed that Criner's eyes were wandering toward distant horizons, that this would be the coach's final season in NFL Europe. Executives from the nascent Extreme Football League (XFL), a stateside football league funded by the WWF's Vince McMahon that was scheduled to kick off in February 2001, had shown interest in hiring Criner to coach one of the league's eight teams for its inaugural season. Now the Claymores' front office was aflame with rumors that these were Criner's last days in Scotland. "He's gone," said one Claymore staffer of Criner. "He'll make more money in the XFL, and he won't have to live in Europe for three months."

As Criner pounded the pavement trying to burn off some nervous energy, Rickey Brady was up in his room and seriously considering going home. His wife, who was back in Norman, Oklahoma, had had surgery on her right knee the day before. It was a simple procedure, but something went wrong. In a panicked phone call late the previous night, she told Rickey she couldn't move two of her toes and would have to undergo another surgery at the same time that the Claymores would be playing the Fire. Just by her quivering voice, Brady knew that his wife was afraid and in pain. Brady loved his wife tragically, which was why this hurt him so much. "It's driving me crazy, not being with her as she's going through this," said Brady. "I really should be there."

Despite his guilt, Brady stuck it out. Three hours before the game, he wandered around the field at Hamden Park, a 52,000-seat stadium in Glasgow where the Claymores and Fire would face off. Brady was distraught and Wuerffel could see the agony in his face. Wuerffel approached Brady and then for five minutes the two opponents knelt down and prayed together. Years from now neither of these players will remember much about the game they were about to play, but they will surely remember this shared moment. "I respect Danny a lot," said Brady. "He's just a real decent person."

Brady had spent the past six years trying to land on an NFL roster.

He had been cut nine times by seven different NFL teams, and had never lasted more than a few weeks on any one. "It's a humbling experience," said Brady. "But going this route makes you appreciate the game a lot more."

Brady was a *Parade Magazine* All-American at Putnam West High in Oklahoma City. He went on to play for his beloved Oklahoma Sooners. In his senior year, he led the team in receptions (35) and receiving yards (536) and was named All-Big Eight. Originally drafted by the Los Angeles Rams in the sixth round of the 1994 draft, Brady was cut after training camp. He was re-signed to the practice squad and eventually promoted to the fifty-three-man roster. When he made his NFL debut on December 24, 1994, Brady became a historical footnote. He was the last Los Angeles Ram, as the franchise moved the next season to St. Louis.

"I really didn't even think about it," said Brady, who became the 761st player to wear the Rams' colors in the forty-nine seasons they were in Southern California. "But that would be the one trivia question I would be able to get right."

Brady was cut by the Rams the following preseason. For the next few summers, he was invited to different camps only to be released or signed to the practice squad. In April 1996, Brady got married to Joanne and the two went on a honeymoon cruise in the Caribbean. After their ship returned to the States and they got off the boat, the Bradys witnessed an ominous sight. The ship, much like Brady's professional career, started to sink. "The day we got back to Oklahoma, Rickey talked to his agent and found out that the Eagles had cut him," Joanne said. "That was rough."

Brady finally grew tired of life on the NFL edge. In August 1996, he signed with the Jets, but after a few workouts, he told coach Rich Kotite that he'd lost his desire to play. All the disappointment had taken a toll on Brady. It was time to walk away.

You couldn't blame him. Brady had been cut so many times he

knew the whole routine—the phone call, the coach's voice-cracking explanation, the pat on the back—by heart. Revered Brian Wiesinger, one of Brady's close friends in Oklahoma City, even prayed for Brady regularly, but it never helped. "At my wedding, I gave all my grooms-men NFL footballs and he put his in his windowsill," said Brady. "He told me once, 'You wouldn't believe how many times I see that foot-ball every day, and I pray for you every time I see it.'"

After leaving the Jets, Brady went back to Oklahoma where he was a volunteer assistant coach at Yukon High. While working with the kids, Brady realized he still wanted to play. When Brady was a rookie with the Rams, he saw mediocre tight ends earn roster spots by long-snapping. He decided that that was his ticket to the NFL. "I needed to put on some weight, put everything I had into it," said Brady, who started his pro career at 246 pounds. "I was going to become a block-ing tight end and teach myself to deep-snap, because I thought the key to my door opening was snapping. I wanted to use snapping to get back into the tight end position."

Brady got his weight up to 270 pounds. He went to Scotland in 1997 and honed his long-snapping skills. After returning from Scot-land, Brady was signed by Tampa Bay after the regular season for a playoff game against Green Bay. That one game, which the Bucca-neers lost and which Brady didn't play in, was the highlight of Brady's professional career. He came back to Scotland for the 2000 season only because he wanted to win a championship and end his career, which had been so difficult, on a high note.

"I really think my playing days are done after this season," said Brady one day on the bus going to practice, his world-weary eyes looking outside at the misty morning in Glasgow. "I've been in this business for a long time and it really takes a lot out of you, constantly traveling and never being with your family. I just want to win a title and then go home to Oklahoma and spend time with my wife and get a regular job. That will be nice."

THE PROVING GROUND

WITH A LITTLE less than three minutes left in the first quarter, the Claymores struck first. Donald Sellers beat his defender to the right corner of the endzone and Daft laid the ball in his hands perfectly from five yards out to give Scotland a 7–0 lead. At the start of the second quarter, Rhein answered when Weurffel hit Kevin Drake for a 13-yard touchdown pass. After the extra point by Manfred Burgsmuller, the game was tied at seven.

With his scraggly blond locks and wrinkle-free face, Burgsmuller cut the image of a twentysomething. But the man was old enough to be the father of many of his teammates. At fifty Burgsmuller was the oldest player to ever play in a professional football game, surpassing Oakland Hall-of-Famer George Blanda, who ended his career at a sprightly forty-eight years three months, and eighteen days. Burgsmuller couldn't hit a field goal much longer than 40 yards, but he was virtually a sure-thing from 35 and in. "I've always thought it's better to be accurate than long," said Burgsmuller. "My coaches feel the same way."

The Fire signed Burgsmuller in 1995 as a marketing gimmick. Back then, Reebok was the main sponsor of the World League and Burgsmuller worked for the company as a representative. The Fire's attendance was flagging at the time, so team executives decided to sign a famous soccer player to try to put folks in the seats. Their first choice was Burgsmuller, who had played for the soccer team German Bundesliga for the past twenty-four years. He had also played for the German national team three times. "Before I joined the Rhein Fire, I knew that the ball was not a round ball but an oval-shaped ball and that these guys were big and tough," said Burgsmuller, who is 5'10" and 152 pounds. "It took some time to get used to kicking a football, but I think I've gotten pretty good at it."

Burgsmuller isn't the only prop that the Rhein Fire used to lure people into the stands. In 1998, a woman named Dolly Buster—a well-endowed German porn star—wiggled and jiggled her way onto the field to toss the coin before a game. Days earlier the Fire had announced that Buster would be on hand for the pregame festivities to entice both fans and reporters to check out what American football was like. It worked. As Buster threw up the coin, a near-capacity crowd belted out a roar so loud that it seemed to rattle the entire city of Düsseldorf. This proved two things: one, gimmicks work as a device to goose Germans to watch American football; and two, there's no better gimmick than having a busty blonde bouncing on the 50-yard-line.

AFTER EXCHANGING PUNTS, Marcus Crandell directed a three-play, 37-yard drive that culminated with a 2-yard scoring pass to backup running back Ben Snell. With 7:35 remaining in the half, the Claymores were back in front 14–7.

When the Fire got the ball back, the offense imploded. On first down, Scotland defensive end Jabbar Threats blindsided Weurffel for a sack, momentarily knocking him out of the game. On second down, backup quarterback Matt Lytle was sacked by end Rasheed Simmons. On third down, it was tackle Michael Mason who nailed Lytle for the loss, forcing Rhein to punt. This was the kind of play from the defensive line that Tomsula had had in mind when he told his players two months ago that they had the chance to be the best in league history. "That's what you can do every series," Tomsula yelled as his players jogged off the field. "Every fucking series."

The half ended 14–7. Though the Fire trailed, panic was not one of the prevailing emotions in the Rhein locker room. The Fire had been a second-half team all season; they had outscored their opponents 73–34 in the fourth quarter alone. "Play our game," Coach Galen Hall calmly told his players in the locker room, "and we'll walk out of here with the win."

On the opening drive of the third quarter, Weurffel found his rhythm. Throwing a variety of screens and quick outs, Weurffel led his team downfield. Facing a 2nd and 9 from the Scotland 10-yard-line, Weurffel was forced out of the pocket by the rush, but the slow-footed quarterback scrambled to his left, broke three tackles, and dove into the endzone for his second touchdown run of the season. A high snap on the extra point left the score 14–13.

The defenses then tightened. Daft couldn't find any open receivers and Wuerffel was mercilessly harassed by the Claymores' defensive line. But Scotland made the game's next big play when defensive lineman Jabbar Threats broke through the line and blocked a Rodney Williams's punt, which was recovered by safety Chris Bayne at the Rhein 13-yard-line. Three plays later, Daft fired a 7-yard touchdown pass to Rickey Brady, who didn't even smile after catching the pass. His mind was back in that Oklahoma hospital. After the game, Brady admitted that he barely remembered making that grab, which gave the Claymores a lead of 21–13 with 4:40 to play in the third.

After two turnovers, the Fire had the ball on their own 17-yard-line. On third and thirteen, safety Marcus Ray knocked the ball out of the hands of receiver Kendrick Nord after Nord caught a pass from Weurffel. Scotland recovered the fumble at the Rhein 8-yard-line, which set up a 23-yard field goal from Hart. Just twenty-two seconds into the fourth quarter, the Claymores were up 24–13.

Weurffel then got hot. First he hit Kevin Drake for a 17-yard touchdown pass, then he linked up with Nord on the two-point conversion pass, cutting Scotland's lead to 3, 24–21, with 10:12 remaining in the fourth quarter. Rhein caught a break four minutes later when Damon Gibson fumbled a punt return. The Fire recovered on the Claymores' 33. Six plays later, kicker Peter Ele-zovic, who kicked long field goals for the Fire, connected on a 38-yard attempt. The score was knotted at 24 with 4:54 remaining.

Instead of going with Crandell at the end of the game, which had been customary in the quarterback rotation, Criner and Alcalde played a gut feeling and instead inserted Daft. Their feeling was that if Crandell threw an interception—which he was prone to do—their season could be over. At first, their decision seemed right. Daft calmly led Scotland up the field to the Rhein 27-yard-line. But then Stecker got stuffed and Daft tossed two incompletions. The drive stalled. Hart attempted a field goal from 43 yards, which was about as far as he could kick the ball under perfect conditions. The kick sailed wide left. There was 1:38 remaining in the game.

"Make this the series of your lives," Tomsula screamed at his defensive line before they retook the field. "This is the season right here, right now, so make it count."

They did. In three plays, Wuerffel threw a 4-yard completion and then was sacked twice, first by Noel Scarlett and then by Rasheed Simmons—Scotland's ninth sack of the afternoon. When Weurffel fell to the ground after the second sack at the 31-yard-line, 1:07 remained in the game. The entire Claymore defense looked toward the sideline to see if Criner wanted to call a timeout. But Criner was nowhere to be found. He was back by the bench consulting with the offensive line. Hesse yelled to defensive coordinator Myrel Moore that they should call a timeout, but Moore didn't respond—that, ultimately, was the head coach's decision. After twelve seconds ticked off the clock, Hesse took matters in his own hands and signaled for the timeout. Fifty-five seconds remained. When Hesse reached the sidelines, Criner asked him what the hell he was thinking.

"I want to win this game, coach," Hesse said.

"I didn't want that timeout," said Criner, who apparently was content with letting the game go into overtime. "I wanted the clock to run."

"Screw that," yelled Finkes. "We're going to do whatever we can to win this game, and that means we had to call the timeout."

Criner walked away, disgusted. Hesse and Finkes were flabbergasted. They simply could not see the advantage of letting time drip off the clock. The Fire could have milked the clock so that less than thirty seconds remained, which would have made a scoring drive nearly impossible. That moment, Criner's ability to manage the clock was questioned by more than a few of his players. With a trip to the championship on the line, Hesse and Finkes didn't think that their coach was up to the task.

After the timeout, Rodney Williams of the Fire boomed a 52-yard punt to Selucio Sanford, who fielded the ball at his 17-yard-line. Sanford drifted left, then cut upfield sharply. He broke one tackle, then two. Then another. He stormed into the open field. He was at the Claymores' 30-yard-line. Then the 40. By the time he reached the Claymores' 45, he was in the clear. He had a wall of blockers in front of him that sealed a route to the endzone. Thirty yards to paydirt. Then 20. The path was still clear. But at the 5-yard-line, Rhein safety Chris Aikens pushed him from behind and Sanford fell to the ground at the two. Thirty-four seconds remained.

On first and goal, Daft handed the ball to Stecker on a sweep to the left, which was stuffed. Stecker lost two yards. Scotland quickly called another timeout. "Tell everyone in the huddle that it's all north and south now," Criner told Daft. "Tell them to come off the ball."

In their huddle, the Claymores' offensive line talked about finishing the game. They didn't want to rely on Hart. "Let's do this," Cavil told his offensive-line mates. "Everyone just get on your man and block. Move him backward one yard—one yard!—and we'll win this thing and get to the World Bowl."

The play was called "Six Crunch." It was a new play that the Alcalde had installed this week. Its virtue was its simplicity: Daft handed the ball to Stecker, and he ran toward Rickey Brady, who lined up on the strong side. Everyone on the line executed simple drive blocks, which meant pushing the defender backward. Stecker was supposed to read where the hole was—whether it was to the inside of Brady or the outside—and put his head down and gain the tough, last yards.

Daft then came to the line and surveyed the field. He called the signals, then handed the ball to Stecker. He saw penetration outside Brady, so he ran to the inside. A Fire linebacker had blitzed in that hole, but he grabbed nothing but air as Stecker cut and spun to the inside. He then put his head down and pushed the pigskin about three inches into the endzone. After Hart's extra point, the Claymores took the lead 31–24. Fifteen seconds remained.

Starting at their 20-yard-line, the Fire had time for two offensive plays. On first down, Weurffel hit Olo Alalare for 14 yards. Seven seconds remained. Weurffel then threw the ball as far as his weak arm could—all of 48 yards—down the middle of the field. Marcus Ray intercepted the pass. The game was over, but Ray didn't go down. A week earlier the Scotland defense had put money into a hat that would go to the first defensive player who scored a touchdown. Now Ray had the ball in his arms and, though the team didn't need the score, he needed the money. For a moment, it looked as if Ray had a chance to earn some coin. But then, the entire defense suddenly quit blocking for Ray, realizing that he could win the kitty. A few Claymores actually fell on the ground and let the Fire take Ray down. "Marcus was trying to take my money," said Finkes. "No way was I going to allow that guy to score. I would have tackled him myself."

As the Claymore fans celebrated the victory, Criner grabbed a microphone that was hooked up to the stadium's PA system. His voice echoed in every nook and cranny of the stadium. "We got one more game to go, but I want to say something to the people in the stands," said Criner. "You were wonderful today and thank you very, very much. This win was for you." The crowd then erupted, making as much noise as 10,150 fans possibly could. Criner had cast a spell on the faithful. They believed. Up in the press box, all the Scottish writers were already busy typing their rhapsodies. They also believed.

IN THE CLAYMORES locker room, there was nothing but joy. "The way it sits right now," Criner told his players, "we're in the World Bowl unless Barcelona beats us by 129 points next week. Hey, Selucio, get in here."

The team then huddled around Sanford, who'd saved the Claymores' season with his long punt return. Players showered him with cold Coors Light and hugged him tightly. This is as good as it gets for a football player. "Let's hear it for Selucio!" yelled Criner.

The room erupted, and the party was on. At the postgame celebration, the team's favorite local musician, Karl Byrne, had written a song for the Claymores. Sung to the tune of Billy Joel's "Piano Man," the chorus went like this:

> *Throw me the ball, you're the quarterback,*
> *Throw me the ball if you're Daft,*
> *Throw me the ball, you're the quarterback,*
> *'Cause the Claymores are kings of their craft . . .*

As Byrne belted out the Claymore chorus, Tate tripped the light fantastic on an elevated stage. He floated as he moved and grooved on the dance floor, and at least for one day, not a single player on the Claymore roster wished he was anywhere else in the world. Tonight, this was no longer NFL Europe. Tonight, this was simply a team going to the championship. This was why they played the game.

28 The Last Night

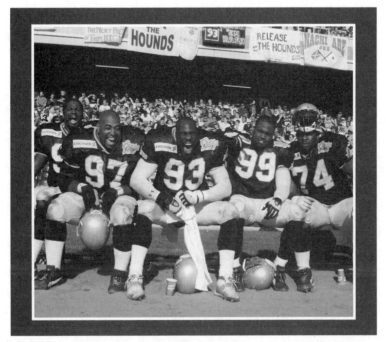

The Claymores' devastating defensive line: (*left to right*) Jabbar Threats, Noel
Scarlett, Rasheed Simmons, Chris Ward, and Antonio Dingle.

Barcelona, Spain. Five Days Before Game Ten

IT IS FOOTBALL'S Eden, a place where the sun always shines,
the food is succulent, and the beautiful people are scantily clad. The
Barcelona Dragons live the good life in the resort beach town of Sitges, which is a half-hour drive south of Barcelona. "I know some guys
on other teams get real homesick during the season," said Brad
Trout, a safety for the Dragons. "But not us. Most of us could stay
here for a very long time."

The Dragons stayed in The Subur, a four-star hotel perched on a nude beach. Following the Spanish tradition of siesta, the Dragons usually finished practice and tape-review by 1 PM—or about three hours earlier than every other team in the league. On any nongame-day afternoon, about half the players took a stroll on the beach, sizzled in the sun, or lolled in the Mediterranean in paddleboats. The other half usually passed the time on a seaside golf course.

As sweet as the day life was in Sitges, the nightlife was even tastier. "The clubs here are amazing," said Trout, who was allocated by the Broncos. "They'll go to four or five in the morning almost every night. The only problem is that some of the clubs are so close to the hotel that guys have to wear headphones when they sleep because it's so loud. But no one's complaining. I mean, where else could you live on a nude beach, play golf all the time, work just a few hours a day, have your own maid, and get paid to do it? It's awesome."

"Everybody wants to go to Barcelona," said Scotland's Jon Hesse. "That's why, year in and year out, they usually have the most talent in the league and why they can get away without practicing as much as the other teams. Guys out there are like, 'Hey, I've been lying on the beach all week and come the weekend I'm ready to knock some guys around.' Whereas we've had about twenty hours of practice during the week, and most of it has been in pads. There are times when I don't want to hit anybody when it comes time to play a game."

One player in the past who benefited from the easy life of Barcelona was Lawrence Phillips, the former Nebraska star who played for the Dragons in the spring of 1999. Coach Jack Bicknell had selected Phillips in the tenth round of the free-agent draft that year and was pleasantly surprised when Phillips showed up at training camp in the best shape of his life. He had shed 30 pounds and tipped the scales at a lean 205. In training camp, Phillips worked hard and kept his mouth shut. He was a model player. "I owe coach Bicknell a great debt," said Phillips. "I was very happy to find out that they drafted me and were going to give me a chance to play. Coach called me and said just come over and play. There was no big speech or anything. He just said, 'You know what you have to do, come over and play,' and that's what I did."

Phillips had been out of football for eighteen months. Ever since his college days at Nebraska, Phillips had been a troubled player. In his junior season, he'd developed a problem with alcohol and a proclivity for settling disputes with his fists—even if his adversary was a female. He was suspended from the team after allegedly dragging his girlfriend down a flight of stairs. Coach Tom Osborne allowed Phillips to return for Nebraska's final game of the 1995 season in the Fiesta Bowl, and Phillips responded. He rushed for 125 yards and helped the Cornhuskers win their second consecutive national title as they crushed Florida 62–14. After the game, Phillips declared himself eligible for the NFL draft.

He was selected by the Rams with the sixth overall pick of the 1996 draft, but in a span of nineteen months he was arrested three times and spent twenty-three days in jail. When Phillips showed up at practice with a hangover one day in 1998, Coach Dick Vermeil lost it. He let Phillips go on the spot, convinced that no matter how hard he tried or how patient he was, he couldn't save Phillips's football soul. The Dolphins then signed Phillips. But after being accused of hitting a woman in a West Palm Beach nightclub, the team severed its ties with the taciturn tailback. Europe was Phillips's final chance to resurrect his dying football career.

At training camp in Orlando, Phillips mostly stayed to himself. He impressed both NFL scouts and his coaches with his explosive quickness and swift cutting ability. He became the talk of the league, prompting ESPN to ask Phillips for a sit-down interview. The first question the reporter asked Phillips was, "Did something happen, did something go wrong, in your upbringing that predisposed you to committing violence against women?" Phillips responded with a small laugh, as he pulled off his microphone and walked out of the room. It was the last interview with an American reporter that Phillips would give during the season.

"The first thing that Lawrence has to do in NFL Europe is to maintain a low profile," said Vermeil a few days before Phillips left for Spain. "That's what LP stands for. Lawrence Phillips is low profile. I've tried to convince him of that for a long time."

When Phillips got to Barcelona, he did just that. He rarely went out. Occasionally he'd play dominoes with his teammates in the lobby of the hotel, but usually he stayed in his room or lay on the beach and listened to music. He also liked to wade in the Mediterranean, the warm salt water was soothing to his beat-up legs. For the first time in his life, Phillips was in an environment that was perfectly suited to him. He practiced, he went to meetings, he ate his meals, and he went to bed early—it was a simple life. And Phillips thrived.

"Lawrence loved to practice," said Bicknell. "Ever time we ran a play, he'd break through for 40 or 50 yards. I'm sure he did that all of his life because I've talked to people at Nebraska and they said he was one of the hardest-working guys they ever had."

With no distractions, Phillips authored a spectacular season. He became the first player in the history of the league to rush for more than 1,000 yards in a season, he was named NFL Europe's MVP, and he led the Dragons to the championship game, which they lost to Frankfurt 38–24. "Without Phillips, that team would not have won two games," said Amsterdam coach Al Luginbill. "If he can learn to run with the right people and stay away from alcohol, he can be all right. But when he abuses booze, he becomes a different personality."

If Phillips's life in the States could have been as basic as it was in Barcelona, he might have had a ten-year NFL career. But after he returned from Europe, the running back's old problems started to surface. He was cut by the 49ers after he reportedly refused to practice. In the end, his frailties overwhelmed his talents. "Lawrence could have been one of the greats," said Scotland linebacker Jon Hesse, who played with Phillips at Nebraska. "But now he's just one of those guys who is a could-have-been. It's really kind of sad."

Glasgow, Scotland. Five Days Before Game Ten

At the end of the season, life in Barcelona was nothing like life in Glasgow. During Scotland's final week of practice, the temperature hovered in the thirties and the rain came down hard each day and night; the sun and the stars hadn't been visible for days. All of this affected the players dispositions. "Even though we're winning games and are going to play in the World Bowl, it's tough to stay upbeat with this weather," said Matt Finkes. "It's awful."

Despite the rain and wind, three obsessed fans came to every Claymores' practice the final week. In fact, this troop of Claymore followers had only missed a handful of practices in the last three seasons. A woman in her sixties and her two sons brought their foldout chairs and sat and watched every afternoon, utterly fascinated by the violent ballet that is football.

Every Claymore player knew the Caufields. Though they usually didn't travel to the away games, the Caufields—the mother is retired, one son is a teacher in his thirties, the other son is a student in his twenties—would greet the Claymores at the Glasgow Airport and they attended all of the home games. They are kind and generous people, always willing to lend a hand. Two years ago, they were helping to carry some equipment bags from the locker room to the practice field when a few players asked them if they'd go across the street and buy them something to drink. Happy to feel needed, they dutifully fulfilled the request and returned ten minutes later with three bags full of drinks. But by the time that Graham Reith, a practice squad wide receiver, got over to the Caufields, all the drinks were gone. Jokingly, Reith asked, "Where's my strawberry milk?" It was a nice sunny day, and Reith thought some strawberry milk would be refreshing. One of the sons then ran back across the street and, five minutes later, returned with some strawberry milk for Reith.

For the next two seasons, at every practice, no matter what the weather, the Caufields brought Reith a carton of strawberry milk. "Now I fucking hate strawberry milk," said Reith, a national player. "I can't stand it."

After every practice for the past two years, Reith and Scott Couper, another national wideout, put down a wager. Standing 20 yards apart, they'd set their helmets in front of them and then take turns trying to hit each other's helmet with a football. The first one to hit the helmet five times won £5. In 1999, Couper was the big winner; at the end of the last practice Reith owed Couper £20. But Couper said he'd wipe the slate clean if he went and kissed "Mums," as Mrs. Caufield was known, square on the lips.

Reith accepted. As Mums shook hands with the players and bade them goodbye and good luck with their NFL careers, Reith slowly walked up to her. Mums extended her hand to shake Reith's, but Reith instead grabbed her by the shoulders. Mums turned her cheek but, not to be deterred, Reith nailed one right on her kisser. About twenty players, all of whom were watching, fell to the ground in laughter. "Easily, that was the best £20 I ever spent,'" said Couper with a laugh.

EVEN THOUGH THE Barcelona game would have no effect on the standings, Criner had his players practice in pads twice during the week. He was trying to convince his team that the game mattered. "We had three goals back in training camp," said Criner at his last press conference of the season in Glasgow. "The first was to win as many games as we can. The second, to make each player as good as we can and give all of them an opportunity to further their career. And the third was to get to and win the World Bowl. Once we get past the next hurdle we can concentrate on that one."

"I don't give a fuck about goals," said Finkes. "We're a beatup team right now. That's why other teams in this league don't practice in pads—just Amsterdam and us. Last year, when I went to training camp in the NFL, my body was really hurting. It will be the same this season. I don't see that furthering my career."

The team's last night in Scotland was Thursday, June 15. Criner knew that many of his players were planning a late night out, so he instituted a 10 PM curfew. So far this season, Finkes had missed almost as many curfews as he'd made. The coaching staff was aware of this, but failed to punish him for one simple reason: They trusted Finkes to be in top form on game day. But that same trust did not extend to the other players. During the season if anyone else on the team missed curfew, they were usually fined. "I think they just know that fining me won't stop me from going out," said Finkes with a laugh. "So they don't bother. But there definitely is a double standard."

On their last night out in Glasgow, Willy Tate agreed to meet Finkes at a bar called Ginty McGinty's at 9:30. The two had talked of this night for the entire season—how they were going to make this an evening to remember, how they were going to raise this night into the realm of myth. Unfortunately, Tate had bumped into Criner at an Italian restaurant in the city's West End just before he was to meet Finkes. "Is everybody on the team ready to play?" Criner asked Tate.

"I think so, Coach," Tate replied. "But I don't know if too many guys are going to make curfew tonight, since it's our last night here and all."

"Well, they'd better," assumed Criner. "Because if they don't, I'll chew some ass and fine them $500 each. Spread the word."

At this point Tate had little choice but to make curfew and stand up Finkes. "Willy dropped far in my estimation," said Finkes later. "He just got scared." Finkes and a host of other players did go out and did violate curfew, but Finkes once again wasn't fined.

Barcelona, Spain. Game Ten

It was Tate who was the main character in the play that changed the Barcelona game. On the first snap of the contest, which was played on a warm spring night at Olympic Stadium, Daft lobbed a perfect pass into the arms of Damon Gibson, who was running free down the left sideline. No Dragon was within 25 yards of Gibson and Daft hit his wideout in stride. Nineteen seconds into the game, the Claymores led 7–0.

After a Barcelona punt, the Claymores' offense moved the ball effortlessly down the field. But on a second-down play from the Claymores' 46-yard-line, Daft faked a handoff to Stecker and took a seven-step drop into the pocket. From his tight end position, Tate stayed in to block. Dragon linebacker Marc Megna, blitzing from the outside, came hard around the corner. Tate saw him and tried to cut-block him, diving at his knees. But Megna jumped over Tate and blindsided Daft, forcing, then recovering a fumble. As Tate jogged back to the sidelines, Criner yelled, "We never cut-block. Never." This wasn't exactly true. All season long, if a blitz was coming off the corner, Tate would cut-block. It had been effective all season, but now that it hadn't worked, he was getting an earful.

"I had a one-two read, where I look inside and then outside," said Tate later. "But their linebacker was hot off the corner and I didn't have time to get to him. It was a huge play for them. If we had gone up 14–0, the game would have been over. Those guys had nothing to play for. They would have packed it in and given up. But I guess I let them back in the game."

The Dragons marched down the field and scored on a 22-yard run by Jesse Haynes, who'd played for the Claymores in 1999. That week he'd made negative remarks about Scotland and Criner that had been posted on the NFL Europe website. Criner saw this and, instead of blaming Haynes, blamed the league. He felt that this league-sponsored trash-talking proved beyond doubt that the suits at NFL Europe didn't give a lick about the Claymores and their minuscule fan base. "Total lack of respect," said Criner. "And I'm pretty sick of it. Jesse says that I stabbed him in the back by not getting him back on my team, but you know what? I would have stabbed myself in the back if I had gotten him. Because if I'd taken Haynes, then I wouldn't have gotten Aaron Stecker and Ben Snell, and they're both terrific."

In the second quarter, Barcelona embarked on an 81-yard drive that was capped by a 4-yard touchdown pass from Tony Graziani to Jermaine Copeland. The previous week against Frankfurt, Copeland had caught 22 passes, breaking Tom Fears's professional record set in 1950 of 18 passes in a single game.

Down 14–7, the Claymores seemed to give up. They played with little passion and lost 28–25. But it wasn't as close as the score indicated; Scotland got a late touchdown on a 2-yard Marcus Crandell run. "We just weren't ready to play that game," said Tate. "Even though the coaches tried, they just couldn't get us up for it. We knew that we were in the World Bowl and we knew that, in the end, this game didn't matter. It showed in the way that we played."

"Learn from our mistakes and become better football players,"

Criner told his players after the game. Though upset by his team's poor play, Criner spoke cautiously. He knew, deep down, that this loss meant nothing. "We didn't play very well, but we still have the biggest game of the season in front of us," said Criner. "Let's prepare this week like we're going to play the best game of our lives next Sunday."

The game was inconsequential to all but Rob Hart. Heading into the contest, he held a 4-point lead over Barcelona kicker Jesus Angoy in the overall points lead for the league's $1,000 bonus. As Hart warmed up before the game, a teammate asked Hart if he wanted him to take out Angoy with a bone-crushing hit. "I'll guarantee you your bonus," he said to Hart. "I'll do it."

The player may have been kidding. Nonetheless, Hart told him not to resort to such tactics. Hart was confident. And even though he had a field goal blocked in the second quarter, he rebounded to hit a 37-yard field goal in the third to seal his points victory. He finished with 55 points, while Angoy had 50. "In the beginning, I figured a guy named Jesus might beat me," said Hart. "But in the end, not even Jesus could get the job done."

Hart let out a good chuckle at this line—a laugh that he will no doubt take all the way to the bank.

29 Sore Foot

Coach Al Luginbill.
Photo courtesy of the Amsterdam Admirals

Düsseldorf, Germany. Game Ten Between the Admirals and the Fire

ABOUT 1,000 MILES away from Barcelona in Düsseldorf, Admirals' head coach Al Luginbill was on the threshold of losing his mind. It had been a long, difficult season for Luginbill, who'd been the head coach at San Diego State from 1989 to '93. His team was 4–5 heading into their season finale against the Rhein Fire and the fans of Amsterdam had already revolted against him. They wanted a winner in Amsterdam, and wanted one now. Two weeks earlier in Amsterdam's final home game of the season against the Claymores, fans brought signs to the stadium that read AL LOSERBILL and AL MUST GO. Unlike fickle American fans, it is rare for fans in NFL Europe to turn on their coach. But they'd turned on Luginbill.

Luginbill had had some memorable moments in his six seasons as the Admirals' head coach. In the 1995 World Bowl between Amsterdam and Frankfurt, fans gave Luginbill a thunderous ovation as he ran out of the stadium tunnel in Amsterdam and was introduced to the home crowd. It had been raining all afternoon and as Luginbill jogged out onto the grassy field, he slipped. He fell to the ground hard, and he didn't bounce right back up. He had dislocated his left shoulder, but that didn't stop him from coaching the game. He told the trainer to put his arm in a sling and Luginbill tried to block out the pain. In spite of his best effort, his team lost the championship, 26–22.

Having coached Marshall Faulk in college and Kurt Warner in Europe, Luginbill's fingerprints were all over the St. Louis Rams team that won Super Bowl XXXIV. (Six alumni of NFL Europe were on the Rams' roster in that Super Bowl season.) But Luginbill has never been able to get his own team to win the big game, and the 1999 season was his first losing campaign in Europe, as his team finished 4–6. It appeared that the Admirals were headed for that same record this season when Amsterdam's Ron Powlus hit tight end Jerry Ross for 5-yard touchdown pass with six seconds remaining in the Admirals' game at the Fire. After the touchdown and extra point, Amsterdam trailed 31–28, setting the stage for the most bizarre moment of the entire 2000 NFL Europe regular season.

Amsterdam attempted an onside kick. Kicker Silvio Dilberto punched the ball to his right. It hit the ground, then popped up high into the air. Just as a Rhein player was about to catch it, an Admiral player hit him. It was clearly interference, and the officials made the proper call. So even though Amsterdam recovered the kick, the play had to be run again because of the illegal contact called on the Admirals.

When he saw the official signal the call, Luginbill slammed down his headset and ran out onto the field. His arms were flying up and down and the expletives that shot out of his mouth were worthy of a sailor in a saloon. Powlus restrained Luginbill, putting him in a bear hug and dragging him back to the sidelines.

For a moment, it looked as if Luginbill had calmed down. The back judge then ran about 40 yards upfield to take his position for the rekick. Suddenly, Luginbill ran up the field after the back judge, sprinting out onto the playing field. Once again, his arms were flailing as he yelled profanities. It looked like he might Woody-Hayes the official.

But before he could throw a punch, his players dragged him off the field. Order was restored and then the Admirals tried another onside kick. It failed and Amsterdam lost. After the game, the referees ran off the field quickly. They didn't want to face Luginbill, who was again jogging after them. When the refs safely made it to their tiny locker room, they locked the door. But Luginbill didn't give up the fight. First he banged on the door with his fists, then he kicked at the door with his foot. He had the eyes of a madman and his hair stuck out like he'd been electrocuted. "You do this to me every time," Luginbill yelled at the refs. "Every time!"

Some ten minutes later, he had cooled down. Reality had set in. Luginbill had a losing record and, as he sat alone on a table in the trainer's room, a big pack of ice on his very sore foot.

30 The Nuclear Bomb

Cornerback Kory Blackwell.

Frankfurt, Germany. Three Days Before the World Bowl

AS WARM SUNSHINE fell on Waldstadion, Matt Finkes and a group of coaches sat on a bench on the west sideline. They watched as the klieg lights shined on the Rhein Fire's quarterback Danny

THE PROVING GROUND

Weurffel. Five cameras and ten reporters circled Weurffel during the World Bowl media day. Weurffel was the one player on either team with the name and the game that was known by football fans across the globe. So the reporters came to him, like moths around a bright light, wanting to know if he was going to be the next Kurt Warner. But Wuerffel's star power also made him a moving target—and it was Finkes who fired the first shot.

"When will somebody tell Danny that he doesn't have to comb his hair like Lenny from "Laverne and Shirley" anymore?" said Finkes to Myrel Moore. "He should be ashamed to leave his home."

Just then, Weurffel turned and looked directly at Finkes. For a moment, their eyes locked, as Wuerffel proffered an expression of disgust. Moore told his linebacker, "Thanks, Matt. Just what we wanted to do. Piss off the best quarterback in the league."

"I can't be sorry about that, Coach" replied Finkes. "My woman wouldn't let me out of the house looking like that. Danny is married. His wife should inspect him before he leaves each morning. He gives Americans in Europe a bad name."

While Finkes took home the day's award for the best trash talking, Aaron Stecker and Duane Hawthorne won more coveted prizes. In a minor upset, the coaches voted Stecker as NFL Europe's offensive MVP. Even though Stecker rushed for a league-high 774 yards and finished second in the league with 11 touchdowns, most of the Clay-mores expected Weurffel to walk away with the MVP trophy. He had thrown a league-record 25 touchdown passes with seven intercep-tions. He had guided the Fire to the best record in the league (7–3) and was the undisputed leader of his team. "I was a little surprised," said Stecker. "But that doesn't mean I don't deserve it. I do."

Hawthorne was named codefensive MVP of the league, sharing honors with Berlin Thunder defensive end Jonathan Brown, who fin-ished the season with a league-high 10 sacks. If not for Brown's

4-sack performance against the Claymores in Week Three, when Brown obliterated backup tackle Jason Tenner, then Hawthorne likely would have won the award outright. Hawthorne was tied for the league lead with four interceptions. But more important than that was the feeling among most NFL Europe coaches that Hawthorne was one of the finest cornerbacks to ever play in the league. "It's nice to get recognized," said Hawthorne, "but hopefully, this is just the beginning for me."

BEFORE THE CLAYMORES took the practice field an hour after media day, Siran Stacy brandished his 1996 World Bowl championship ring to his teammates. He wanted the young players on the team to realize that this game meant something. "I wanted everyone to know that they could get themselves one of these if they play well on Sunday," said Stacy. "I think it worked. Everybody was like, 'My God, that thing is huge.' "

Though most of the players were still jet-lagged from their Glasgow-to-Barcelona-to-Frankfurt trip, they had an exceptional workout. The reason was obvious: Twelve scouts from various NFL teams watched the practice closely. The scouts came to Frankfurt to assess the talent of the two World Bowl teams, hoping to discover a gem or two. "Having those scouts watch the guys really turned up the intensity," said Moore. "They are now really playing for something. Namely, a championship and their future."

It wasn't just scouts who came to Frankfurt. NFL commissioner Paul Tagliabue and five NFL owners made the trip overseas as well, along with executives from almost every NFL team. They traveled to the game to show their support for the league.

The World Bowl didn't always get this much attention. At the inaugural World Bowl in 1991, only a handful of NFL owners and execu-

THE PROVING GROUND

tives were at Wembly Stadium in London to watch the London Monarchs take on the Barcelona Dragons. The feeling then among the NFL brass was that the league could fold at any moment. But those execs that did show up were treated to something special.

The game itself was ordinary. Quarterback Stan Gelbaugh led the Monarchs to a 21–0 victory. When London won, the players went up into the stands and celebrated with their fans—something that has never happened in the NFL. The Monarchs ran around Wembly carrying the trophy over their heads, dancing to blaring music, and waving the Union Jack around as if it were their very own (only four players on the team were non-Americans). There were 61,108 fans in attendance—which was 838 short of the attendance at the first Super Bowl in Los Angeles in 1967—and they lingered long after the game was over. Twenty-five minutes after the final gun, only 1,000 fans had left the stadium.

The victory was especially gratifying for the Monarchs because of the tough living conditions they'd endured for the season. In 1991, the Monarchs lived in hundred-year-old, vacant university dorms, which were a £30 ($45) cab ride from London. The dorms had showerheads at shoulder level, no telephones in the rooms, one television in each lounge, next to no heat, even less hot water, and, as a sole source of entertainment, a fraying dartboard. To kill time, the Monarchs had a dart tournament almost every night. They played all kinds of darts: backward darts, blindfolded darts, and lucky darts, in which outside linebacker Danny Lockett would suddenly bury the darts as hard as he could into a wall and everybody in the room would duck to avoid getting punctured.

But the tight living conditions fostered a strong sense of team unity on the Monarchs during that first season. As they ran laps around Wembly after taking the championship, every smile was genuine, every hug heartfelt. It was sports at its finest.

THE NUCLEAR BOMB finally detonated. At practice three days before the World Bowl, Matt Finkes felt as if some of the black players on the team had turned against him. "The looks that came my way today were incredible," said Finkes. "It was as if I was the devil incarnate."

The problem stemmed from an incident that occurred in Barcelona on the night after the Claymores lost to the Dragons. That evening, thirty-five Claymore players went out in Barcelona to a place called the Baja Beach Club, which was situated smack on the Mediterranean. Criner had arranged for a bus to shuttle the players from the team hotel to the club and then back to the hotel. Criner instituted a 10 PM curfew and sternly instructed his players not to break it. He wanted everyone on that bus when it left the club at about 9:30.

Once the team got to the beach-side club, the drinks came fast and furious. The bartenders were doling out Long Island iced teas, on the house. By 9:15, most of the team had decided that they wanted to stay late and blow off curfew. Finkes then gathered the team together in an upstairs room and said they should take a vote. "If there are a lot of guys who want to stay, then we should just stay and tell the bus driver to wait," said Finkes. "But if there are guys who want to go, then we'll all just go." The players voted overwhelmingly to stay. What was Criner going to do, suspend the entire team?

Not everyone, though, was pleased with this decision. Cornerback Kory Blackwell started telling a few of the players, "Finkes doesn't care about you. He's got his own agenda, and he's not a team player."

Minutes later, word got back to Finkes that Blackwell was talking behind his back. Finkes then hunted Blackwell down, prepared to do whatever it took to shut him up. Blackwell saw him coming, then ducked outside. Finkes eventually found him in front of the club.

"Kory, don't stab me in the back," said Finkes. "You got something to say, you say it to me."

The next morning, the argument continued. Finkes saw Blackwell as the team was walking toward the team bus. Blackwell, who the night before had called Finkes the "white devil," flashed Finkes a ferocious look. Now Finkes could feel the heat of his own anger. "If you want to resolve this right now, let's do it," yelled Finkes at Blackwell outside of the bus. "Otherwise you get your ass in that bus, go sit in the back, and shut your fucking mouth." The entire team was watching, and Blackwell then upped the stakes. "I'll kill you, motherfucker," he said. "I'll do it."

Finkes just laughed and stepped into the bus. But now, less than fifty-six hours before the biggest game of the season, the Claymores were a fractured team. Some of the black players clearly supported Blackwell; many of the white players were solidly behind Finkes. The issue of race relations is something that affects nearly every professional football team, but it's a topic that coaches rarely discuss. The reason? Coaches, generally speaking, consider it taboo to talk about it openly because that would give the issue even more prominence, thereby creating even more racial division. "Coaches don't want to stir up the pot when it comes to race," said Finkes. "They want to leave it alone and hope it doesn't destroy the chemistry of the team. But I'd say it has really hurt our team chemistry. I think we all play hard, but it's not like we're playing for each other. We're playing for ourselves."

At one point in the season Criner was so concerned about the issue of race that he told a reporter who was asking players questions about the racial divide that he could no longer talk to his players. Criner even told his public relations director to inform that reporter that if he came to practice he'd be arrested for trespassing. He also said through his public relations director that if he saw that reporter in the hotel speaking with his players he'd try to have him arrested—

for what, precisely, was never made clear. But it was evident that a certain amount of Nixonian paranoia, especially when it looked as if the Claymores season was caving in, had gripped the coach when it came to this issue. "I won't tolerate inappropriate questions," Criner said. "And when a reporter asks questions about race, that's crossing the line. Players shouldn't be worrying about that."

So by ignoring the issue, Criner and the Claymore coaching staff let it fester all season long. A day before the World Bowl, however, there was a sense among the players that healing was finally starting to take place. Realizing that he had been out of line, Blackwell approached Finkes in the team hotel and apologized. "That's not what I'm all about," said Blackwell to Finkes as the two stood together in the lobby. "I'm angry at myself for being angry at you."

"I accept your apology, Kory," replied Finkes. "Just don't ever do that again—to anyone." Finkes then walked away, never to speak to Kory Blackwell again. On the bus the next day, as the team drove toward Waldstadion to play in the World Bowl, white players and black players sat side-by-side for one of the few times all season. It may have seemed like a little thing, but it meant a lot. The racial problem hadn't magically disappeared, but for one game, one night, the players acted as if they were color blind.

31 The Kick

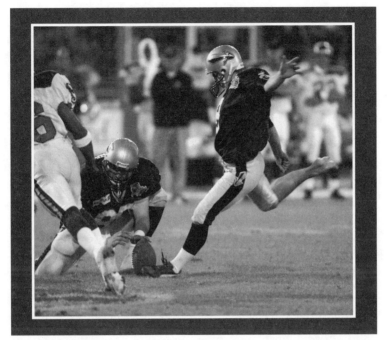

The fateful kick: Willy Tate on the hold, kicker Rob Hart about to make contact.

Frankfurt, Germany. The World Bowl

TWO HOURS BEFORE World Bowl 2000 kicked off, Duane Hawthorne was in the locker room getting dressed when Jerry Jones sidled through the door. The Cowboys' owner had come to Frankfurt to check out his players—six allocated Cowboys were playing in this game. Jones was also there to congratulate Hawthorne in person on his sterling season. "Duane is one of the best corners to ever play in this league," said Richard Kent, the Claymores' defensive-backs coach. "He's got tremendous man-to-man skills."

Hawthorne played his college ball at Northern Illinois. After getting bypassed in the NFL draft, he was signed by the Cowboys as a free agent prior to the 1999 season. He had a strong camp and was the only undrafted free agent to make the Cowboys' roster. After a few cornerbacks went down with injuries, Hawthorne became a starter—albeit a picked-on starter. "Other teams would come at me all the time," said Hawthorne. "But I think I handled it pretty well."

By the end of his first NFL season, Hawthorne had three interceptions—the most by a rookie defensive back for the Cowboys since Everson Walls in 1981. A few days after the '99 season, Hawthorne was at his apartment in Dallas when Dave Campo, the Cowboys' head coach, called Hawthorne and told him he wanted to see him immediately. When they met, Campo asked Hawthorne what he thought of NFL Europe. "I don't know the first thing about it, Coach," replied Hawthorne. "But if you think I should go over there and play, then I'll do it. I'll do whatever you want."

What Campo wanted was for Hawthorne to get more game experience and improve his route-recognition skills. So Hawthorne went to Scotland and became a poster-child for how NFL Europe can groom players and prepare them to flourish in the NFL. "We are all very proud of you, Duane," Jones told Hawthorne as he shook his hand. "You've done wonders for yourself and you've represented the Cowboys very well. Thanks for all your hard work."

Hawthorne, who is twenty-three but has the face of a teenager, then smiled brilliantly, his teeth sparkling like a row of piano keys. It was the perfect way to begin the championship evening.

ALONG WITH THE NFL heavies who spent the week pressing the flesh with the players and European fans, every NFL Europe coach and general manager attended the World Bowl. All the powerful forces of professional football were converging on Frankfurt. "With everyone watching us, we know we have a chance to make an impact," said Tate. "Everyone has been a little sharper this week in practice and in film study."

For fans who like to rub shoulders with players, the World Bowl is definitely their kind of place. At media day, a small throng of Claymore faithful walked onto the Waldstadion field and took pictures of their favorite players. They got autographs and shot the breeze with them for more then thirty minutes. "The access we have to the players is incredible," said Ian Carey, a statistician who lives in Edinburgh and is an ardent Claymore supporter. He'd attended fifty-three out of Scotland's last fifty-six games, both at home and on the road. "And the players are great, too," said Carey. "They'll go out of their way to say hello and thank me for coming out to support them. It's one of the league's best attributes."

The World Bowl will never enjoy the pomp and circumstance of the Super Bowl, but it does have one thing that Super Bowl never will—a unique sense of connectedness between fan and player.

OUTSIDE WALDSTADION, the party, as usual, began four hours before kickoff. About 1,000 fans from Scotland made the trip to Frankfurt and many of them were dressed in kilts. Criner and a few Claymore front-office personnel had donned kilts to attend a few functions earlier in the day. At one point, Criner spied some fans across the lobby at the team hotel in Offenbauch, a suburb that was twenty minutes from Waldstadion. The coach was in cheery mood, and he couldn't resist the temptation to shock his flock of followers. So right there, in the bright lights of the lobby, he lifted up his kilt and mooned everyone in eyeshot. (True Scots—and Criner fancies himself one—don't wear anything under their kilts). After revealing his lily-white bum, the coach was all smiles as he mingled with fans. He felt ready to conquer the day.

About 15,000 fans had made the three-hour drive from Düsseldorf to Frankfurt to cheer on the Fire. The remaining 23,000 fans in attendance were mostly from Frankfurt and the surrounding area. Because the Galaxy faithful view the other German teams as their sworn enemy, virtually all of these fans supported the Claymores. For the first time all season, Scotland would have a decided home-field advantage as one of the loudest crowds in all of sport would be behind them.

In the Claymores' locker room minutes before the game, not much needed to be said. Ever since the players first sat in the Harley Hotel ballroom in Orlando three months before, their sights had been set on this moment. Now it was staring them in the face. For the ten minutes before the Claymores were to run out onto the field, no one said a word. Everyone was in his own world—the coaches, the players, even the trainers. Sure, this wasn't the Super Bowl, but it was a championship game that would be seen in forty different countries around the globe. In this locker room, at this moment, there was nothing more important in the universe than this game.

"You have a chance to do something special," Criner finally said, breaking the silence. "Have fun. Enjoy this moment, because you'll remember it for the rest of your lives. Play our style of football and play with class and poise. Now, let's go out there and kick some ass." The locker room erupted, as if all the pent-up emotion exploded in one cataclysmic moment. The dream was now stirring in their heads, and all the Claymores felt ready to make it come true.

In the Rhein locker room before the game, Coach Galen Hall spoke softly as he told his players to carry a big stick. "Within your grasp is something you'll remember forever," said Hall. "I'll promise you that when you come in here after the game, after we win, you'll experience one of the best feelings of your life. And have some fun. It's a game you've prepared for all your life. Just go out there now and play it better than they do."

When the Claymores emerged from the catacombs of the stadium, they were greeted by their biggest cheer of the season. More than 35,000 souls had collected on this night and they were whipped into a froth, screaming and blowing whistles so loud that the noise could be heard from a half-mile away. Energized, the players jumped around wildly as they sprinted out onto the field. "That was incredible," said McElmurry later. "I've never experienced anything like it."

Scotland lost the coin toss and kicked off. Right away, problems ensued. On the kickoff return, cornerback Hurley Tarver grabbed the facemask of the Fire's Steve Fisher and was flagged for a 15-yard penalty, giving Rhein the ball on Scotland's 45-yard-line. After an incompletion, the Claymores had to take a timeout because they didn't have the right personnel on the field. Two plays later, Scotland was flagged again, this time for an illegal substitution. Four plays after that, the Claymores again committed the same violation. Early on, they looked very much like a minor-league team. The Fire moved quickly down the field, but their drive stalled at the Claymores' 5-yard-line. Manny Burgsmuller then came on and kicked 21-yard field goal to give the Fire a quick 3–0 lead.

But in three plays, the Claymores answered back. Starting at their 25, Stecker gained nine yards on a sweep to the outside. Then Daft hurled a 30-yard, wobbling pass to Tate, who leaped high to make the grab. On the final play of the drive, Stecker took a handoff right up the belly of the defense. Starting at the Fire's 36-yard-line, Stecker broke five tackles in his most spectacular run of the season. He even carried one defender on his back as he rammed into the endzone, giving the Claymores a 7–3 lead.

In the second quarter, the team exchanged field goals to make the halftime score 10–6 in favor in the Claymores. During the intermission, the Claymore staff felt good about the game. Their defense was dominating and their offense was producing just enough. Now the question was whether or not they could hold on. When Criner gathered the team around him, he tried to raise their emotions. "Turn it up, now," he yelled. "Stay after them and let's go get ourselves a ring."

When quarterback Marcus Crandell jogged back out onto the field, he fully expected to play in the second half. Criner had told Alcalde that he didn't use Crandell in the second quarter because Daft only got three snaps in the first, and he wanted to see what Daft could do with more playing time. But Crandell would never enter the game. "It wasn't until afterward that I found out that Criner had supposedly suspended me for the game," said Crandell later. "I warmed up on the sidelines before both the second and fourth quarters expecting to play, but he never put me in. Even in the locker room, Criner never told me why I didn't play. It was just bizarre and totally unfair."

On the eve of the game, Criner had set a 10 PM curfew. Most of the players spent the evening lounging by the pool at their hotel in Offenbauch, so they could be in their rooms by 9. Crandell was one of those players, and he was in his room well before bedcheck. But at about 9:55, a young woman, whom Crandell had met a few days earlier, appeared in the lobby and started asking people where she could find Crandell. One of the Claymores coaches saw this and immediately went to Crandell's room to warn him that he shouldn't allow this young lady to enter his room, as that would be a violation of bedcheck. It was about 10:05 when the coach pounded on Crandell's door. The quarterback answered and the two talked for five minutes. While they were chatting, the young lady appeared. Crandell, who wasn't romantically interested in the woman, told her to leave. She did, then Crandell told his coach good night and went to sleep.

Criner, who refused to speak about the incident and never privately explained his actions to Crandell, then suspended his quarterback for the World Bowl. This hurt more than Crandell's feelings. Allocated to the Claymores by the Kansas City Chiefs, Crandell was hoping to impress Carl Peterson, the Chiefs' general manager and a friend of Criner, and a few other Kansas City front-office people who had traveled to Frankfurt to see Crandell play. (It was no coincidence, Crandell and many others felt, that he would be released by Kansas City shortly after the Claymores' season was over, even before the start of training camp.) "I didn't do anything wrong," said Crandell. "I wish somebody could have explained to me why I wasn't allowed to play. I think I was owed at least that much."

Over the years, the alternating of quarterbacks has usually proved to be a formula for failure in both college and professional football. But in Europe, because the season is short and the team with the best defense usually wins the championship, the rotation of quarterbacks is common. This season, the Claymores didn't hit their groove until Alcalde made the difficult decision to insert Crandell in two quarters of each game. Scotland was in a nice rhythm with their quarterback rotation—Daft was steady and took what the defense gave him, Crandell was the gambler who went for the big play—but now that rhythm was gone. And nobody really knew why except for the tight-lipped Jim Criner.

SCOTLAND CAME OUT flat in the third quarter. Daft overthrew wide receiver Selucio Sanford over the middle and the Claymores went three-and-out on the initial possession of the half. But Scotland's defense was still in control of the game. Wuerffel's first pass of the second half was intercepted by McElmurry, who returned the ball to midfield. Daft then threw two beautiful balls to Rickey Brady and

Sellers, both for first downs. Then at the 18-yard-line, Daft dropped back to pass. But just as his arm moved forward to unleash the ball, he was blindsided by Fire defensive end Derrick Ham. The ball flew forward about three yards, then dropped to the ground. For four seconds, everyone just stood around, thinking that the play was over. Suddenly realizing that the whistle hadn't yet blown, Rhein's Larry Fitzpatrick jumped on the ball. It was ruled a turnover.

If Daft hadn't gotten hit, he most likely would have thrown a touchdown to Donald Sellers, who was open by 10 yards in the middle of the endzone. At that point, with Scotland's defense dominating the game, an 11-point lead might have been insurmountable.

The Scotland defense again held, forcing another Fire punt. But on the Claymores' next possession, Daft again fumbled after getting sacked by Ham. Daft had plenty of time to get rid of the ball, but couldn't find anyone open. The turnover gave the Fire possession of the ball at the 18-yard-line, but again Rhein came away empty when Burgsmiller's 29-yard field-goal attempt hit the right upright and bounced backward. Scotland still had a 4-point lead with seven minutes left in the game.

The Claymores desperately needed a first down to give their defense a breather, but Daft was in a funk. Many players and coaches wanted Criner to insert Crandell, but the coach stubbornly stuck by his earlier decision and kept his second-string quarterback on the bench. Daft proceeded to overthrow two passes and Stecker was thrown for a five yard loss. Scotland had to punt.

The Claymore defense was gassed. They had been on the field for most of the steamy night. "We were definitely getting fatigued, but we felt like if we could just hold them one more time, and keep them out of the endzone, then we'd win the game," said Finkes. "We just knew that the offense wasn't going to do anything and that basically it was up to us. But that's the way we wanted it."

THE PROVING GROUND

On their final drive of regulation, the Fire started at the Claymores' 46-yard-line after a poor punt by Ballantyne. Running back Pepe Pearson then took control. First he ran for 11 yards. Then six. Then another six. After a long Weurffel completion and a short run, the Fire had the ball at the Claymore 3-yard-line. It was second and goal. Two minutes remained.

The Claymores' defense was playing with as much heart as it had displayed all season, but it wasn't enough. First Pearson carried for two yards. Then, on third and one, Pearson ran off tackle and dove into the endzone with 1:19 remaining. The Fire now led 13–10.

This was not the position the Claymores wanted to be in. All season long, even going back to Orlando, the offense had struggled in the two-minute drill. But now the game and the championship would be won or lost on the right arm of Kevin Daft.

Damon Gibson fumbled the kickoff, but he was able to recover the ball at his 18-yard-line. Daft then hit Stecker over the middle for eight yards. Then, after a short completion, he found Sellers over the middle for 13 yards to Scotland's 46-yard-line. Forty-nine seconds remained. Three plays later, Daft again hit Sellers, this time for 12 yards to Rhine's 42-yard-line. Thirty-three seconds remained.

From his press-box vantage point, Alcalde believed a draw play to Stecker would work. Rhein's defensive ends were charging hard off the corner and their linebackers were either dropping straight into coverage without checking Stecker or they were blitzing around the ends. So Alcalde made a gutsy call and told Criner to call the draw. But it was stuffed for only a 3-yard gain. The Claymores quickly called a timeout. Seventeen seconds remained.

When Daft came over to the sideline to speak with Criner, he had an air about him, a comportment, that the young quarterback hadn't shown all season. Much to the surprise of everyone on the sideline, he looked as if he was actually confident that he would get the job done. This look, the determination on his face, was something that Daft had acquired only in the last few weeks. This was what the maturation of a quarterback looked like—this is why NFL Europe exists.

Daft jogged back onto the field. He called the count and then took a seven-step drop into the pocket. He scanned the field, then rifled what was clearly his best pass of the season. He drilled the ball into the arms of wide receiver Selucio Sanford, who was cutting across the middle, 17 yards downfield. As soon as Sanford was tackled at the Fire 23-yard-line, Daft signaled for Scotland's final timeout. Eight seconds remained.

When Daft got to the sidelines, he wanted one more play so he could take a shot at the endzone and the win. Confidence was coursing through his veins. But Criner decided to play it conservative— that's what old school coaches do in such a situation—and have Hart attempt a 40-yard field goal. "I just don't want to take the chance of not getting a field try out of this," Criner said to Daft. "We're going to kick."

Rob Hart did not have an NFL-caliber leg. On field-goal attempts of 39 yards or less during the season, he had connected on six out of seven. But on field goals that were 40 yards or more, the English kicker was just one out of four. Despite having the odds stacked against him, Criner sent his 25-year-old kicker trotting onto the field. The championship hung in the balance.

All week long, the players had been talking about the $2,000 bonus that everyone would receive for winning this game. Every player on the losing team would get a check for $1,000. To these players, some of whom were a paycheck away from poverty, this was an enormous amount of money. "The cash award seems to be on everyone's mind," said Hawthorne a few days earlier. "I don't think it will necessarily make us play harder than usual, but it just ups the stakes.

THE PROVING GROUND

For some guys, especially the ones who probably aren't going to make it in the NFL, the extra money could really help them out when they get home."

Hart lined up for the kick. The center was Rickey Brady and the holder was Willy Tate. Both of these players were veterans, old-hands whom Criner had purposefully sought out before the season for moments like this. Just before Brady snapped the ball, Galen Hall instructed his team to take a timeout. He wanted Hart to contemplate the kick.

For as long as he could remember, Hart had played out this moment in his mind—what it would be like to have a chance to kick a field goal as important as this. In all of his boyhood reveries he had made this kick, had watched the ball sailing through the uprights. He teammates would swarm him, and together they would leave the field as champions. This was how it was in his dreams ever since he started playing the sport in his early teens. And once, when he was a junior at Murray State, Hart had lived out his fantasy. Against Eastern Kentucky, on a cool autumn afternoon in Richmond in 1996, Hart nailed a 36-yard field goal on the last play of the game to give his team a 17–14 win. "That was the highlight of my career," said Hart a few days before the World Bowl. "I'd love to be put in that sort of situation again. That's what every good kicker wants: to have the game decided by his own foot."

Now here Hart was, wandering around the field, alone, during the ninety-second timeout that Rhein had called. No one wanted to speak to him and disrupt his concentration. He had made kicks this long all season in practice, but even Criner knew that the odds were against Hart connecting. Now the game was Hart's to tie or to lose.

The Claymores lined up. The snap went to Tate. He fielded it cleanly, then put the ball down on the grass. He spun the laces perfectly, so they faced away from Hart, a soccer-style kicker. Hart took three steps, then solidly connected with the ball. It easily cleared the line of scrimmage, then flew through the night, climbing high into the dark sky.

Right away, Hart knew the kick had the distance. He'd struck the ball in its sweetspot and it had leapt off his foot. But there was one problem: The kick was nearly blocked by a Fire defender rushing around the right edge of the line. The ball missed his fingertips by less than three inches, but the rush affected Hart. He could sense it coming and it had caused him to hurry his kick, which sailed wide-left. The game was over. Paradise was lost.

The missed field goal set off a wild celebration on the Rhein side-line. Players cried and danced and hugged. On the Claymores' side-line, no one was more distraught than defensive end Rasheed Simmons. He had ran onto the field and collapsed on the 22-yard-line, inconsolable. A few Scotland players tried to get Simmons to leave the field—there were still four seconds remaining—but he refused to get up. As Weurffel took a knee to kill the clock, Sim-mons lay on the wrong side of the line of scrimmage, sobbing. This hurt—a lot.

Hart was equally dejected. As soon as he missed the kick, Tate grabbed him hard and hugged him. "This loss wasn't your fault," Tate told Hart. "We lost as a team."

When Tate got to the sideline, he found Finkes. The two embraced for twenty seconds. They had become as close as any two players on the team in the past three months, and now it was all over—except for their friendship. "It was a hell of a season," Finkes told Tate. "I'll never forget it."

Neither would Jaime Baisley, a linebacker for the Fire. When the final gun sounded, Baisley grabbed the World Bowl trophy, held it above his head, then sprinted across the field to a section of the stadium where the Fire fans sat. With confetti raining down and fireworks crackling above, Baisley high-fived fans and let a few of them touch the trophy. He then handed it around to his teammates, who had congregated there to share the moment with the fans who had supported them throughout the season. For a few minutes, as the players drank in the adulation, it was as if the Fire had won a game that was as royal as the Super Bowl.

"THERE ARE NO excuses," said Hart after the game, his eyes red and puffy. "There is no easy explanation. I just blew it. Words can't describe just how awful I feel at this moment. As a kicker, you have limited opportunity in every game that you play, and the reason you play football is to have the chance I was given tonight. To blow that chance is a sin, as far as I'm concerned. I am paid to make kicks like that and the fact that I didn't make it means that I have let the whole team down. It doesn't matter to me that we had other opportunities to win the game. When my chance came, my duty was to take it, and I feel so bad that I have cost these players their chance at lifting the World Bowl trophy."

Sports legacies can be cruel. Ralph Branca of the Brooklyn Dodgers throws one pitch—"the shot heard 'round the world"—that is hammered into the Polo Grounds seats by the Giants' Bobby Thomson on October 3, 1951, and every other pitch of Branca's twelve-year career is almost forgotten in an infamous instant. Scott Norwood of the Buffalo Bills misses a 47-yard field goal at the end of Super Bowl XXV, a kick that would have beaten the New York Giants, and the rest of Norwood's outstanding career becomes an afterthought.

In the press room after the World Bowl, one reporter dubbed Hart's miss "The Scottish Norwood." Though the missed kick will not haunt Hart as devilishly as Norwood's failure, it will no doubt take some time for the young English kicker to recover from it. "Rob would give his right arm to have made that kick," said Criner. "And I don't think that's an exaggeration."

When Criner spoke with the press after the game, he looked like a man who hadn't slept in weeks. His eyes were baggy and his words fell flat. There had been speculation prior to the World Bowl that Criner would retire from NFL Europe immediately after the game if the Claymores won. But on this day, he wasn't ready to retreat to the wilds of West Yellowstone just yet.

"This is such a tough loss to take," said Criner, his voice cracking only for the second time this season. "But I just have to deal with this and take some time to reflect on whether I will come back to Scotland next season. This defeat is so painful that I will have to take a long time to make up my mind. I hope you understand."

In NFL Europe this season, 17 of the 30 games played were decided by six or fewer points, so it really wasn't surprising that the World Bowl would come down to the last play of the game. But that didn't take the sting away from the Claymore players, who still sat on the front steps at Waldstadion ninety-minutes after the World Bowl had ended. As they waited for their coach to finish his postgame meal, the team crouched under the shimmering stars. Soon they would head home to the States, going in different directions to different homes, different teams, and different futures. But as they waited on the floodlit steps, exchanging home phone numbers, no one voiced any regrets. Though the season sometimes seemed longer than the last day of school, almost every Claymore believed that the experience in NFL Europe had enriched his life. "I can't believe it's all over," said Tate. "There were times during the season when the end couldn't came fast enough, but now that it's finally over, I wish it could go on."

THE PROVING GROUND

When Criner finally appeared, he shepherded his team through the pale moonlight and onto the bus. The coach then hopped into his rental car and drove into the darkness. The bus followed, and the Scottish Claymores were on their way home. All that was left behind were footprints on the proving ground.

Afterword

JIM CRINER

Less than two months after the 2000 season, Jim Criner became the third NFL Europe coach to jump to the XFL, joining Rhein Fire's Galen Hall and the Amsterdam Admirals' Al Luginbill. Before Criner defected to the new league, where he would coach the Las Vegas franchise, he had some bitter words for NFL Europe executives. He felt that Scotland had been repeatedly slighted in the flesh-peddling game that is the allocation of NFL players.

"Three years in a row allocated players were taken away from me and given to other teams," Criner claimed. "It goes back to Jon Kitna. He was coming to Scotland but Oliver Luck [the former president of NFL Europe] took him away and gave him to Barcelona. The situation this past year was also unfair. The league got our ex-players Kevin Drake and Jesse Haynes to say negative things about us in a press release. Why single out Scotland? All that stuff adds up. I think NFL Europe is a wonderful thing, but sometimes people who don't know a great deal about football get involved and make things hard for those of us who are on the front line. It wears thin after awhile.

"In Scotland, a fresh approach from a new man at the helm may, in the long term, be in everyone's best interests. The best thing that can happen for the Claymores is to have a fresh face. I'm only stepping aside after having done some things to improve the product on the field. I may have made some enemies, but I'm excited about the future. I would love to have left having given the fans a championship instead of a second-place trophy, but being part of building something new has been very rewarding to me, and very special."

VINCE ALCALDE

The Claymores' offensive coordinator joined Criner's staff in Las Vegas in the same coaching capacity.

RICHARD KENT

The Claymores' defensive-backs coach returned to Scotland for the 2001 season. He occupied the same position under new Claymore head coach Gene Dahlquist.

MYREL MOORE

Moore, the Claymores' defensive coordinator, retired from coaching after the 2000 NFL Europe season.

JIM TOMSULA

The Claymores' defensive line coach returned to Scotland for the 2001 season.

The Players

NACHI ABE

In late July 2000, Nachi Abe was signed to a ten-day contract by the Atlanta Falcons to help promote Atlanta's August 5th game in Tokyo against the Cowboys. Abe made a quick impression on Falcon's coach Dan Reeves. "He came in, told the players how honored he was to be a member of our football team and to represent us in Japan," Reeves said. "He got all the single guys excited because he told them that he would introduce them to beautiful Japanese girls."

AFTERWORD

Early in the fourth quarter of the game, Abe raced downfield on a Falcons' kickoff. Then he suddenly came face-to-face with kick returner Michael Wiley. "I was surprised I had such a clear shot at him," said Abe, who had four plays at tight end and several kickoffs. Wiley nearly shrugged off Abe, but the powerful Japanese tight end kept hold long enough to trip him up. It was his first and last NFL tackle.

"Abe jumped right in on kickoffs, ran offensive plays, and did a great job for us," said Reeves. After his ten days were up, Abe was released. He hoped to return to the Claymores for the 2001 season.

TREMAYNE ALLEN

Allen, a backup tight end for the Claymores, was selected by the Los Angeles Extreme with the 368th overall pick of the XFL expansion draft.

JON BALLANTYNE

Ballantyne, the Claymores' punter, was waived by the Browns in the 2000 preseason. He was hoping to punt for an NFL Europe team in the 2001 season.

CHRIS BAYNE

Bayne, a safety, was cut by the Dolphins in the 2000 preseason. He was selected by Criner and the Las Vegas Outlaws with the 76th overall pick in the XFL expansion draft.

KORY BLACKWELL

Blackwell, a cornerback, was cut by the Raiders in the 2000 preseason. He was selected by Criner and the Las Vegas Outlaws with the 21st overall pick in the XFL expansion draft.

RICKEY BRADY

Brady, a tight end, was cut by the Cowboys in the 2000 preseason. He was selected by Criner and the Las Vegas Outlaws with the 37th overall pick in the XFL expansion draft.

BEN CAVIL

Cavil, an offensive tackle, was selected by the New York/New Jersey Hitmen in the XFL expansion draft.

SCOTT COUPER

Couper, a national wide receiver for the Claymores, thought long about retiring from football after the 2000 season. "I've been at this for a long time," said Couper after the World Bowl loss. "I've been playing since 1995. It may be time to hang it up."

But the more Couper thought about it, the more he realized he couldn't walk away just yet. So he decided to return to the Claymores for the 2001 season. "If we win the World Bowl this season, I'll definitely retire," said Couper. "But if we don't, well, who knows?"

MARCUS CRANDELL

After being cut by Kansas City before training camp, Crandell signed with Green Bay, where he was beat out by Danny Weurffel for the third-string quarterback position in 2000. He was selected by the Memphis Maniacs with the third overall pick in the XFL expansion draft. "This is actually going to be the first time since I got out of college that I've really gotten a real shot at competing for a job," said Crandell, who was very much looking forward to playing the Las Vegas Outlaws and getting a chance to go up against his old coach, Jim Criner.

AFTERWORD

SCOTT CURRY

Curry, a starting tackle for the Claymores, injured his knee in the third week of training camp with the Packers. But Green Bay's medical staff was at first unable to identify what precisely was wrong with Curry's knee because MRI tests didn't reveal any damage. When Curry's knee remained sore after six weeks on the sidelines, team doctors operated and found that a small chunk of bone had fragmented from his knee. They removed the fragment. Curry then missed the season on the injured reserve list, but was healthy for the Packers minicamp in the spring of 2001. "I'm just glad we finally found out what was wrong with my knee," Curry said.

KEVIN DAFT

Daft was in the Tennessee Titans players' lounge with quarterback Billy Volek in late August 2000 when Daft was summoned to meet with the offense coaches. Daft and Volek had been in a heated battle for the Titans number-three quarterback job. In the third game of the preseason, against the Eagles, Daft was given a chance to start. It was Daft's misfortune that he had to face the Eagles' starting defense for the first quarter of the game. Philadelphia blitzed early and often and rattled the young quarterback, hurrying Daft into a 1-of-8 passing night for eight yards. He was sacked twice and thrown to the turf several more times.

When Daft sat down with his coaches, he was given the somber news: they were going with Volek. Daft was cut. "It was a difficult decision to make, but Billy made it hard on us from the start," coach Jeff Fisher said. "It was very competitive." Fisher went on to say that he didn't believe Daft's chances had been harmed by playing in Europe while first-year offensive coordinator Mike Heimerdinger was installing a new playbook in Nashville.

Daft was signed by San Diego during the 2000 season, but was then released. Atlanta picked him up and will give him a look in the 2001 preseason.

ANTONIO DINGLE

Dingle, a defensive tackle, was selected by Criner and the Las Vegas Outlaws with the 28th overall pick of the XFL expansion draft.

MATT FINKES

Finkes, a linebacker for the Claymores, was cut by Jacksonville in the 2000 preseason. He was then selected by the Chicago Enforcers with the 136th overall pick of the XFL expansion draft.

JASON GAMBLE

Gamble, a guard for the Claymores, was cut by Jacksonville in the 2000 preseason. He was selected by the Orlando Rage with the 109th overall pick in the XFL expansion draft.

DAMON GIBSON

Gibson, a wide receiver for the Claymores, was selected by the Los Angeles Extreme with the 256th pick in the XFL expansion draft.

ROB HART

In the offseason, Hart, the Claymores' place kicker, moved from Bath, England, to Glasgow so he could work on his kicking year-round with Claymore coaches. He was planning to return to the Claymores for the 2001 season and hoped to redeem himself for his heart-breaking miss in the 2000 World Bowl.

DUANE HAWTHORNE

Hawthorne, a cornerback, spent the 2000 season on the roster of the Dallas Cowboys. He saw action in 14 games and made four tackles.

Hawthorne spent most of his time on the scout team, but Cowboy coaches still believed that Hawthorne could someday blossom into a starter. "When I came back from Europe my body was really worn down," said Hawthorne. "I think it affected my play. But if I had to do it over again, I'd go back to Europe in a second. It really helped my career."

JON HESSE
Hesse, a linebacker, went to the Falcon's 2000 training camp, but injured his neck soon after camp started. After consulting with doctors, who told Hesse that he was just one hit away from serious injury, he retired from football. He and his wife, Amy, live in Lincoln, Nebraska, where Heese is now a financial planner.

MICHAEL MASON
Mason, a starting defensive end for the Claymores, was selected by Criner and the Las Vegas Outlaws with the 53rd overall pick of the XFL expansion draft.

BLAINE MCELMURRY
McElmurry, who played safety for the Claymores, was cut by Jacksonville in the 2000 preseason. At last report, he was considering applying to medical school.

DEON MITCHELL
Mitchell, a backup wide receiver for the Claymores, was selected by Criner and the Las Vegas Outlaws with the 396th overall pick of the XFL expansion draft.

SULECIO SANFORD
Sulecio Sanford, who was allocated to the Claymores by Chicago, had

a strong 2000 training camp with the Bears. He flourished on punt returns and seemed to make a highlight-kind-of-catch at every practice. But then he injured his knee. At first the Bears thought the injury would keep Sanford out for just a month, but it turned out to be much worse. He was lost for the season.

"We thought enough of Sulecio that when it seemed just a three-week or four-week injury, we had every intention of carrying him [on the roster]," Bears coach Dick Jauron said. "We felt he could still come back and compete for a spot. He was doing that well."

Sanford is hoping to make the Bears squad in 2001.

NOEL SCARLETT

Scarlet, a defensive tackle for the Claymores, was released by the Patriots in the 2000 preseason. The Chiefs then signed Scarlett to their practice squad, only to release him midway through the season. Late in 2000, he was picked up the Cowboys and, according to Dallas coaches, he will be given every chance to make the 2001 squad.

BEN SNELL

Snell, a backup running back for the Claymores, was selected by Criner and the Las Vegas Outlaws with the 325th overall pick of the XFL expansion draft.

AARON STECKER

Aaron Stecker was a backup running back and kick returner for the Buccaneers during the 2000 season. His stats were modest: 12 rushes for 31 yards; 29 kickoff returns for 663 yards (22.9 per return). Stecker had an explosive 2000 preseason, running several balls back for touchdowns during scrimmages and running one ball back 78 yards during an exhibition game against the Dolphins. Tampa coach Tony Dungy believed that Stecker could have a long career as the team's kickoff returner, as long as Stecker could learn to combine his aggressive approach with the team's scripted style.

"When I first started returning kicks, whatever hole I saw I'd just hit it," said Stecker. "But then the coaches started telling me to look at a certain guy for his block and to run off his butt or whatever. Usually I just catch the ball and run to wherever I want to. And I was successful that way. So now I think I have to go back to doing what helped me get on this team and that's just run wherever I feel and hopefully a big return will happen."

DONALD SELLERS

About three months after leaving the Claymores, Sellers, a wide receiver, was arrested in Gilbert, Arizona, and charged with sexual misconduct with underage girls. Sellers was arrested and accused of raping one teenage girl, having intercourse with three others, and molesting a fifth. He was released from custody and, despite the gravity of the charges, was selected by Criner in the XFL allocation draft with the 92nd overall pick. In February Sellers drove his pickup from Las Vegas to Phoenix to stand trial. On that drive, just outside of Phoenix on Arizona State Route 93, Sellers lost control of his vehicle and crossed into oncoming traffic. His pickup was hit by another car and then flipped, ejecting Sellers. He was pronounced dead at the scene. He was twenty-six.

BRIAN SMITH

After suffering a devastating knee injury in Week Seven against Barcelona, Smith had reconstructive surgery in Birmingham, Alabama. A linebacker who was allocated to the Claymores by the Falcons, Smith then spent the next eight months rehabilitating his knee in Birmingham. His spirits never wavered. "I believe I'll be back playing in the 2001 NFL season," said Smith. "I'm working about six hours a day trying to get my knee back in shape and I'm on schedule to be ready to go for training camp. I've never given up hope."

HURLEY TARVER

Tarver, a backup cornerback for the Claymores, was selected by Criner and the Las Vegas Outlaws with the 108th overall pick of the XFL expansion draft.

WILLY TATE

Tate, a tight end and long-snapper for the Claymores, was the surprise of the Oakland Raiders' 2000 preseason camp. When Oakland's long-snapper Adam Treu went down with an injury, Tate was called into camp as an emergency backup. He proceeded to catch a touchdown pass in a preseason game and made several other nice grabs. Ultimately, though, when Treu returned to action, the Raiders gave Tate his walking papers. "A few guys ahead of me would have had to spontaneously combust for me to have made that team," said Tate.

Tate was again prepared to begin life after football. That's when he got another phone call. This time he had been informed that he had been selected by the Chicago Enforcers with the 281st pick of the XFL expansion draft. The Enforcers held their five-week training camp in Orlando. During camp, his roommate was none other than Matt Finkes. "We're having a great time down here," said Tate from Orlando. "It's the Claymores all over again. But this time we don't have go to Europe to play and the money is a little bit better."

CORDELL TAYLOR

Taylor, a backup cornerback for the Claymores, was selected by the San Francisco Demons with the 22nd overall pick of the XFL expansion draft.

AFTERWORD

RYAN TAYLOR

Taylor, a backup linebacker for the Claymores, was placed on the Cleveland Browns' injured reserve list in early November after fracturing a fibula in a loss to the New York Giants. Taylor had played on special teams and was the team's only linebacker in their "dime" defense.

Despite his injury, Taylor had a lasting impact on the Browns' season. In a practice drill midway through the season, he rushed quarterback Tim Couch, who wasn't supposed to be hit. When Couch threw the ball, his thumb hit Taylor's helmet on his follow-through. As a result, Couch broke his thumb and was lost for the season. Taylor, who had spent all of the previous season on the Browns' practice squad, said he was just trying to play hard. "It's a competitive situation and I was trying to make an impact," said Taylor. "But you have to be smart. The quarterback is the key player on your team and I should've laid off of him. I was just coming on the blitz and trying to make my move on the running back and I put my hand up to block the ball."

Couch harbored no bad feelings for Taylor. "I talked to Ryan and he felt really bad," said Couch. "He was kind of down about it. I told him I had no hard feelings and not to worry about it. It was just one of those things."

Acknowledgments

Writing a book, like preparing a feast for thousands, is not a solo effort. I received a tremendous amount of help in cooking up this main course you now hold in your hands.

My beautiful wife, Sara Anderson, should have her name on the cover. Not only did she encourage me to push forward with the project even though I had to leave for Europe just three weeks after we were married, but she also line-edited the manuscript. She did this with an uncommon grace and a deftness that will no doubt carry her far in the magazine business. She also helped turn a jumbled mess of a manuscript into an organized whole. Thank you, SP.

This endeavor never would have gotten off the ground without the considerable efforts of Steve Livingstone, the public relations director of the Scottish Claymores. Steve showed enthusiasm for the idea from the beginning and spent countless hours with me telling me stories about life in NFL Europe. After the season, Steve was deservedly promoted to general manager of the Claymores.

Thanks also to Marc Resnick, my editor at St. Martin's Press. Marc had a clear vision for the book and helped sculpt the manuscript with his fine touches. Mark Zitzewitz, an eternal friend and a future statesman in the great state of Minnesota, also lent an elegant editing hand. Dave McRitchie, a photographer who, in my estimation, is the coolest guy in Glasgow, generously donated pictures to what he thought was a worthy project. My agent for this book, Scott Waxman, helped cultivate the idea and always offered encouraging words. The crew at *Sports Illustrated*—especially David Bauer, Larry Burke, and Richard Demak—graciously gave me time off and always provided me with rock-solid advice. And the players and coaches of the Claymores tolerated my presence and questions with class and

ACKNOWLEDGMENTS

patience. Specifically, I am indebted to Matt Finkes, Willy Tate, Jon Hesse, Rob Hart, Antonio Dingle, Rickey Brady, Donald Sellers, Blaine McElmurry, Marcus Crandell, Jon Ballantyne, Ben Cavil, Brian Smith, Scott Curry, Myrle Moore, Jim Tomsula, Vince Alcalde, Richard Kent, and, lest I forget, Deep Throat.

I encountered a few roadblocks in the process of my reporting, but because of the people just mentioned, I will always have fond memories of my time in Scotland with the Claymores.